MADISON'S NIGHTMARE

Madison's Nightmare

HOW EXECUTIVE POWER THREATENS
AMERICAN DEMOCRACY

Peter M. Shane

The University of Chicago Press ★ *Chicago and London*

PETER M. SHANE is the Jacob E. Davis and Jacob E. Davis II Chair in Law at the Ohio State University Moritz College of Law.

The University of Chicago Press, Chicago 60637
The University of Chicago Press, Ltd., London
© 2009 by Peter M. Shane
All rights reserved. Published 2009
Printed in the United States of America

18 17 16 15 14 13 12 11 10 09   1 2 3 4 5

ISBN-13: 978-0-226-74939-6 (cloth)
ISBN-10: 0-226-74939-8 (cloth)

Library of Congress Cataloging-in-Publication Data
Shane, Peter M.
   Madison's nightmare : how executive power threatens American democracy / Peter M. Shane.
       p. cm.
   Includes bibliographical references and index.
   ISBN-13: 978-0-226-74939-6 (cloth: alk. paper)
   ISBN-10: 0-226-74939-8 (cloth: alk. paper)
   1. Executive power—United States—History. 2. Separation of powers—United States—History. 3. Representative government and representation—United States—History. 4. United States—Politics and government—21st century. I. Title.
   JK516.S435 2009
   320.473'04—dc22   2008040188

Contents

Preface

Our Constitution was founded on the radical hope that good government design can so constrain the ambitions of public officials as to protect the American public from tyranny and abuse. Instead of constrained ambition, however, Americans have become increasingly accustomed to governmental audacity. Whether it is a President running foreign policy behind Congress's back, Congress impeaching a President for lying about his sexual affairs, or the Supreme Court effectively deciding a presidential election through a dubious application of equal protection law cut from whole cloth, we seem to have abandoned checks and balances for something very different. At this point, that "something" looks more and more like a virtually unchecked presidency, nurtured too often in its political aggressiveness by a feckless Congress and obsequious courts. A handy mnemonic for this phenomenon might be "Guantanamo" or "Abu Ghraib," but, as a constitutional lawyer, what I call it is "presidentialism." The increasingly assertive claims to unilateral presidential authority, accompanied by the occasional overreaching of the other two branches of government, add up to the subversion of constitutional checks and balances that I have dubbed "Madison's Nightmare."

Chapter 1 of this book introduces the perfect storm convergence of executive power and partisan aspiration that have produced our current predicament. It lays out three foundational points. The first is the critical role intended for checks and balances in our constitutional system. The second is that the 1981–2009 campaign for policy dominance by the right wing of the Republican Party, no matter what branch is involved, has involved a radical attack on our constitutional system's impetus toward consensus and accommodation. Finally, I will explain how a coincidence of contemporary political circumstances combined with our constitutional structure has enabled this attack to proceed as effectively as it has, especially in exploiting the historic trend toward increased executive power, in order to take the form of aggressive presidentialism we have experienced since 1981.

Chapter 2 will then analyze the legal debates that surround the current growth of presidential power. The 2006 confirmation battle concerning Supreme Court Justice Samuel Alito brought to many citizens' consciousness the fact of a disagreement among constitutional scholars and practitioners about something called "the unitary presidency." That debate, however, is not generally well understood. The legal argument in favor of presidentialism is constitutionally baseless, and this chapter seeks to explain why.

Chapters 3–6 then turn from legal doctrine to government practice. Proponents of expansive executive power typically argue that the presidency they envision is more likely to operate in the national interest than a presidency fully accountable to courts and Congress. I seek to show why this is false.

Chapter 3 looks at the making of foreign and military policy, with special reference to our national experience in Vietnam and Iraq. In both cases, the presidents involved were allowed to proceed, in effect, under the presidentialists' view of how the executive branch should operate. Yet, the history of both wars shows how presidentialism is quite likely to degrade the quality of executive branch decision making because it breeds a degree of isolation, defensiveness, and ideological rigidity that will predictably undermine the soundness of presidential decisions.

Chapter 4 looks at national security policy making, with a special focus on the "Bush 43" Administration. It argues that presidentialism is likely to degrade the quality of decision making for a special reason, by eroding government attorneys' conscientious attention to the law, which is supposed to operate as a check on abuses of government power. Historians wondering why government lawyering broke down at critical points during policy deliberations after September 11 are likely to find the ideology of presidentialism very much at work.

Chapter 5 explores the rule of law theme further. It explains how contemporary presidentialism has embraced an especially thin view of what the rule of law entails. This tendency is exhibited in the Bush 43 Administration's treatment of executive privilege and, most dramatically, in the proliferation of presidential signing statements raising constitutional objections to statutes that the President is signing into law.

The most novel post-1981 context for presidentialist initiative has been the assertion of presidential control over domestic regulatory policy making. Presidents do not have as wide a constitutional scope for domestic policy initiative as they do in foreign affairs and are not afforded the same discretion to proceed largely in secret. Presidents have thus not yet succeeded in consolidating executive power over domestic policy making as effectively as they have with regard to policy making over military and foreign affairs. Chapter 6 explores how Presidents Reagan through Bush 43 have, nonetheless, sought to extend such control and how, if they and their successors prevail in this campaign, presidentialism is likely to undermine not only the rule of law, but democratic accountability more generally.

Chapter 7 synthesizes the analysis of earlier chapters by contrasting the models of democracy and the rule of law embedded in presidentialism and its more appealing counterpart, constitutional pluralism. It concludes by laying out a series of concrete steps that Americans can take to reassert the vigor of checks and balances and curb the extreme presidentialism that our perfect storm has wrought.

I did not start this project thinking that my end result would be a book about the Administration of George W. Bush. Indeed, I started to lay out the themes and arguments of this book in 1994. But the Bush 43 Administration has so perfectly demonstrated what I feared would be the dangers of aggressive presidentialism that this presidency has become the laboratory for illustrating many of my key points. I emphasize, however, that the risks of presidentialism remain even as the Bush 43 Administration recedes into history. Americans of all political stripes should want an emphatic return to the pluralistic government of checks and balances that was Madison's dream.

I have been at work on this book for what I consider to be an embarrassingly long time. My regrettable pace, however, did give me the opportunity to develop and try out the themes and many key arguments of this book over a series of articles and book chapters. None of my prior writings appears intact in this book, but occasionally, especially when it comes to chronicling specific events, I have found it useful to incorporate portions of earlier-written prose. I am grateful to the publishers of the following works for permission to do so:

Deliberative America, 1 J. Pub. Deliberation, Art. 10 (2005), available at http://services.bepress.com/jpd/v0l1/issl/artl0/.

Disappearing Democracy: How Bush v. Gore *Undermined the Federal Right to Vote for Presidential Electors*, 29 Fla. St. U. L. Rev. 535–585 (2001).

Independent Policymaking and Presidential Power: A Constitutional Analysis, 57 Geo. Wash. L. Rev. 596–626 (1989).

Learning McNamara's Lessons: How the War Powers Resolution Advances the Rule of Law, 47 CASE W. RES. L. REV. 1281–1304 (1997).

Political Accountability in a System of Checks and Balances: The Case of Presidential Review of Rulemaking, 48 ARK. L. REV. 161–214 (1995).

Powers of the Crown [Review of JOHN YOO, THE POWERS OF WAR AND PEACE: THE CONSTITUTION AND FOREIGN AFFAIRS AFTER 9/11 (2005)], 68 J.L. & POL. 702–707 (2006).

Presidential Signing Statements and the Rule of Law as an "Unstructured Institution," 16 WM. & MARY BILL RTS. L. REV. 231 (2007).

Presidents, Pardons, and Prosecutors: Legal Accountability and the Separation of Powers, 11 YALE L. & POL'Y REV. 361–406 (1993).

Public Information, Technology, and Democratic Empowerment, in PETER M. SHANE, J. PODESTA, AND R. LEONE, EDS., A LITTLE KNOWLEDGE: PRIVACY, SECURITY AND PUBLIC INFORMATION AFTER SEPTEMBER 11 (Century Foundation Press, 2004).

Reflections in Three Mirrors: Complexities of Representation in a Constitutional Democracy, 60 OHIO ST. L.J. 693–709 (1999).

When Interbranch Norms Break Down: Of Arms-for-Hostages, "Orderly Shutdowns," Presidential Impeachments, and Judicial Coups, 12 CORNELL J.L. & PUB. POL'Y 503–542 (2003).

Curious readers can also find in the articles cited yet more extensive footnotes documenting many of the points made in the analysis that follows.

I have also, in a couple of spots, borrowed thoughts and a few sentences from work written in collaboration with Professor Harold H. Bruff, my partner for two decades in developing the only law school casebook on separation of powers law, *Separation of Powers Law: Cases and Materials* (Carolina Academic Press, 2d ed. 2005). Hal is a never-failing source of insight and critique, and, although I have tried to pirate only my own sentences from our book, it is a testament to the depth of our joint initiative that we can no longer always tell whose words are whose. I am grateful to Hal for all that he has taught me and for his reciprocal willingness to use our words and allow me to use them, whoever may first have coined them.

I likewise wish to thank a special group of people, who have had a profound impact on my thinking over the years about separation of powers issues. My ideas on checks and balances first took shape in the Justice Department Office of Legal Counsel (OLC), then under the leadership of John Harmon, Larry Hammond, and Larry Simms—three of the finest lawyers, I am confident, ever to serve the American public. Among my academic colleagues, I will always be especially indebted for the friendship and insight of Cynthia Farina, Jerry Mashaw, and Peter Strauss, along with the late Thomas Sargentich. The premature passing of Tom, an especially close friend during our years together working at OLC, has robbed not just the academy, but the nation as a whole of one of its wisest voices on the nature of constitutional government. I would also like to express my deep thanks to my University of Chicago Press editor, David Pervin, for reading this manuscript so carefully and offering invaluable suggestions. My friends and former colleagues Bert Rockman and William Keech also offered generous and insightful readings, as did two anonymous reviewers, whose comments significantly improved the work. The Ohio State University, through both the Moritz College of Law and the Mershon Center for International Security Studies, also provided numerous forms of tangible and intangible support and encouragement as I completed this project. Of course, I remain responsible for such deficiencies of analysis or expression that may remain.

My greatest debts are owed to Martha Chamallas and Beth Shane, who have shaped my perspective on much more than the Constitution. It is to Martha and Beth that I dedicate this book.

1

Madison's Nightmare: How the Federal Government Became Unchecked and Unbalanced

When the Constitutional Convention adjourned in September, 1787, James Madison made a fateful choice. He resumed his place in the Congress, still sitting in New York City, rather than returning immediately to his life and home in Virginia. In New York, Alexander Hamilton asked for Madison's help in penning a series of anonymous essays intended to persuade the New York ratifying convention to vote affirmatively on their Philadelphia handiwork. Madison was Hamilton's fourth choice of a collaborator, one New York luminary having turned him down, another having proven inadequate to the task, and one—John Jay—falling ill.[1] Madison joined in the project eagerly, however, even asking George Washington to help arrange for reprinting the texts in Virginia.[2]

November 22, 1787 marked the publication of Madison's first contribution. As Publius—the identity assumed jointly by Hamilton, Jay, and himself—Madison began his essay, *Federalist* No. 10, by identifying the issue perhaps closest to his heart. "Among the numerous advantages promised by a well constructed union," he wrote, "none deserves to be more accurately developed than its tendency to break and control the violence of faction."[3] He was specific in his definition of faction: "By a faction, I understand a number of citizens, whether amounting to a majority or a minority of the whole, who are united and actuated by some common impulse of passion, or of interest, adverse to the rights of other citizens, or to the permanent and aggregate interests of the community."[4] Factionalism, in Madison's view, was thus not a matter of numbers, but of motivation and orientation. A majority or a minority would be a faction whenever animated by considerations of passion or self-interest above genuine public concern.

Faction was not a new theme for Madison. He foreshadowed his views in an April 1787 enumeration that he prepared of the "Vices of the Political System of the United States."[5] Gearing up intellectually for the Philadelphia deliberations that would commence a month hence, he argued that "the great desideratum in Government"[6] was the control of faction. The challenge before America was to create institutions strong enough to mediate effectively among society's competing interests and achieve the public interest for all without unleashing the prospect that new structures would themselves tyrannize the people.

Madison is generally credited as the lead architect of our constitutional design. Animated by his vision of checks and balances, the founders prescribed an intricate network of new institutions, all holding the others to account through carefully distributed powers and chosen through a variety of different methods designed to prevent any one faction from dominating. Through the winter of 1787–1788, as Madison hurriedly worked through his twenty-nine contributions to *The Federalist*, he must have taken no small satisfaction from the intelligence, even the elegance, of their collective achievement.

Madison's hopes for the new nation must also have been sustained by the remarkable display of statesmanship in which he had participated in Philadelphia. Madison famously opined in *The Federalist* No. 51, "If men were angels, no government would be necessary."[7] But, in retirement, he reflected that "there never was an assembly of men, charged with a great & arduous trust, who were more pure in their motives, or more exclusively or anxiously devoted to the object committed to them, than were the members of the Federal Convention of 1787."[8] He had thus seen that, even if divinity is beyond human attainment, our political leaders, properly motivated and organized, could put aside partisan differences and rise to great occasions. The institutional scaffolding that the Constitution erected might even nurture and reward that spirit.

Let us imagine, though, even as he completed his writings as Publius in March 1788, there came a chilly Manhattan night when James Madison's sleep grew fitful. Let us imagine that, perhaps in a moment of unconscious self-doubt, he began to envision the future with a prescience exceeding even that of Benjamin Franklin. In this dream, as I imagine it, Madison began to conceive not the restrained chief executive for which the Framers planned, but an ambitious and overreaching presidency, nurtured too often in its political aggressiveness by an irresponsible Congress and overly deferential courts. A spirit of presidentialism, not republicanism, had become the national government's animating principle. The new electoral college system, designed to promote wise leadership and worthy character, had somehow become a tool for entrenching the power of an ideologically narrow elite. Rather than cultivating the spirit of consensus that animated 1787 Philadelphia, the parties in power, in this alarming dream, routinely cast aside habits and processes born of mutual respect and accommodation in order to advance an all-too-inflexible factional agenda. Surely, this would have been Madison's worst constitutional nightmare. The good news, for Madison, is that he probably never had such a dream. The bad news is that the dream I am hypothesizing would have foreseen all too accurately the real government of the United States of America, especially as it functioned during the Reagan through George W. Bush years.

For the last quarter century, the checks and balances of American government have been increasingly battered by the merger of two powerful currents. One is the gathering concentration of power in the hands of the federal executive, a trend nurtured since the New Deal by Presidents both Democratic and Republican, although at different rates of acceleration. The second current has been the relentless campaign of the right wing of the Republican Party since 1981 to steer the capacities of our national government toward the fulfillment of a conservative social, economic, and foreign policy agenda. Together, the growing concentration of executive power and the campaign for partisan predominance have produced an era of aggressive presidentialism, a theory of government and a pattern of government practice that treat our Constitution as vesting in the President a fixed and expansive category of executive authority largely immune to legislative control or judicial review. This constitutional perfect storm has put the design of our democratic republic at risk, upending many of the norms and informal institutional practices that have helped to sustain the Madisonian checks and balances in our national government, at least since the end of World War II.

The campaign for partisan predominance has sometimes entailed the assertion of congressional or judicial power in constitutionally dubious ways—most notably, the impeachment of President Clinton and the Supreme Court's decision in *Bush v. Gore*. Its gravest implications for day-to-day governance, however, arise from the conjoining of partisanship with the attempted aggrandizement of presidential authority. In order to further its revolutionary policy ambitions, the Reagan Administration developed a more aggressive theory of presidential power than any prior Administration had propounded. In its hands, and during the Administrations of both Presidents Bush, presidentialism took unprecedented new forms, challenging historic conceptions of both legislative and judicial power. The ideological zeal with which these Presidents and their supporters pursued their constitutional vision fully exemplifies the spirit of partisan passion and narrow self-interest that Madison located at the heart of faction.

This is not to let the Clinton Administration off the hook. Even as it disavowed aspects of right-wing constitutional interpretation,[9] the Clinton Administration found some of its tenets congenial for accomplishing its own ends. U.S. participation in the spring 1999 NATO air campaign against Serbia was based on claims of presidential authority arguably more dubious than any since the end of the Vietnam War. After the Republicans took control of Congress in 1994, President Clinton likewise made claims for the presidential control of domestic regulatory policy making that were nearly unprecedented in substance and certainly unparalleled in volume—hoping, no doubt, to reassert his relevance on the national political stage.

The Clinton-era developments illustrate one of the great dangers of presidentialism—its resistance to contraction. The usurpation of authority works as a one-way ratchet. Even if only some Presidents advance executive power unduly as a matter of partisan ideology, all Presidents, whenever their power is challenged, will be tempted to embrace their predecessors' more audacious claims as sources of legal authority and strike out on their own. Unless somehow rebuked, the example of any President asserting authority without a genuine constitutional basis thus becomes historical precedent for the next President committed to the practice of presidentialism whether as a matter of ideological commitment or mere political calculation.

As recent history has unfolded, it is the legal theorists working for our most recent Republican Administrations who have most vigorously championed presidentialism as an accurate reading of what our constitutional Framers historically intended. It is not. Other presidentialist legal thinkers, including advocates for presidentialism under Democratic Administrations, have argued that presidentialism is such good governmental practice that either we should read the Constitution in a more modern vein in order to mandate presidentialism or we should welcome practices of legislative and judicial deference to the President that allow government to behave in a presidentialist fashion. The historical record, however, does not bear out the claims for presidentialism as good practice. If we look at the functioning of our national executive when behaving most consistently with the tenets of presidentialism, we frequently find that the assumption of unilateral presidential authority prompts a narrowness in consultation, and a defensiveness and rigidity in outlook, that degrade the quality of executive decision making. Furthermore, as might have been predicted, presidentialism operates as an ethos of government in a way that undermines other critical values, such as allegiance to the rule of law and respect for coequal branches and divergent political outlooks. As discussed in chapters 4 and 5, the results, made dramatically manifest in the "Bush 43" Administration, have included dangerously irresponsible government lawyering and a fetishizing of presidential prerogative in ways that defy common sense and the public interest. When presidentialist practice is analyzed clearly, it seems to rest on ideas about democracy and the rule of law that are unattractive and deeply unpersuasive.

Of course, the nation sometimes benefits from unilateral presidential action—Washington's proclamation of neutrality, Lincoln's Emancipation Proclamation, and the resolution of the Cuban missile crisis are but three celebrated examples of the many undoubtedly available. But the realization of these benefits does not require anything like the wholesale adoption of aggressive presidentialism, either as constitutional theory or prevailing government practice. In all but the most exceptional circumstances, searching congressional oversight, robust presidential accountability to the rule of law, and a pluralist approach to policy development within the executive branch are all consistent with the level of executive branch energy we need in order to thrive as a nation.

The ambitions of the unilateral presidency cannot be squared with either the presidency envisioned by our Constitution or contemporary needs. Its proponents may argue that the historical conception ought to be replaced with a new unilateral presidency because a more autonomous, less fettered presidency actually works better in the national interest than does a presidency subject to strong checks and balances. But time and time again, it has become evident that Presidents, left relatively unchecked by dialogue with and accountability to the other two branches, behave disastrously. The new unilateral presidency is thus not appealing either as constitutional interpretation or as good institutional design. To put the point another way, the Framers got this right. It is now critical to restore checks and balances to robust health and reinvigorate American democracy so that no narrow faction of the American polity can dominate policy making throughout all our institutions of national government.

Checks and Balances and Democratic Legitimacy

At the heart at our founders' design for a new republican form of government is a web of political institutions structured to hold each other accountable. As Madison explained, it is not enough for the security of liberty that the constitutional text provide for three separate and distinct branches of the national government. It is not sufficient that legislative, executive, and judicial powers should each, in the main, be concentrated chiefly in just one of those branches. Power, he wrote, "is of an encroaching nature" and must "be effectually restrained from passing the limits assigned to it."[10] The separation of powers, in other words, is essential to liberty, but cannot preserve itself without checks and balances.

In the Framers' hands, the key institutional imperative was to structure the national government so that each branch, acting under the influence of foreseeable ambitions and incentives, would keep both itself and its co-ordinate branches within their respective constitutionally assigned roles. In Madison's famous words, protection against tyranny "must be supplied, by so contriving the interior structure of the government as that its several constituent parts may, by their mutual relations, be the means of keeping each other in their proper places."[11] Applying this thought to the new presidency, we would not have to worry about monarchy, because Congress and the judiciary would hold executive ambition in check.

In operation, the new institutional design required some complex calculations. The Framers had to position the branches of the new government to achieve a careful balance of autonomy and interdependence. Examples abound: The President has unilateral authority to establish diplomatic relations with other nations, but cannot make treaties without Senate consent. Congress may oversee the operations of the executive branch, but cannot create or modify administrative authority without enacting a statute subject to presidential veto. The Constitution protects the independence of the federal judiciary with guarantees of salary protection and lifetime tenure for individual judges, but gives Congress the authority to delineate the courts' actual jurisdiction.

Among the most important powers of each branch are the authorities each holds to review the exercise of power by the others. The President, for example, reviews legislation through his veto power and can countermand the exercise of judicial authority by his power of pardon. Congress has not only investigative power with which to review both the President and the judiciary, but exclusive power to impeach and remove any officer of the United States, thus giving it the authority to review, and respond to, individual wrongdoing by federal office holders. The courts have power to review both executive and legislative acts through cases properly brought within their jurisdiction, including the power to nullify, where necessary, the unlawful acts of the other branches. In general, the manner in which each branch deploys its checking powers is entirely within its exclusive discretion.

At the same time, in order that the branches not use their autonomous checking powers with undue disregard for the prerogatives of their coordinate branches, each branch had to be put in a position of partial institutional dependency. For the most part, each branch needs the acquiescence, if not actually the agreement of, the other two branches in order to work its will. Thus, Congress cannot easily legislate without presidential agreement. It cannot execute the laws once passed. Likewise, the President is dependent for most of his initiatives on key officials whom the Senate must confirm and on appropriations that Congress must enact. For its part, the judiciary does not execute its own judgments and depends on Congress for both appropriations and the delimitation of its jurisdiction. Through the combination of the branches' autonomous powers and what might be called their "collaborative powers"—powers that cannot be exercised effectively without the cooperation of other branches—each branch was given both positive incentives to cooperate and weapons to retaliate against uncooperative conduct.

In addition to the prophylactic virtue of constraining power, this system promised an affirmative virtue—fostering deliberation. The multiplicity of institutions, each with different constituencies, organizational structures, modes of selection, and internal decision making processes, would insure that the nation would embark on no program of public policy without the examination of that policy from a wide array of perspectives. This was crucial to the Framers partly for the general reason that, all things being equal, it is better to make important decisions through careful consideration, rather than rashly and without discussion. But a second point was also critical. The Constitution tried to insure that, in the process of deciding upon national affairs, all affected interests would have a genuine opportunity to be heard and to have their interests accounted for in a collective determination of the public interest. In Alexander Hamilton's words: "The oftener [a] measure is brought under examination, the greater the diversity in the situations of those who are to examine it, the less must be the danger of those errors which flow from want of due deliberation, or of those missteps which proceed from the contagion of some common passion or interest."[12] Deliberation among numerous parties embodying a diversity of interests was thus essential to decision making consistent with the public good. In contrast, decision making based on "some common impulse of passion, or of interest," would be tainted by the spirit of "faction"[13] that Madison so decried. The web of new governmental structures was designed, in sum, to help insure that policy outcomes represented something other than "an unjust combination of the majority of the whole."[14]

The Framers called their theory of legitimate government "republicanism." In modern parlance, we recognize their republicanism as an extraordinary advance in both the theory and practice of what we would today call democratic legitimacy. Governments rule legitimately when the relative few who exercise the power of the state are morally entitled to rule. It is the implicit claim of democratic systems that democratic governments are morally entitled to govern because, to the maximum extent possible, democracy promotes two political virtues. First, it fosters a life of autonomous citizenship, in which people experience themselves as free political actors, participating meaningfully in the project of collective self-governance. In its American version, this experience embraces not only the right to vote, but to petition the government, to stand for office, and to associate freely for public, as well as private purposes. Second, democracy respects equally the interests of all citizens, all of whom are entitled to receive full and fair consideration in the making of public policy.[15] Because the very premise of democracy is the presumed moral equality of all persons within the polity, no one's interests can properly be excluded from the community's concern as laws and regulations are adopted that either restrain the scope of individual activity or provide for the distribution of public or private resources.

The special genius of the American Constitution lies in the realization of its Framers that such full and fair consideration of all citizens' interests requires a multiplicity of legitimating mechanisms. That is, the Framers might have provided for a system that relied for legitimacy entirely on a single factor, namely, the electoral accountability of government officials. But they did not. Alternatively, they might have provided for a system that relied entirely on wise and public-minded deliberation, without recourse to popular sentiment. They did not do that either. Instead, they combined elements of what we would now call both representative democracy and deliberative democracy into a unique set of "republican" institutions. These checking and balancing components combine elements of both representative and deliberative legitimacy, while preventing any branch from overstepping its constitutionally assigned bounds. Checks and balances thus operate as both shield and sword for liberty. They protect against the overweening ambition of any one branch of government, while affirmatively supporting the values of political freedom and equal consideration that render government just.

Constitutional Culture and the Modern Attack on
Checks and Balances Norms

Of course, neither fair deliberation nor even the more general hobbling of government's tyrannical impulses, was the Framers' sole objective. First and foremost, they wanted a government that would work and that would work effectively to advance the "permanent and aggregate interests of the community" in both domestic and international affairs. From that standpoint, any government of separated powers poses obvious difficulties. Because a monarchy revolves around a single source of authority that embodies the sovereign power of the state, it can act quickly on behalf of the nation. This is not so for America. In the United States, it is the people who are sovereign, and there is no one source of official authority that is charged with acting unilaterally on their behalf. The Framers thus gave us a form of institutional interdependence that helps to check tyranny and that orients the system toward consensus, but at a price. Their system inevitably entails delays in decision making and a bias in favor of gradualism.

Norms or habits of institutional cooperation are essential to enable a government of this kind—a government of separated powers—to achieve its multiple potential virtues. It is not merely foreseeable, but intended, that the three branches of government experience tension and competition. Friction, to some extent, is a sign of the system at work. But life cannot be all friction. As the British Prime Minister Lord John Russell famously put the point: "Every political constitution in which different bodies share the supreme power is only enabled to exist by the forbearance of those among whom this power is distributed."[16] A system of separated powers, in other words, works only if every branch is committed to effective governance and is willing to hold back from deploying its powers to their extreme theoretical limits. In a separation of powers system designed to embody checks and balances, where powers are allocated to each branch precisely with the purpose of rendering each branch vulnerable to the discretion of the others, some degree of institutional self-restraint is imperative.

To put this point another way, no paper plan for the operation of government can ever be sufficient in and of itself to guarantee the responsible exercise of power, even if it is a plan built on thoughtfully designed checks and balances. A paper plan for government can operate in vastly different ways depending on its participants' commitment to the values that animate that plan and their allegiance to those values in the form of norms or implicit, but widely recognized, rules and customs. Consider, for example, if Congress had early determined on a custom that legislative votes to override presidential vetoes would be automatic—that all members of Congress, on pain of expulsion, would agree to override any presidential veto, irrespective of which members actually voted for the original bill. Such a custom would have all but eliminated the President's capacity to influence the design of legislation. Likewise, what if Presidents automatically pardoned all criminal defendants of their particular party or Congress decided that judges who rendered unpopular decisions were, for that reason alone, guilty of a "high crime or misdemeanor," warranting removal from office? Such practices would have enervated what we now think of as judicial independence. When we bring these possibilities to mind, it becomes evident that it is not only or even primarily the existence of checks and balances on paper that preserves liberty against government ambition; it is the web of attitudes, beliefs, and informal practices surrounding implementation of the Constitution that gives life to the document's underlying purposes. We can call this web of attitudes, beliefs, and practices our "constitutional culture."

Ordinarily, at least four factors in the American system coincide to produce the culture of self-restraint that averts any serious breakdown of government. One is the internalization within each institution of norms of deference for the core capacities of the other two branches. The history of federal court jurisdiction provides a powerful case in point. The past two centuries are replete with examples of the federal judiciary rendering decisions antagonistic to the views and interests of the elected branches of government. The judicial invalidation of President Truman's seizure of the steel mills and the overturning of anti-flag-burning laws are two well-known historical illustrations. Yet, the elected branches have rarely retaliated in any significant way. The President has rarely—and never in modern history—refused to enforce or recognize judicial orders. Congress, despite numerous proposals to do so, has never ousted the courts from all jurisdiction to decide a category of cases in which Congress, from a political standpoint, would probably prefer judicial silence. It seems impossible to explain the forbearance of the elected branches from substantially curtailing federal jurisdiction in such controversial areas as abortion, school prayer, or desegregation unless we regard that self-restraint as a sign of our elected officials' allegiance to the near inviolability of the judicial function as conveyed by Article III of the Constitution. This is what I mean by a habit or a norm of deference.

A second factor is a common belief in the legitimacy and necessity of active, problem-solving government. Frequently, even amid deep policy disagreement between the executive and legislative branches, public policy compromises emerge in the solution of public problems because both elected branches are committed to demonstrating their capacity to respond in some constructive way to public challenges. Powerful examples from the 1990s include tax and budget reform under President George H. W. Bush and welfare reform under President Clinton. In each case, an ideologically reluctant President went along with congressional initiative out of a felt imperative to respond to a widely perceived public problem and to share in the credit for its solution.

Third, each branch—but each of the elected branches especially—has historically been motivated to represent a broad range of public opinion on critical issues. Even when the elected branches disagree significantly on public policy, each has usually been motivated to seek the approval of a wide spectrum of American voters. This impulse was significantly evident in President Clinton's judicial nominating strategy, in which he worked with a Republican-controlled Senate to confirm potential judges who were notably centrist in their views, and in the Republican Congress's 1996 enactment of line-item veto authority, which threatened to empower a Democratic President, but which was perceived to be widely popular among the national electorate.

Finally, each branch of the government is structured internally so as to promote deliberation, thus increasing the likelihood that multiple points of view will be heard and given time to help shape long-term policy outcomes. Congress, for example, is divided into two houses, which must concur in a legislative proposal in order that it be enacted. The length of terms and the geographical basis of representation is different in the two houses, which, originally, were also selected by different methods. The judiciary consists of a Supreme Court and lower courts through which legal interpretation evolves in a highly formal, multivocal way. Article III of the Constitution gives those judges who officiate over the courts authorized by that article lifetime tenure, insuring that, at any given moment, the judiciary is populated by judges whose pre-judicial careers exhibit a variety of ideological and political predispositions. Even the constitutional text describing the executive branch, the most unitary of the three branches, contemplates that the President may seek advice from the heads of "departments." Deliberation was an intended feature of the new government through and through.

Government lawyers, if they perform their jobs well, play a central role in maintaining the ethos of deliberation that was the Framers' hope. Decision making is most effectively deliberative if it involves a wide variety of perspectives, each shedding light on whatever issue is under discussion.[17] In formal deliberative settings, such as an argument before the Supreme Court or debates on the floor of Congress, contending perspectives are literally embodied in different human beings, all physically present and asserting their various points of view. Decisions within the executive branch, however, are most frequently made in a potentially more insulated environment. The only voices literally present in a particular policy conversation may be those of a high-level presidential appointee, some lower-level presidential appointees, and civil servants who are most directly accountable to these presidential appointees. In such settings, it would require some form of special self-discipline for those immediately involved in the decision to actually concern themselves with perspectives and interests other than the partisan agenda they likely all share. This is especially so for the vast majority of decisions that will never be reviewed in Congress because they are too low-visibility and that will never be reviewed in court because they do not affect the specific interests of identifiable individuals in a way that would ordinarily entitle them to call those decisions into question through litigation.

Seen in this light, a critical function of the law in operation—the law as embodied for the executive branch in judicial opinions rendered by the courts and statutes enacted by Congress—is to make manifest the range of interests and concerns that would not otherwise be vigorously articulated when key decisions are made. It is precisely in this way that the rule of law is a fundamental day-to-day check on the spirit of faction in government affairs. Executive branch lawyers, residing in every agency of government, make this check real because they advise on virtually every important administrative decision and focus decision makers' attention on whatever law is relevant. When the executive branch in 2009 attends, for example, to the Voting Rights Act of 1965[18] or the 1969 National Environmental Policy Act[19] or the Supreme Court's 1974 decision in *United States v. Nixon,*[20] the Administration can, in a sense, hear the multiple voices of earlier times that themselves had to reach consensus in order to create binding public policy. These voices are virtually, even if not physically present, and their recognition can serve as a buffer against the more immediate passions of partisanship or the undisciplined pursuit of self-interest. Conscientious lawyering insures that contending perspectives are brought to bear whenever current decision makers act, and is thus a critical element in preserving the democratic legitimacy of American government.

The attack on checks and balances between 1981 and 2009 can very much be seen as an assault on a constitutional culture built on checks and balances norms. Each branch has been deploying its powers with increasing disrespect for its coequal branches, and the escalating institutional conflict between President and Congress most especially has created a level of mutual disregard that would have been essentially unthinkable at any prior moment in modern times. It is important to be clear on what is new about this. It is not unprecedented for one branch of government to chafe against restraints imposed by others or even to undertake initiatives pressing the edges of its constitutional prerogatives. The overall system has some capacity to self-correct for such tensions. If, however, one looks at the historic points of greatest tension among the branches—Andrew Jackson's battle against the National Bank, the impeachment of Andrew Johnson, or the attempted court-packing of President Franklin Roosevelt—they have generally been characterized by an impulse that is absent from the current trend. In refusing to sign legislation that would recharter the Bank, Jackson was standing fast against an institution widely regarded as supporting the interests of creditors against the interests of the more numerous, but less moneyed classes. Congress enacted the Tenure in Office Act hoping to provoke Andrew Johnson into a violation of law that would provide formal grounds for impeachment, but its plain motivation was Johnson's opposition to Reconstruction, which Congress had helped impose in order to end white caste rule in the South. Roosevelt proposed court-packing, an obvious challenge to the political independence of the Supreme Court, in response to what he regarded as the Court's unwillingness to legitimate legislative and executive measures designed to relieve the Depression and for which the elected branches enjoyed a popular mandate. Thus, each of these earlier assaults on conventional ways of doing business was arguably in the attempted service of more democracy. Even though checks and balances were compromised by such earlier interbranch battles, the challenges to business as usual tended to be supportive of the very aspirations for democratic legitimacy that checks and balances are also supposed to advance.

The impulses behind recent breaches of interbranch accommodation, however, were decidedly antidemocratic. Consider, for example, the 1995 budget showdown between President Clinton and Congress. Congressional Republicans threatened to withhold funding from the executive branch entirely unless President Clinton relented on a series of budget priorities that had been the core of his successful 1992 campaign for the presidency.[21] Congress has the formal authority to defund the entire executive branch because the Constitution vests the power of the purse in Congress without any express textual limitation. The problem is that, if any Congress takes this authority to extremes, the power to hobble the courts and all but dismantle the entire executive branch could obviously undermine one of the Constitution's fundamental organizational premises, namely, that the government consists of three coequal branches. Nonetheless, the 1995 Republicans did not relent in their demands until the nation sustained two across-the-board shutdowns of government agencies, in November and December, 1995, of seven and twenty-one days, respectively.[22] Congress and the President finally agreed in April 1996 on appropriations for Fiscal Year 1996, which had actually begun on October 1, 1995.[23] Congress could hardly argue that its position was in service of democracy; on every issue drawn between them in this debate—funding for education, environmental protection, Medicare and Medicaid—majority public opinion favored the President's position.[24]

Another conspicuous example of the antidemocratic assault on the culture of checks and balances consists of the impeachment and trial of President William Jefferson Clinton. The December 1998 House vote for Articles of Impeachment brought together two key subplots designed to terminate the Clinton presidency.[25] One was the Whitewater investigation, a prolonged special prosecutor investigation into a nearly impenetrable series of allegations regarding the peripheral involvement of President Clinton and his wife, Hillary Rodham Clinton, in a series of Arkansas business dealings dating back to the late 1970s.[26] Twelve people ultimately were convicted of a variety of offenses in connection with the Whitewater real estate venture and the related failure of the Madison Guaranty Savings and Loan Association. After an investigation that lasted more than six years, it was ultimately determined that neither of the Clintons should face any charges relating to the Whitewater matter.[27]

The second subplot (or combination of subplots) involved allegations against Clinton for sexual misconduct. These stemmed originally from a suit initiated by Paula Jones, a former Arkansas state employee, accusing President Clinton of allegedly sexually harassing her in 1991, when Clinton was still governor of Arkansas. Clinton's claim that Presidents ought to be immune, while in office, from civil lawsuits arising from alleged misconduct that occurred prior to taking office as President was rejected in May 1997 by the U.S. Supreme Court.[28] As the Jones suit proceeded in a federal district court in Arkansas, Jones's lawyers were tipped that, from 1995 to 1997, President Clinton had engaged in an extramarital sexual relationship with Monica Lewinsky, a former White House intern. In January 1998, both Lewinsky and President Clinton denied the affair, and the Special Division of the D.C. Circuit responsible for appointing and overseeing independent counsel extended Kenneth Starr's jurisdiction to consider whether Lewinsky and others had perjured themselves or suborned perjury in connection with the Jones case. A day later, President Clinton denied his relationship with Lewinsky in a videotaped deposition.

Although the trial court ultimately dismissed *Jones v. Clinton* on a motion for summary judgment, Starr subpoenaed President Clinton to testify in front of a federal grand jury. During that testimony, Clinton acknowledged his affair with Lewinsky, but denied that he had lied or withheld evidence or urged others to do so. Less than a month later, Starr submitted to Congress an extensive report concluding that Clinton had perjured himself. On September 11, the House voted to release the report, and on October 8, voted 258–176 for an impeachment investigation that resulted in the House Judiciary Committee's approval of four Articles of Impeachment, mostly by straight party-line vote. On December 19, the lame-duck House passed one article alleging grand jury perjury by a vote of 228–206, with five Democrats supporting the article and five Republicans opposing it. An obstruction of justice article passed 221–212, but likely would have been defeated if the vote had been held upon the January 1999 seating of the 106th Congress, in which the Democrats held five more seats. The two other articles, alleging perjury in the Jones deposition and misstatements in Clinton's written responses to Judiciary Committee questions, were both rejected. On February 12, 1999, the Republican-controlled Senate voted to acquit Clinton by votes of 55–45 on the perjury count and 50–50 on the obstruction of justice count; no Democrat voted for either article. The Republicans, who would have needed 67 votes to prevail, could not achieve a clear majority on either article, even in a Senate in which they held 55 seats.

House Republicans might well have said that their pursuit of President Clinton did not transgress any express legal limitation on their impeachment power, but, as with the 1995 budget showdown, the Republican Congress was risking, perhaps even seeking, the destabilization of a coordinate branch of government through the deployment of its formal powers to an extreme degree. It could not credibly be asserted that Clinton's alleged misconduct put either the welfare of the nation or the strength of our constitutional system at risk. Not surprisingly, the Republicans never managed to arouse anything close to majority public support for the impeachment,[29] and President Clinton's approval ratings rose to astonishing peacetime levels as the proceedings against him intensified.[30] Although the impeachment failed, the diversion of the President's time, energy, and attention in defending against such an effort was dangerous, and the episode stands as an ominous institutional precedent for seeking to remove a President based all but entirely on partisan animus.

A third example of the spirit of faction undermining the constitutional culture of institutional self-restraint is the Supreme Court's strange role in determining the outcome of the 2000 presidential elections. While it is virtually certain that a plurality of Floridians who cast their ballots for President thought they had voted for Vice President Al Gore, after a month of legal wrangling and contested recounts mandated by the Florida Supreme Court, the right-wing-dominated U.S. Supreme Court called a halt to the vote counting, virtually directing that the Florida—and thus national—election be awarded to Bush. The Supreme Court initially involved itself based upon an utterly bogus legal issue and then resolved the case as it did based on entirely novel and substantially implausible legal reasoning. As a consequence, *Bush v. Gore* will perhaps stand forever as the Court's most striking expression of contempt for modern democratic norms.

Although much can be and has been said by way of critiquing the Court's opinion, its most conspicuous defect from a checks and balances perspective is the majority's willingness to abandon the Court's prior commitment to one of its most important norms of self-restraint, the political question doctrine. Even though the Court has the authority to overturn actions by the elected branches, it has long recognized that the constitutional order works best if some constitutional matters are authoritatively left to be resolved by those branches. In this respect, *Bush v. Gore* can be instructively compared to *Nixon v. United States,*[31] in which the Court confronted a challenge by an impeached and convicted federal judge to the procedures by which the Senate had removed him from office. Rather than taking evidence in plenary session, the Senate had delegated that function to a committee. The Senate as a whole met only to review the Committee's report and to hear such arguments as Judge Nixon was prepared to offer on his own behalf. Nixon argued to the Supreme Court that this procedure denied him his constitutional right to be "tried" by the Senate, as the Constitution says.

The Supreme Court unanimously determined that it would not intervene in the matter. The majority, speaking through Chief Justice Rehnquist, held that the constitutional sufficiency of Senate procedures for adjudicating impeachment controversies was a matter to be resolved exclusively by the Senate itself. The constitutional vesting in the Senate of "the sole Power to try all Impeachments" was deemed "a textually demonstrable commitment of the issue [by the Constitution] to a coordinate political department."[32] That is, the Court concluded that the Constitution meant for the final resolution of this particular legal question to lie outside the judiciary.

Moreover, the majority said, the word "try" in Article I of the Constitution was too vague and general to yield "judicially manageable standards" for what would amount to a constitutionally sufficient trial.[33] In other words, the Justices insisted that they could not work out a sufficiently stable and predictable definition of the verb "to try," against which to measure whether Judge Nixon had actually gotten a trial; it was as if the Constitution had used a word like "cute" or "tasty," about which there could be infinite argument. This was unmistakably dramatic testimony to the Court's determination to respect Congress's impeachment authorities. Nine Justices determined that, for purposes of enforcing Article I of the Constitution, federal judges—people who conduct trials for a living—were unable to determine in a sufficiently rigorous way what ought to count as a "trial."

Nixon v. United States rests on sound institutional judgment. Impeachment is the sole constitutionally designated process for achieving judicial accountability for wrongdoing. It would have appeared an unseemly conflict of interest for the Court to have reserved to the judiciary the power to oversee that very process. But the argument for the Court eschewing involvement in the 2000 presidential election was surely even more compelling. For sitting Supreme Court Justices to adjudicate which person shall be entitled to name their successors does unmistakable violence to constitutional checks and balances. Article II of the Constitution and the Twelfth Amendment, which create our system of presidential elections, quite plainly embody a textually demonstrable commitment to Congress of the power to resolve all issues related to the proper tabulation of electoral votes. Indeed, Congress has enacted a detailed statutory scheme to make just that process possible.

Of course, Congress may not have conducted itself any better than the Court; this was, after all, the Clinton impeachment Congress. But, even if Congress messed up, even if it cut deals behind closed doors, and even if it failed to deal reasonably with Florida's difficulties in achieving an accurate count, a simple fact remains: if the people of the United States were unhappy with Congress on any such account, those members of Congress deemed responsible could have been voted out of office. No such recourse against unelected judges is possible. One could hardly imagine a set of decisions in which democratic accountability is more important than those involved in the legitimate political resolution of an election contest. By contrast, despite the ineffable odor of partisanship that hangs over the Court's opinion in *Bush v. Gore*, there was no politically appropriate response to be levied against the responsible Justices themselves. The Court that decided

Nixon v. United States should surely have known better—every Justice in the *Bush v. Gore* majority was already on the Court and voted for the result in *Nixon v. United States*.

Bush v. Gore corresponds with the other episodes described because it stands as an astonishing departure from institutional norms with regard to interbranch relations. Never before has the Supreme Court directly implicated itself in the political selection of the authorities in charge of another branch of government. It will be an enduring source of shame to our legal system that, in resolving a dispute over the world's most important elected office, the Supreme Court penned an opinion in which our national commitment to democracy—indeed, the very word, "democracy"—does not appear.

The Most Dangerous Attack on Checks and Balances:
Iran-Contra and Modern Presidentialism

The episodes just recounted were detrimental to American democracy, but do not represent partisan ambition in its most dangerous form. That distinction belongs to the marriage of partisan ambition with the long-term and bipartisan trend toward increasing executive power. With the end of World War II, the advent of the cold war and its national security preoccupations launched a steady accretion in unprecedented presidential authority. In the aggressive presidentialism of the Reagan Administration, America finally saw what would happen when the bipartisan ambitions of America's Presidents became fully conjoined with the political agenda of a zealous political faction.

The Iran-Contra scandal is perhaps the most crystalline example of the consequences. To understand the constitutional magnitude of Iran-Contra, we must remember that Congress is able to secure its position as coequal with the executive and the judiciary because it has three key authorities: its control over "the purse," its powers of legislation, and its authority to investigate. Congress would hardly be a serious counterweight to the other two branches without these powers. Any attempt by another branch to circumvent entirely this triumvirate of powers would obviously breach an implicit norm of interbranch deference. It is likewise critical to note that, despite the President's pivotal role on the international stage, Congress's combined arsenal of fiscal, legislative, and investigative powers is no less important in foreign than in domestic affairs. Congress has the express power to regulate foreign commerce. It regulates immigration and defines offenses under international law. The ratification of treaties and the appointment of ambassadors require the Senate's assent. Congress has the power to provide for the support of our military and to declare war. And, of course, there may be foreign policy ramifications, both direct and indirect, to Congress's exercise of legislative powers in the domestic arena, as well as in its exercise of its fiscal authorities.

Between 1984 and 1986, the Reagan Administration committed a significant assault on all of these powers—legislative, fiscal, and investigative—in an attempt to oust Congress from foreign policy making influence with regard to Nicaragua. Congress, in line with clear public sentiment, had proscribed the use of military or intelligence appropriations to aid military forces (the "Contras") seeking to overthrow the government of Nicaragua.[34] In a stunning three-pronged attack on Congress's authority in this area, the executive sought to raise money for the Contras independently of Congress (in evasion of Congress's fiscal powers), facilitate that fund raising through arms sales that flouted applicable federal law (in evasion of Congress's legislative powers), and to lie about it, even under oath (in evasion of Congress's investigative powers).

In November 1986, while denying that the deals represented a trade of "arms for hostages"—American hostages held by radical Islamic groups in Lebanon with ties to Iran—President Reagan confirmed reports that the United States over the previous two years had facilitated six sales of antitank missiles, antiaircraft missiles, and spare parts for missile systems to Iran[35] that were unlawful under various statutes regulating the international sale of arms.[36] National Security Council (NSC) staff facilitated the diversion of profits from the arms sales to the support the Contras.[37] In brief, NSC staffer Lt. Col. Oliver North helped set up a nominally private company through which to funnel proceeds from the arms sales to the Contras—funds that belonged to the United States and could lawfully be spent pursuant only to an appropriation or other legal authority.[38] No such authority had been enacted. When the web of operations became public, North and a host of other officials, including National Security Adviser John Poindexter and former National Security Adviser Robert McFarlane, lied to Congress, destroyed evidence, and unlawfully withheld information from investigators.[39] Seven officials were convicted of these crimes, although the convictions of North and Poindexter were set aside on the ground that the cases against them were tainted by evidence that they had supplied voluntarily to Congress under a grant of immunity.[40] A prolonged independent counsel investigation came to an end in 1993, after President

George H. W. Bush, following his loss in the 1992 elections, pardoned six high officials who had either been convicted of Iran-Contra offenses or were under continuing investigation.

All of this might be dismissed as an isolated scandal without lasting political implications except that executive branch Republicans in subsequent Administrations were all but unrepentant about it. President Reagan's Vice President and successor, George H. W. Bush, adopted a remorseless view of the events, signaling a clear lack of understanding as to their constitutional significance. Specifically, he embraced the view of Oliver North that efforts to bring legal accountability to those involved in the scandal were merely attempting to "criminalize policy differences." For its part, the George W. Bush Administration appointed two of the officials who admitted to misleading Congress in this affair to significant policy positions: Elliot Abrams became Deputy National Security Adviser and John Poindexter was named Director of the controversial Information Awareness Office at the Defense Advanced Projects Research Agency, perhaps the most important government agency for funding basic and applied research for the Department of Defense. It is clear that Reagan's conservative successors actually regarded the Iran-Contra scandal as acceptable executive branch behavior.

But there is an even larger point to be made here. As serious as may be abuses of power by both Congress and the Supreme Court, it is the President who, at the start of the twenty-first century, poses the most profound threat to our checks and balances system. First, as Iran-Contra demonstrates, it is the President who has the greatest capacity to act in secret and without the assistance of the other two branches. Had details of the Iranian arms deal not leaked through a foreign journalist, we may never have learned of the Reagan Administration's assault on Congress's appropriations and foreign affairs powers. In contrast, the impeachment of Bill Clinton and *Bush v. Gore* were ignominious, but public events. Thus, to the extent that transparency fosters accountability, it is the executive branch with its ability to operate secretly that is the most worrisome.

Second, both Congress and the judiciary have to muster collective majorities to accomplish their bad ends. Before another impeachment as irresponsible as the Clinton impeachment occurs, there will again have to be 218 votes in the House to support it. Presidents can mobilize their staffs much more easily than Speakers can mobilize legislative majorities. A majority on a federal appellate court or on the Supreme Court may be easier to muster than a majority in Congress, but courts are inherently restrained by the knowledge that they cannot execute their own judgments—it is the executive branch and the legislative branch that would have to implement. Although this is an imperfect institutional check to be sure, judicial awareness of this limitation poses at least some impediment to irresponsible action by the courts that the executive does not confront. Judicial interference with checks and balances is a less worrisome prospect also because courts lack the power of initiative that rests with the elected branches. They cannot file their own cases.

And the President is the most dangerous branch for two other reasons, as well. All of the impediments I have mentioned to congressional and judicial action in defiance of checks and balances are institutional weaknesses, as well, in mustering an effective response to presidential usurpation. Time and political inertia are invariably on the side of whichever branch can deploy its independent resources with the least encumbrance. And, of course, to the extent secrecy is not the President's most pressing concern, he has an administrative and military apparatus potentially at his disposal that neither Congress nor the courts can match. In terms of mobilizing efficiently and effectively for deleterious ends, the President has profound institutional advantages over the other two "coequal" branches.

It is also worth underscoring that the dangers of presidentialism do not confine themselves to foreign affairs. Foreign and military affairs provide the ripest context for presidentialism because the Constitution confers on the President more robust powers in foreign than in domestic affairs, and, in foreign and military affairs, the President often acts in relative secrecy. Yet, as the nation saw during the Bush 43 Administration, a President determined on a course of domestic policy—such as forestalling all government regulation aimed at addressing global climate change—can pursue such a policy largely without regard to the other branches through a combination of strategic appointments and bureaucratic discipline. Under the theory of the unitary presidency, explored in chapter 2, the President can effectively make environmental policy in this way, even though the Constitution gives the President no authority at all with regard to the domestic health and environmental welfare of the American people.

The Campaign against Deliberative Legitimacy and Its Causes

Each of the critical episodes I have recounted involved a destabilizing and antidemocratic initiative by a branch of the national government while in the control of the current, very conservative generation of Republican Party leadership. Former White House Counsel John Dean has suggested a link between the GOP's embrace of unbridled executive power and an

authoritarian personality style that may be drawn to right-wing ideology.[41]
It is not hard to spin other hypotheses centered in ideology and psychology. It could be argued there is a link between the GOP's business orientation and its comfort level with a style of leadership that emulates corporate
values of hierarchy and command. It is not hard to see a paternalistic, even
masculinist strain in the practice of presidentialism that might appeal to
party members ill at ease with changing gender roles in American society.

Without discounting these possibilities—they are not at all mutually
exclusive—it may be more plausible to trace the roots of our current quan-
dary to institutional and structural causes. I say this for two reasons. First,
there is truly no necessary link between political conservatism per se and
assaults against checks and balances. Indeed, traditional conservatism
might well be expected to be hostile to recent extreme claims of executive
power, as shown by the prominence of such conservative commentators as
Bob Barr, John Dean, Mickey Edwards, and Bruce Fein among the Bush 43
Administration's most vocal critics. Second, there is nothing ideologically
pure about the right wing's embrace of presidentialism. Between 1994 and
2001, with a Democrat in the White House and Republicans in charge of
Congress, congressional assaults on the prerogatives of the presidency were
brutal. It was Republican right-wingers who drove both the 1995 budget
showdown and the Clinton impeachment. Thus, while it is fair to say that
the dominant constitutional outlook among conservative legal thinkers has
clearly been antagonistic to checks and balances, the embrace of "presidentialism" by party leaders seems at least as much a matter of opportunism
as conviction.

For these reasons, my hypothesis is that the repeated willingness of the
Republican Party's most conservative elements to embrace the constitutional theory of presidentialism is rooted primarily in historically contingent
institutional circumstance, including the changing social and ideological
character of the party. Political scientists have documented that, since the
1970s, the diversity of each major political party's base has declined, "reducing internal conflicts and making more unified party voting more likely."[42]
Each political party, especially in the House of Representatives, has moved
closer to the voting preferences of its ideological base—so much so that
there is little overlap in voting behavior between "moderate Republicans"
and "conservative Democrats," especially in the House.

Yet, the phenomenon has not been identical for both parties. The Republican shift to a base of support that is more rural, more affluent, and
more disproportionately white has given that party an activist base that is
far less likely than the Democratic base to embody substantial divergences

of economic, social, and cultural interests. Thus, although the general drift of the Democratic Party has been decidedly liberal, the dynamics of those areas in which the Democratic Party holds dominance—New York or Chicago, for example—pose significantly greater challenges for the party in mediating differences among its core constituents. The party has even tried, while moving leftward, to hold on to its well-organized pro-business constituencies, and has been more successful than the Republican Party at attracting the involvement of minorities or the poor. As a result, norms of deliberation and consensus building are inescapable elements of Democratic political strategy; the party cannot afford any of its contentious constituencies to regard itself as utterly neglected. Republicans, by contrast, have prospered by insisting on a level of party discipline that simply would be impossible without a far more homogeneous base of party activists.

The Republicans Party's increasingly narrow ideological base and homogeneous constituency[43] reinforce the attractiveness of its conservative thought leaders' opposition to constitutional views that embrace dissent, deliberation, pluralism, and accommodation. Between 1995 and 2006, the Republican leadership of the House of Representatives showed little flexibility in dealing even with intraparty dissent, and abrogated much of the 1994 "Contract with America" designed to curb what Republicans then said were Democratic abuses of majority power.[44] The mutual reinforcement of party demographics and a narrow ideology that is hostile to deliberative democratic legitimacy is what signals that the breaches of interbranch norms reflect a genuine political tendency, and not just a series of unconnected political misadventures.

This might not matter, especially if conventional avenues of political competition made the matter easy to correct. But they do not. The judiciary, of course, is not elected and possesses lifetime tenure. Thus, even if outrage over *Bush v. Gore* were more widespread, no electoral retaliation against the majority Justices would be possible. Perhaps more important is the fact that the antimajoritarian composition of the Senate and the antidemocratic bias it lends to the electoral college system play greatly into the hands of an ideologically narrow-banded party that is widely dispersed geographically. That is because the U.S. population that resides in Republican-dominated states resides in states that are smaller and thus overrepresented in Congress, especially in the Senate.

The 2000 presidential election proved the point dramatically. Each state currently casts one electoral vote for each of its Senators and one for each member of the House of Representatives. Thus, of the 271 electoral votes credited to George W. Bush in 2000, sixty represented the Senate-based electoral votes coming from each of the thirty states he won. Yet, the population of those states accounts for slightly under half of the total U.S. population.[45] A more democratic electoral account—albeit one still overrepresenting the smallest states—would give each state a slate of electors based only on its seats in the House of Representatives, which is more reflective of population. Giving the District of Columbia only one elector, equivalent to the minimum number of House members accorded to every state, the electoral count under this method would have been 225 for Gore to 211 for Bush, rather than 271 for Bush and 266 for Gore. In other words, Gore lost not because we have an electoral college, but because we have an electoral college that is so profoundly malapportioned by state population.

The 2002 Senate elections confirmed the pattern. The Republicans took fifty-one seats. However, the population they represented—crediting them with half the population in those states in which the Senators belong to different parties—comprised only 44.6 percent of the U.S. population that lives within the fifty states. Indeed, even in losing their Senate majority in the 2006 midterm elections, Republicans managed to hold forty-nine seats, even though their Senators in the 110th Congress represent only 36.2 per cent of the U.S. population that lives in the fifty states. In short, the more widespread geographical distribution of the Republicans, despite their narrower ideological appeal, assures them disproportionate influence in both the executive and legislative branches. For this reason alone, it is not surprising that President George H. W. Bush was not fatally handicapped by the Iran-Contra affair and that public displeasure over the 1995 budget battle and impeachment did not cost Republicans control of Congress in 2000, 2002, or 2004.

Checks and balances—the design principle adopted by the Framers of our Constitution—are intended to promote consensus and accommodation in the formulation of national government policy. While led by the Republican right wing, each branch of the national government during the last quarter century has contributed to an erosion of checks and balances in favor of solidifying right-wing Republican policy control, most especially in the form of an increasingly unilateral presidency. The GOP was facilitated in its pursuit of this vision by antidemocratic structural features of the national government, namely, the makeup of the Senate and of the electoral college. Recent elections have shown that these features do not make GOP control inevitable, but they do insure that the states in which the Republican Right is strongest do have entrenched disproportionate influence.

Many Americans hoped that the 2006 midterm election would suffice to correct the system, but the inability of the Democratic Congress to impose meaningful controls on the Iraq War, despite its huge unpopularity, proved the contrary. At least, the Republican loss of majority control in both Houses of Congress positioned congressional Democrats to be far more assertive in conducting oversight, thus seeming to restore one kind of institutional check glaringly absent for the previous six years. But this misses a crucial point. The right-wing assault on checks and balances has accelerated what has actually been a bipartisan trend in aggrandizing executive power. The fact that Bill Clinton did not preposterously claim constitutional authority for his own version of aggressive presidentialism does not belie this trend. The groundwork has been laid for an executive branch dangerously excessive in its exercise of effectively unchecked power, no matter who is in the White House.

Democrats may well think this is not a bad thing. After so many years of aggressive right-wing executive policy making, America might benefit from an equally aggressive presidency dedicated to increasing social equality, addressing critical issues of health care financing and environmental protection, and repairing America's reputation abroad. Democrats must surely be tempted to think that. But looking at the unilateral presidency in action shows us that the growth of executive power is all too likely to produce dysfunctional government, no matter which party is in control. Adopted as an ethos of government, aggressive presidentialism breeds an insularity, defensiveness, and even arrogance within the executive branch that undermines sound decision making, discounts the rule of law, and attenuates the role of authentic deliberation in shaping political outcomes. One may believe—as I do—that the overall direction of American public policy in recent years has been dreadful and still value accommodation and consensus building as part of the process of changing that direction. The post–World War II American presidency is quite strong enough to do the job without making outlandish claims for near-monarchical executive authorities.

The next chapters explain why the Constitution does not support our extreme contemporary presidentialism and explore the harm to government that results from its practice. In the final chapter, I conclude with an overall perspective on the implications of presidentialism for democracy and a set of recommendations for how to move the country back toward more robust checks and balances. Some of those recommendations will speak to changes within government that judges and elected officials could implement in fairly straightforward fashion now. But these will not be enough. If the contemporary assault on checks and balances is most deeply attributable to a convergence of institutional structures and political circumstances that rewards the spirit of factionalism and enables presidentialism to succeed as a political strategy, then an adequate response must look to a combination of those institutional design issues that preoccupied James Madison and considerations of cultural context that give life to institutional design. Madison's first contribution to Hamilton's project concluded with the promise, "In the extent and proper structure of the Union, . . . we behold a republican remedy for the diseases most incident to republican government."[46] Our contemporary challenge is to find democratic remedies for the ailments of twenty-first century American democracy.

2

Checks and Balances
in Law and History

The presidency is both a political institution and a constitutional office. Hence, the proper scope of presidential power is a question not only of politics, but also of law. The campaign to "imperialize" the presidency has been a campaign fought not only in the Oval Office or in the halls of Congress, but also in courtrooms, lawyers' offices, and scholarly law reviews. Because of the law's complexity, however, this is a battle whose terms are not always transparent.

Part of what makes the legal debate complex is that it is multilayered, but not symmetrical. On one side of the debate are *presidentialists,* advocates of what former Vice President Al Gore has perhaps most famously criticized as "the unilateral executive."[1] They interpret the constitutional design as creating a largely autonomous executive branch, in which the President enjoys a robust range of inherent authorities, both foreign and domestic, which are beyond the power of Congress to regulate or the authority of the courts to review. If they are right, then we are legally required to have a unilateral presidency, unless the Constitution is to be amended.

On the other side are those who might most accurately be called the constitutional *pluralists.* Pluralists interpret the checks and balances system to emphasize the roles that the Constitution assigns to the multiple institutions of our national government in holding each other to account. In the pluralist view, the scope of permissible presidential initiative depends very much on the actions of Congress and the courts.[2]

There is, however, a potential disconnect between the debates over constitutional theory and the realities of actual government practice. Assume that the presidentialists are right and the President is legally entitled to exercise unilateral authority over a wide range of domestic and national affairs. In theory, such a President would be entitled to decide unilaterally to create a form of governance that was highly consultative with Congress and open to significant debate within the executive. If the President has unilateral power, he could unilaterally decide he wants to behave in a politically pluralist fashion.

The converse is also true. Even if the Constitution permits Congress and the courts to check the presidency, they are not legally compelled to do so. In exercising their own discretion, judges and legislators may choose to be so deferential or so acquiescent toward the President that the pluralist presidency in operation could look a lot like the unilateral presidency that the presidentialists prefer. There is thus an important distinction to be drawn between a description of the presidency in terms of the powers that formally attach to the office—what might be called "the legal presidency"—and a description of the presidency in terms of how particular Presidents decide to deploy those formal powers—which we can call "the behavioral presidency."

It is just on this point, however, that the contest between presidentialism and pluralism is asymmetrical. In general, Presidents want more, not less unilateral power. Presidential performance is typically measured by accomplishment, and the pace and volume of accomplishment for which Presidents can take full credit can be diminished to the extent that Presidents have to take the time to accommodate Congress and the courts in bringing their initiatives to fruition. Presidents' lives are easier, politically speaking, the more authority they can wield without accountability to the other two branches. Thus, if the presidentialists are right about the nature of the *legal presidency,* they will almost certainly get their way in terms of the operation of the *behavioral presidency.* A President who is legally entitled to exercise power unilaterally will almost surely want to use that power to consolidate, not to diffuse presidential authority—and we will have a unilateral presidency in both theory and operation. Under a presidentialist regime, it is not clear how or why public pressure to conduct executive branch affairs in a more pluralist mode would have any effect.

On the other hand, even if the pluralists are right about the law, Americans still run a never-ending risk of an excessively unilateral executive. That is because both Congress and the courts have significant incentives to defer to Presidents, even when they technically have authority to hold Presidents in check. Congressional members from the President's party may be deferential to preserve what they perceive to be the overall strength of their party. Congress may prefer to keep public attention focused on the President with regard to hard policy decisions, so that Congressional members of either party do not pay a price at election time for unpopular outcomes. This is a common explanation, for example, of why Congress tends to be so quiescent in presidential military adventures.

For their part, courts become involved in disputes over executive authority only episodically and are anxious about decision making in areas where they might lack expertise or could be perceived as intruding in policy making, as opposed to legal interpretation. Judges, moreover, are well aware of the limits that exist to their remedial powers should they decide an Administration is violating the law. In extreme cases, they may defer to the President out of concern that judicial aggressiveness will simply be met by defiance. Although not uttered in a contest over executive power, the reported remark of Andrew Jackson, "John Marshall has made his decision, now let him enforce it,"[3] looms large in the folklore of interbranch relations. In more mundane contexts, courts are simply aware that even formal compliance with judicial judgment may entail little change in the actual operation of the executive branch. The Supreme Court, for example, issued a much-celebrated decision in 2007 rejecting the positions of the Environmental Protection Agency under George W. Bush (a) that the EPA lacked legal authority to regulate carbon emissions from motor vehicles, and (b) if the EPA had such authority, it could nonetheless decline to exercise its authority on general grounds of regulatory prudence. The Court held that, to the contrary, the EPA not only had authority to regulate carbon emissions from motor vehicles, but that it was legally required to issue such regulations unless the agency formally determined—notwithstanding the overwhelming scientific consensus to the contrary—that greenhouse gases do not promote global climate change.[4] Although EPA staff, in the wake of this rebuke, promptly drafted a proposed rule on motor vehicle emissions that would have responded to the Court's manifest impatience, EPA Administrator Stephen Johnson announced that the EPA would not issue a proposed rule, but confine itself to something called an "Advance Notice of Proposed Rulemaking."[5] An ANPRM is basically a public announcement that an agency is thinking about thinking about something, and it represents the most preliminary step possible in a formal regulatory process. Getting from an ANPRM to a final rule typically requires years, which means the Supreme Court's opinion will have had no impact whatsoever on regulatory policy in the George W. Bush Administration. Courts, aware of the potential for such passive-aggressive defiance of judicial power, may be reluctant on that score to act confrontationally against an executive branch well positioned to resist.

Thus, even if the pluralists are legally right, their legal arguments are not going to be enough to assure that the legislative and judicial branches produce healthy checks and balances against an overweening President. Widespread acknowledgment among both public officials and the electorate of the pluralists' legal correctness can assure no more than that the subject of presidential power will be acknowledged as a legitimate subject for permanent dialogue and negotiation among the three branches of government, as well as among the American people themselves. As it happens, the pluralists do have the law on their side—but the American people cannot relax. We can still wind up with a dangerously ambitious version of the presidency, simply by political default. Without both institutional reforms and continuing public vigilance, the behavioral presidency will continue to conform to the presidentialist model even if pluralism is accepted as the accurate description of the legal presidency.

So, what is the law? There is a fundamental starting point on which everyone agrees. Namely, the President can derive legal authority to perform official acts from only two sources, the Constitution of the United States or statutes enacted by Congress. The authorities derived from the Constitution, including such powers as the pardon power or the power to make treaties, are the "inherent" powers of the President. Inherent powers do not need to be implemented by legislation. Especially in domestic affairs, however, the President gets most power elsewhere. Congress delegates power to the executive branch through its own constitutional prerogative to "enact all laws necessary and proper" for carrying the authorities of the legislative branch into effect. These are the statutory or "delegated powers" of the federal executive.

To understand delegated powers, consider, for example, that Article I authorizes Congress to regulate interstate commerce.[6] For example, if Congress believes that interstate commerce is being conducted in a way that causes excessive air pollution and wants to do something about it, the Constitution allows Congress to achieve its goal through any legislation that is "necessary and proper" to carry the regulation of interstate commerce into effect to prevent air pollution. Congress may then choose, as its means of "regulation," to vest power in the executive branch to reduce air pollution through subsidiary regulations, fines, or administrative orders. Congress (as it does) could allow the EPA to issue rules imposing limits on particular pollutants, to levy penalties for noncompliance, and to issue orders against polluters requiring various forms of cleanup or pollution reduction. Congress, in effect, would be hiring the executive branch to use its various tools to carry out Congress's purposes. If it does so, the executive will now enjoy delegated power over air pollution. In fact, given the vast scope of statutory authority of this kind that Congress has enacted, a modern President enjoys profound influence over the regulation of our economy, health, safety, and public welfare. Although the President's inherent powers, generally speaking, address none of these things, Congress has given the President a major role.

Against this background, there now exist two especially hot debates concerning the constitutional powers of the President. The first concerns the scope of the President's inherent authority to oversee the implementation of those powers that Congress alone has delegated to the executive branch. In other words, how much constitutionally based inherent power does the President have to determine how the executive branch's congressionally delegated powers get implemented? For example, if Congress gives the executive branch authority to regulate air pollution, may it definitively vest authority to decide air pollution policy in the head of EPA, or may the President always countermand the EPA Administrator in cases of disagreement? May the President even reassign the EPA's task to another agency if the President so prefers? The second focuses on the degree to which the President enjoys constitutionally inherent powers in foreign and military affairs that are completely beyond congressional control. The "unitary presidency" debate is really a debate about the first issue. The furor over warrantless electronic eavesdropping by the National Security Agency is an example of the second debate. The question at stake in the surveillance debate is not about the President's supervisory powers over the executive branch, but whether his commander-in-chief or foreign policy powers permit him to engage in warrantless electronic surveillance for national security purposes even when Congress has made such surveillance unlawful. Of course, people's views on the two sets of issues may coincide. Presidentialists are likely to advocate both a broad understanding of the President's inherent and fully autonomous foreign affairs and military powers and complete presidential control over statutory authority conferred on the executive bureaucracy by Congress. Pluralists will likely take the opposite tack. But the two debates do involve different sets of legal considerations, and it is helpful to keep them separate in understanding how the relevant law is best interpreted.

What the "Unitary Executive" Debate Is Really About: The President's Inherent Powers over the Federal Bureaucracy

One way to begin clarifying the debate over the "unitary executive" is to explain what the key question is *not*. It is not, despite the explicit contrary claim of presidentialism's most forceful advocates, "whether the Constitution rejected the 'executive by committee' established by the Articles of Confederation in favor of a 'unitary executive' in which all administrative authority is centralized in the President."[7] The answer to *this* question is obviously affirmative. No one has ever suggested that the administrative authority vested by the Constitution in the President is vested in anyone else. The question is, what is the scope of that inherent administrative power?

A clear analysis of this question requires understanding another key, but indisputable point. That is, when Congress assigns a task to the executive branch, whether that task be profound or trivial, Congress must inevitably be understood to give to the executive branch some range of discretion in implementing that task. By "discretion," the law just means "room for judgment," a zone within which the executive branch gets to figure out its own best sense of how to get something accomplished. The legal idea of discretion is easy to understand from even our most common everyday experiences. If you hire people to help clean your house, you probably let them decide which room to start in, which tools and products to use, and how to use those tools and products most effectively. You leave these matters to their discretion. But, if you hire people to help clean your house and they purport to sell it instead, you fire them, sue them, or have them arrested. You argue that they acted illegally—outside their discretion—and have breached their authority.

Administrative discretion is somewhat more complex than this because it almost always comes in two varieties that may well overlap. One form of discretion is *managerial*. If the executive branch has been assigned a task, say, building a dam, Congress has thus committed the executive to pursue a legislative goal, perhaps water conservation or energy production, but it has specified fairly clearly how that goal is to be achieved. All that needs to be determined now is how to accomplish the assigned task—building the dam—in the most efficient or effective way from a purely instrumental point of view. Whether we ought to have a dam is not for the President to decide. His task regarding the dam is not to make policy, just to get the job done.

The other kind of discretion is *policy* discretion. Embedded in the administrative decisions that have to be made—decisions how best to implement the authority Congress has delegated—are questions with implications regarding public values and the overall philosophy of government. Imagine, for example, that Congress has delegated authority not "to build a dam," but rather, "to promote water conservation." Some federal agency would then have to make decisions about the relative merits of building dams, issuing regulations limiting the use of water under particular circumstances, or financing a massive advertising and public education campaign designed to induce voluntary reductions in personal water use. Some of the decision about which tools to adopt will be instrumental; policy makers will try to predict, that is, just how much water conservation will result from these methods. But other bases of decision will implicate competing public values. Regulation might be preferred to dam building in order to avoid the collateral environmental impacts of dam building. Or, an Administration may prefer a program of public education instead of administrative rules because it opposes the regulatory impact on individual freedom. These judgments, even if delegated to an administrative agency, would not be judgments of effectiveness, but rather, judgments about philosophy.

The Constitution charges the President to "take care that the laws be faithfully executed."[8] This means, according to Supreme Court precedent and common usage, that the President may not suspend the operation of a statute that Congress enacts. The President may not direct that a law be violated unless that law unconstitutionally impinges on his own constitutional powers.[9] Thus, when a statute mandates a specific duty to be performed by the executive, then the President or another member of the executive branch must typically perform it. The Faithful Execution Clause also seems to imply, again according to Supreme Court precedent and common usage, that the President must be able to intervene should any member of the executive branch who is charged with performing a duty violate the law in the course of doing so.[10] If an officer of the executive branch is guilty of failing to do his or her job or is violating the law, then the President must be able to get rid of them. If the President cannot do so personally, then it must be possible at least through someone whom the President can fire if *that* person fails to supervise others properly. Otherwise, the President has no mechanism through which to make sure that laws are, in fact, executed faithfully.

All of this is uncontroversial. The debate begins when it comes to the exercise of discretion. What would happen, for example, if Congress wants the executive branch to issue a pamphlet within six months informing the public about the latest knowledge on AIDS? Issuing that pamphlet is a "ministerial duty." That is, it is something that the executive branch is legally bound to do. The President may not decide that an AIDS pamphlet will not see the light of day. Let's take the example one step further, so that Congress wants the Surgeon General of the United States or the head of the Centers for Disease Control or some other expert to be the final editor of that pamphlet, in order to make sure that it is consistent with the best science advisable. Here is where the *presidentialists* and the *pluralists* divide. Presidentialists argue, either because of the Faithful Execution Clause or because of the clause that vests "the executive power" in the President, that only the President is constitutionally qualified to be the final editor of the pamphlet or to determine who the final editor shall be.[11] Presidentialists interpret the Constitution as giving the President inherent administrative power to control the exercise of *any and all* discretion that Congress vests in any officer of the executive branch, including policy discretion. That is the presidentialist claim for the unitary President—that the President is constitutionally in charge of the exercise of any or all policy making discretion that Congress may delegate to anyone within the executive branch.

Pluralists would argue for the contrary position. The President, they would say, has no inherent power with regard to the protection of public health. The power he enjoys is limited to the power vested in him by Congress, plus his general inherent power to make sure that other officers of the United States are executing their statutory authority lawfully. If Congress chooses to give the President complete policy control over the contents of the AIDS pamphlet, fine. But Congress is not compelled to do so by the Constitution. Outside those particular subjects that are independently within the President's inherent powers, such as issuing pardons or making treaties, the degree of policy control the President may exercise is up to Congress, which is limited, in turn, only by the Constitution's constraints on the scope of national legislative authority. Because the President has no relevant inherent authority to protect public health, Congress would be acting within its authority in giving final policy control over the AIDS pamphlet to another member of the executive branch. The President must be able to discharge that person if he or she is not performing the assigned task or publishing pamphlets that Congress has not authorized. But, so long as the President, in this sense, is able to take care that the pamphlet law is faithfully executed, he has no other *constitutionally mandated* role.

This pluralist position on the scope of the President's supervisory authority is neither a radical limitation on the President's influence nor a harbinger of potential policy making chaos within the executive branch. The President has plenty of ways to insure that administrative officials act in ways consistent with his policy preferences. To begin with, subject to the

Senate's power to confirm, the President appoints all the principal officers of the executive branch, in addition to many key subordinate officers, not all of whom even require Senate confirmation for their appointments. Such appointees, and the officials who report to them, will surely start from a position of sympathy toward the President's policy views. Second, all executive branch officials need the President's support for their various missions, especially in the budget process. Routine disregard for White House policy views is an unlikely management choice for an agency head determined to advance his or her agency's position in the Administration. Moreover, for those officials who are subject under law to "at will" discharge by the President, the President may dismiss an official who bucks the President's directions, so long as the President is willing to pay any political cost for firing subordinates who may have their own reservoirs of support in Congress, the press, or the public at large.

The difference between the pluralist and presidentialist positions does, however, make two important differences in practice. One difference is that the pluralist position explains why Congress is entitled to create so-called independent agencies, such as the Security and Exchange Commission, the Board of Governors of the Federal Reserve, or the National Labor Relations Board. Even though these are entities within the executive branch, the tasks they perform are based entirely on authorities delegated by Congress, and Congress may structure the agencies to prevent the President from exercising his own supervisory control over their policy discretion. The organizational detail that makes these agencies "independent" is that Congress has provided, by statute, that the President may not discharge the agency heads accept for good cause. Put bluntly, the President is not entitled to fire "independent" administrators just because he does not like their policy views, and the Constitution does not mandate otherwise.

The second practical difference is subtle, but also significant. Congress frequently determines that centralizing policy oversight in the President makes institutional sense, and most policy making officials in the executive branch are not protected by statutory guarantees of their policy independence. Because the pluralist position does not prohibit Congress from investing the President with statutory authority or allowing him to control the policy discretion of other administrators, it recognizes that, if Congress so pleases, it may allow the President complete policy control over the discretion it vests in the EPA, the Department of Labor, or any other agency. But even in such cases, it is reasonable to assume that how the President exercises his discretion will depend on whether he thinks he owes that discretion to Congress in the first place. If Presidents know that they enjoy significant policy discretion chiefly at the sufferance of the legislative branch, they are likely to behave in a way that is more attentive and accountable to Congress. It is this sufferance and the norm of deference that the presidentialists reject, holding instead that the President's discretion over Administration is rooted in the Constitution and not in powers granted by Congress.

An episode that illustrates the difference in presidentialist and pluralist involves the dispute that emerged in early 2007 between Congress and President George W. Bush over the firing of nine U.S. attorneys. Although the White House and Justice Department initially asserted that the discharges were performance-based, documents shortly emerged suggesting that the firings were politically motivated and that nearly all the U.S. attorneys in dispute were highly regarded.[12] Committees of the House and Senate subsequently moved to acquire White House documents and testimony from both current and former staffers in both the Justice Department and the White House, in order to determine if any aspect of the dismissals was unlawful or otherwise improper. The White House, for its part, resisted full disclosure, largely on the basis that Congress's inquiry would interfere with inherent presidential powers with regard to U.S. attorneys. In a letter to the chairs of the Judiciary Committees in both the House and Senate, White House Counsel Fred Fielding wrote that the focus of their inquiry "seeks information relating to the President's powers to appoint and remove U.S. Attorneys—authority granted exclusively to the President by the Constitution."[13]

In fact, the authority granted to the President to appoint and remove U.S. attorneys is conferred upon him by statute,[14] not by the Constitution. The President does have authority to fire U.S. attorneys on grounds of policy, but only because Congress has not provided otherwise. Had the White House acknowledged that Congress enjoyed authority, within its own discretion, to limit the President's powers to remove U.S. attorneys, it might well have acted less peremptorily in dismissing the officials, and it might have resisted less aggressively congressional inquiries into the legality of the discharges. A President accepting the pluralist view would not have permitted the discharge of the U.S. attorneys, except for reasons that the President would be willing to share with Congress and the public. Pluralism emphasizes the importance of mutual accountability among holders of governmental power, and Presidents are likely to behave more accountably if the pluralist position prevails.

Guided by its presidentialist view, however, the Bush Administration was not going to admit or accept Congress's claim to authority. The White

House moved to stave off congressional inquiry into the reasons behind the nine disputed firings and thus to forestall any congressional inquiry into whether U.S. attorneys should be statutorily protected from "at will" discharge. The political victory may have been incomplete because furor over the firings helped elicit the resignation of Attorney General Alberto Gonzales, who was the Cabinet member most directly involved. On the other hand, the episode could be seen as a victory for presidentialism insofar as the President's stance on the scope of the legal presidency went without effective challenge.

In sum, the issue dividing presidentialists and pluralists is whether the President's constitutionally based administrative powers include the authority to take over or command all policy making discretion that Congress has delegated to anyone within the executive branch, even on subjects as to which the President otherwise has no constitutional power at all. For example, the President has no inherent authority over the environment; when Congress gives anyone in the executive branch delegated power over the environment, does the President have inherent authority to tell that official what to do? Likewise, the President has no inherent authority over the economy; when Congress gives anyone in the executive branch delegated power over the economy, does the President have inherent authority to tell that official what to do?

From where in the Constitution could the President derive the power to tell every official in the executive branch what to do? There are only two plausible sources. One is the President's obligation to "take Care that the laws be faithfully executed." The second is the "executive power" that Article II vests in the President. The presidentialist argument is that, when the founders gave the President executive power, they envisioned complete control over policy discretion, and that control is vested in the President by either the Vesting Clause or the Faithful Execution Clause.[15]

Based solely on the text of the Constitution, pluralists clearly have the edge. As a textual matter, requiring the President to take care of the faithful execution of the laws hardly seems to imply room for inserting his own policy discretion. The clause is derived from the ban on the executive suspension of statutes that appears in the English bill of rights[16] and clearly implies the faithful execution of Congress's will, not the President's. The only real text-based argument the presidentialists seem to have is a supposed inference that the phrase "executive power" implies the precise power they believe that the President possesses. In other words, if the phrase "executive power" was originally defined to include "the power to control all policy making discretion that Congress delegates to anyone within the executive branch," then the presidentialists would be correct that the Constitution gives the President an inherent and exclusive power, not susceptible to legislative limitation, to control all policy making discretion that Congress delegates to anyone within the executive branch.

The Constitution's drafters and ratifiers, however, simply did not conceptualize the President's discretion in policy terms. To the extent that the executive was thought to enjoy discretion in carrying out domestic law, the discretion that contemporaries anticipated pertained to what we would now categorize only as managerial accountability. The executive was to keep within lawful bounds, spend public funds carefully, and deal with problems evenhandedly. When Hamilton or Madison discusses government administration in the context of the *Federalist Papers,* it is not in terms of policy orientation, but rather in terms of whether administration will prove "good" or "bad." Merit, not policy, was the criterion for judging administration.[17]

Moreover, and this is the crucial point, whatever commitment the founding generation had to centralized management did not translate—even in the late eighteenth century—into a model of executive policy control over all administration at the state or federal level.[18] In 1789, the first Congress created, by statute, four civil administrative establishments—the departments of War, of Foreign Affairs, of the Treasury, and of the Post Office. Congress's treatment of the four agencies reflected lengthy deliberation and, of particular import, displayed differing understandings of the extent of executive power in relation to each agency. Two of the departments— War and Foreign Affairs—were understood to be assisting in the implementation of presidential powers vested specifically by the Constitution and, in the statutes creating them, were explicitly denominated "executive departments." The statutes that organized those departments sketched their departmental organization and their duties only in broad terms, and Congress anticipated that the President would exercise broad independence in supervising these departments.

It is clear from the debates surrounding the Treasury Department, however, that the character of Treasury was not perceived to be executive in a manner akin to the departments of War and Foreign Affairs.[19] First, unlike the other departments, Congress did not label the Treasury as an "executive" department. Congress went to great length to specify the Treasury's structure, creating a number of fiscal officers with reporting responsibility to the Secretary. Most tellingly, the first Congress treated the Secretary of the Treasury as if that official's administrative obligations ran to Congress as well as to the President. The most important debate regarding the Secretary centered around a proposed duty "to digest and prepare plans for the improvement and management of the revenue, and for the support of public credit."[20] This wording is nearly identical to the charge to the financial officers authorized under the Articles of Confederation.[21] Some in Congress were alarmed that this parliamentary duty would so involve the Secretary in legislation as to undermine the authority of the House; others saw the charge as undermining the President's power to propose legislation. Nonetheless, Congress conferred this duty upon the Secretary, essentially borrowing a description of the Secretary from this country's former, short-lived parliamentary system.

The implications of this analysis were borne out in practice. For several years, Alexander Hamilton, the first Secretary of the Treasury, performed the functions of the House of Representatives Committee on Ways and Means, which the House created in 1789, but suspended the same year. The House reappointed the Ways and Means Committee only upon Hamilton's retirement from the Treasury. Congress's newly asserted independence in fiscal affairs was not thought to imply any intensification of presidential responsibility for the Treasury. As late as 1823, the Attorney General advised the President that, far from the President being constitutionally obligated to correct an allegedly improper settlement by the Treasury Department of an individual's claim for reimbursement, it would be legally impermissible for the President to substitute his judgment for that of the accounting officer.[22] The vision of an air-tight executive establishment under unlimited presidential control that is conjured by presidentialists thus cannot be matched by the early history of administrative practice.

Noted historian Forrest MacDonald has gone so far as to say that the Constitution, as adopted and implemented in 1789, actually marked the repudiation of the separation of powers principle, having involved the legislative branch so far into the affairs of the executive, and vice versa.[23] The observations, however, of former Stanford University President Gerhard Casper may come closer to the mark. Casper regards late eighteenth-century government decision makers as not having had before them any single, coherent vision of a "separation of powers" principle either to adopt or to reject. Instead, they were intent on structuring an administrative apparatus that would be but one version of a government of largely separated powers.[24] So long as they avoided the sin of commingling all of the legislative, executive, and judicial power in a single branch, the Framers believed they had respected the philosophical demand for separation; the states, equally faithful to the separation of powers principle, could allocate constitutional powers somewhat differently and still be true to that same general philosophy. The aims of the structure on which the Framers settled were functional, to balance the need for effective, coordinated administration with the need to protect against tyranny. It was thus that our system of checks and balances was born.

The presidentialists' contrary historical argument is made chiefly by (1) identifying bits of constitutional text that could conceivably be read as supporting a strong presidency, and then (2) confirming, by recourse to various quotes and documents, that various members of the founding generation read these bits of constitutional text in the presidentialist manner.[25] With due respect to the energy devoted to this enterprise, it is utterly acontextual. The managerial "President" extolled in the late eighteenth century was just not conceptualized in the policy terms as are now understood by modern presidentialists. Thus, no matter how "unitary" the original presidential office was intended to be, and no matter how many founders can be quoted as having uttered the word "unitary," the unitariness of the President's originally designed powers cannot logically add up to the contemporary version urged upon us by the presidentialists.

The Supreme Court's understanding of the constitutional presidency takes the pluralist view. The leading modern decision is *Morrison v. Olson*,[26] which upheld the constitutionality of the now-defunct independent counsel provisions of the Ethics in Government Act passed by Congress in 1978.[27] After Watergate, Congress enacted the independent counsel law to help fend off the conflicts of interest latent in executive branch criminal investigations of high-level executive branch officials and leaders of the incumbent President's election campaign. Until its expiration in 1999, the Act was triggered whenever the Attorney General received specific information in support of an accusation that one of the officials covered by the act had committed a federal felony. Upon getting such a report, the Attorney General had ninety days to investigate. Unless the Attorney General could conclude that there was no meritorious reason for further investigation or prosecution, he or she was bound by the law to apply to a special panel of the U.S. Court of Appeals for the District of Columbia Circuit to appoint an "independent counsel" or special prosecutor. The court would then appoint the independent counsel, who would continue the investigation and prosecution, should one be merited. Within the executive branch, the independent counsel could be removed only by the personal act of the Attorney General, who could fire the independent counsel "only for good cause, physical or mental disability (if not prohibited by law protecting persons from discrimination on the basis of such a disability), or any other condition that substantially impairs the performance of such independent counsel's duties."[28] In short, the independent counsel would be an executive branch official appointed by another branch of government, the courts, and no one within the executive branch would have supervisory authority over the independent counsel's exercise of policy discretion.

Theodore B. Olson, a former Assistant Attorney General (and later Solicitor General) who was the subject of an independent counsel investigation in the mid-1980s, objected on constitutional grounds to both of these features. Because, according to Olson, criminal prosecution was an executive function, the vesting of executive power in the President implied that he had to have influence over the appointment of the official, and he could not constitutionally be denied supervision of his policy discretion. By a vote of 7–1, in an opinion by the late Chief Justice Rehnquist, the Court rejected both of these propositions. Because the independent counsel was subject to removal by the Attorney General, the Court deemed her to be an "inferior officer." The Constitution, noted the Court, explicitly allows Congress to authorize the appointment of inferior officers by "courts of law." Given Congress's concern about conflicts of interest, Rehnquist wrote, "the most logical place to put [the appointing authority] was in the judicial branch."[29] As for the removal provision, its constitutionality was not to be settled simply by labeling the prosecutor an executive officer. "[T]he real question," Rehnquist wrote, "is whether the removal restrictions . . . impede the President's ability to perform his constitutional duty. . . ."[30] The Court answered this question summarily: "Although the counsel exercises no small amount of discretion and judgment in deciding how to carry out her duties under the Act, we simply do not see how the President's need to control the exercise of that discretion is so central to the functioning of the Executive Branch as to require as a matter of constitutional law that the counsel be terminable at will by the President."[31] In other words, depriving the President of direct control over the prosecutor's "discretion and judgment" did not interfere with the President's ability to fulfill any role the Constitution actually assigns to him. It follows that the power ascribed to the President by the unitary presidency theory simply does not exist.

Morrison v. Olson represents a powerful statement as to the limits of presidential authority. The kind of administrative activity at stake in this activity—criminal prosecution—was certainly known to the Framers of the Constitution. If the Framers had in mind a definition of "executive power" that gave the President constitutional authority to control all policy making discretion that Congress delegates to anyone within the executive branch, that definition would necessarily have extended to the control of all policy making discretion inherent in prosecuting the criminal laws that Congress enacted. The Court's correctly determined, however, that policy control over criminal prosecution is historically not part of the "executive power" constitutionally vested in the President, even though criminal prosecution was a government function well known to the Framers. For presidentialists to argue in the face of that history that the Framers nonetheless implicitly prohibited congressional delimitation of presidential authority over matters they could hardly have envisioned—such as the Nuclear Regulatory Commission or the Federal Communications Commission, for example— is utterly fanciful.

In short, the Constitution simply does not command the unitary presidency in domestic affairs that the presidentialists imagine. How unitary the presidency should be in terms of supervising the administration of domestic affairs is legitimately a matter of debate and decision within Congress; if the President exceeds the boundaries Congress sets, courts are entitled to enforce those limits against him. The "unitary presidency" of presidentialist theory is a myth.

What the Warrantless Surveillance Debate Is Really About: The President's Inherent Foreign Policy and National Security Powers

In December 2005, the *New York Times* revealed that, since 2002, the National Security Agency (NSA) has engaged in a presidentially authorized program of domestic electronic surveillance of phone calls by Americans.[32] Not surprisingly, proponents of presidentialism argued that the President was fully empowered to authorize this program. But it is important to make a distinction between the issues at stake in the case of national security surveillance and the theory of the unitary presidency. The issue is not presidential policy supervision of subordinate administrators' discretion delegated by Congress. Congress had not delegated any discretion of this kind; on the contrary, the Foreign Intelligence Surveillance Act of 1978[33] (FISA) made such blanket surveillance unlawful. The issue instead is whether the President can break the law as enacted by Congress. More precisely, does the President possess sufficient constitutional authority in the realm of national security that he may conduct a program of electronic surveillance in direct contravention of a congressionally enacted statute?

It is difficult to overstate the audacity of the Administration's position, which has an infamous pedigree. In 1977, Richard Nixon, having resigned the presidency in disgrace three years earlier, expressed the view that

Presidents are not confined by statutory law when it comes to their national security initiatives. "When the President does" something he believes to be in the best interests of the nation, Nixon said, "that means that it is not illegal."[34] At the time, Nixon's view was widely reviled, even ridiculed, discredited by revelations regarding not only Watergate, but also the unjustified surveillance of civil rights leaders, warrantless covert searches ("black-bag jobs") aimed at antiwar dissenters, and Nixon's misuse of the CIA and Internal Revenue Service for political ends. It was in this context of violations of American rights that Congress passed FISA in 1978. Despite this history, the Bush Administration's legal position regarding the NSA more or less resurrects the Nixon view with a vengeance.

In deciding what the Constitution allows Presidents to do in foreign and military affairs, it is helpful to start by noting the three general approaches we could possibly take, at least in principle. The presidentialist position—the Bush 43 Administration position[35]—is that the Constitution, in essence, allows the President to do virtually anything he likes in foreign and military affairs, subject only to the qualifications and exceptions that are spelled out clearly in constitutional text. The supposed textual source of this authority is, once again, the vesting of "executive power" in the President by Article II of the Constitution. According to presidentialist theorists, the scope of executive power is to be measured according to the powers associated in 1787 with the British monarchy, which, they claim, is the measure of what the Framers understood to be "executive power."[36] Thus, for example, according to the presidentialist view, the President has plenary power to interpret the meaning of American treaty obligations.[37] He has authority not only to make treaties—which Article II makes explicit—but also the power to abrogate treaties unilaterally.[38] He has virtually unlimited authority to protect national security through intelligence gathering and the management of sensitive information.[39] Perhaps most boldly, the most aggressive of the presidentialists insist that the President may deploy U.S. military force at will, without prior congressional authorization of any sort.[40]

One alternative to this position would assert just the opposite. That is, the "executive power" Vesting Clause might be interpreted to have no content at all beyond conveying the precise executive powers articulated in the remainder of Article II. On this reading, except in emergencies that preclude prior congressional action, the President would not have any powers in foreign or military affairs beyond the roles that Article II explicitly assigns to him and what Congress authorizes pursuant to its own legislative powers. This could logically be called the "congressional supremacy" position.[41]

From the standpoint of legal argument, both the presidentialist theory and the congressional supremacy theory have the attraction of being fairly simple. Applying either theory to specific disputes may entail the usual problems associated with interpreting the Constitution's often vague or arcane phrasing. But each is founded on a straightforward conviction about what the Framers intended to achieve by vesting the President with "executive power." Each theory thus yields a straightforward way of assessing the legality of any presidential claim to inherent authority. The problem, however, is that neither of these theories or the policy judgments that inform them can square neatly with constitutional text and our early constitutional history.

Consider, first, the presidentialist theory. If vesting the President with "executive power" were enough to give him all monarchical authorities not otherwise trimmed back by other constitutional text, much of Article II would be inexplicably redundant. For example, Article II confers power on the President "to require the opinions in writing of the heads of departments," as basic an executive function as one could imagine. The British Crown was surely entitled to demand the opinions of its ministers. If the "executive power" Vesting Clause itself gave the President all the powers normally associated with the British Crown, it would be redundant for Article II to then state specifically that the President could require the opinions in writing of the heads of departments. We see this same problem in foreign affairs. The executive powers of the monarchy certainly entailed the power to receive ambassadors and public ministers from other nations. Yet, that specific executive power is explicitly conferred on the President by Section 3 of Article II, notwithstanding the general vesting of "executive power" in Section 1. Again, if the "executive power" Vesting Clause itself gave the President all the powers normally associated with the British Crown, explicitly giving the President power to receive ambassadors and public ministers would be a mere repetition of power already conferred. In short, critical provisions within Article II would be superfluous if the vesting of "executive power" already had the effect of giving the President the full range of British monarchical powers, subject only to the few exceptions stated explicitly in the text. If it was assumed that the President inherently had such power, it would be odd for the Framers to restate explicitly the very same powers.

Moreover, and this is the more fundamental historical point, it is inconceivable that the revolutionary generation—despite their disappointments with weak executive government in the 1780s—would have unreservedly re-embraced the full power of a monarchy, subject only to the fairly limited number of express checks on executive power that are spelled out in constitutional text. Professor John Yoo, a strong presidentialist and former Justice Department official, has conceded that Federalists urging ratification of the Constitution publicly elaborated arguments that the new President would not have powers anything like those of the king. Professor Yoo seeks to dismiss such arguments, however, as deliberate exaggerations of monarchical power deployed to make the presidency seem less powerful than it really was.[42] This response, however, completely misconstrues the nature of constitutional interpretation. The Constitution derives its meaning not from the unarticulated intentions of those who drafted the text, but from the ways in which the text was understood by those who voted to ratify the Constitution and make it law. That is because the Constitution was not a binding document at the conclusion of the Federal Convention in Philadelphia, but became one only after adopted in state conventions. To the extent historical understanding is to guide our contemporary reading of the Constitution, then, we need to reflect on how the members of state conventions ratifying the Constitution understood the document on which they were voting. The text of the Constitution is itself the best guide to the ratifiers' understanding, but it is legitimate also to draw evidence from pamphlets and essays supporting the Constitution that may well have influenced their view of the document. Seen in this light, what makes the *Federalist Papers* so important is not that its authors helped draft the Constitution, but rather that the arguments in the *Federalist Papers* were apparently decisive in winning support for the Constitution in the New York ratifying convention. Whether Alexander Hamilton was insincere in his public descriptions of the new President's powers does not change what his text actually said. The arguments he made publicly were the arguments on which the ratifiers relied. To the extent the *Federalist Papers* were influential, they thus informed their readers that the President's powers were not to be measured against those of the English Crown. It is inconceivable that the ratifiers intended to approve a presidency comprising the powers of the monarch annotated with just a few asterisks, as it were, when no such interpretation was offered to them.

On the other hand, there does seem to have been an early consensus among the Framers and in the early Congresses that the President's constitutional powers in foreign and military affairs did extend beyond those authorities that the Constitution articulates with precision. To take arguably the least controversial example, no one has doubted the inherent authority of Presidents to direct covert intelligence gathering against foreign powers, even though the Constitution never mentions it. Moreover, in a famous speech to the House of Representatives in 1800, John Marshall, then

Congressman and later Chief Justice of the United States, declared: "The President is the sole organ of the nation in its external relations, and its sole representative with foreign nations. . . . The [executive] department . . . is entrusted with the whole foreign intercourse of the nation. . . ."[43] Marshall succinctly articulated what has generally been agreed: the President has unique authority to voice to other nations what is the foreign policy of the United States. The Constitution does not spell out either of these powers; yet, there seems never to have been any doubt that the President of the United States would possess them. And indeed, both Congress and the Court have generally deferred to this norm and granted the President considerable autonomy and forbearance in the conduct of foreign policy.

If we are searching for an understanding of the Constitution faithful to original intent, neither the straightforward presidentialist theory nor a straightforward congressional supremacy theory suffices. The reason for this is simple: Although the Framers and ratifiers probably did understand that the vesting of executive power conveyed to the President some range of authority beyond the precise functions enumerated in the constitutional text, there was no common categorical understanding of what those powers were in either domestic or foreign affairs. The implicit inherent powers I have just mentioned—the authority to spy on foreign governments and to articulate American foreign policy—were probably well understood and little feared, because neither had any direct implications for the rights and liberties of American citizens. Beyond that, however, there was substantial disagreement. The vesting of executive power in the President is thus most accurately understood as giving him a discrete set of specific powers on which the founding generation would have agreed, plus such powers as might be ratified later by common law constitutional interpretation and by an unfolding history of institutional practice. Even with a written Constitution, the British idea that institutional norms might evolve over time into constitutional understandings would have been familiar. To us, the idea that the text of the Constitution does not settle all by itself exactly how narrow or how broad are the authorities of our government leaders can be disquieting. But this is probably the most plausible account of what the founding generation actually had in mind.

The depth of disagreement among the Framers over the scope of the President's foreign affairs powers is well dramatized by the dispute between Alexander Hamilton and James Madison about President Washington's authority to issue his famous Neutrality Proclamation of 1793. Notwithstanding the 1788 Treaty of Alliance with France, President Washington proclaimed, on behalf of the American government, that "the duty and interests of the United States require that they should with sincerity and good faith adopt and pursue a conduct friendly and impartial towards" France, on one hand, and Great Britain and its allies, on the other, who were in a state of war.[44] His proclamation further declared that citizens of the United States would render themselves liable to punishment or forfeiture under the Law of Nations and would forfeit the protection of the United States against such punishment or forfeiture, should they commit, aid, or abet hostilities against any of the warring powers. Congress, however, had not authorized the President to make such a statement.

Hamilton and Madison's dispute over the Neutrality Proclamation is critical to understanding how the founders thought about foreign affairs issues, not only because each had a hand in drafting the Constitution, but because each was an author of the *Federalist Papers* that continue to stand as the Federalists' authoritative attempt to define for the public what they were being called upon to ratify. Five years after that project, using the pen name Pacificus, Hamilton vigorously defended the President's authority to issue his proclamation, arguing that the Neutrality Proclamation did not change American treaty obligations in any respect and specifically did not alter or abrogate the treaty of alliance with France. It stood merely as a "manifestation of the sense of the government, that the United States are, *under the circumstances of the case, not bound* to" come to France's aid in its war with England.[45] Announcing the American position thus fell properly to the President: "As the *organ* of intercourse between the nation and foreign nations; as the *interpreter* of the national treaties, in those cases in which the judiciary is not competent, that is, between government and government; as the *power,* which is charged with the execution of the laws, of which treaties form a part; as that which is charged with the command and disposition of the public force."[46] In short, Hamilton was asserting that Washington was acting with the authority that falls within the executive power of the President, which consists of all the executive power possessed by the government of the United States, subject only to the "exceptions and qualifications"[47] that the Constitution spells out. No such exceptions or disqualifications prevent the President from making a statement that Pacificus regards as a measure necessary and appropriate for maintaining the peace.

James Madison, under the pen name Helvidius—presumably chosen to honor the Roman stoic who argued that the emperor could act only with consent of the Senate—wrote five public letters that disputed Hamilton on virtually every point. Madison strongly attacked the position that sovereign powers of war and peace are presumptively lodged in the executive. Madison cited a variety of then-contemporary writers on international law and political theory to the effect that "the powers to declare war, to conclude peace, and to form alliances, [are] among the highest acts of the sovereignty; of which the legislative power must at least be an integral and preeminent part."[48] In Madison's view, it was therefore absurd to regard a mechanism for congressional involvement in foreign affairs, such as the requirement of Senate concurrence in treaties, merely as an exception to a general rule that foreign affairs are to be handled by the executive. Instead, Madison said treaty making should be viewed as lawmaking and, according to Madison, the President's involvement in treaties should be regarded as an exception to the predominance of legislative power in making law.

As for the specific powers granted to the President concerning foreign affairs, Madison found none of them relevant. The fact that the President is limited to serving as commander-in-chief demonstrated, to Madison, that policy making on the critical issue of war was regarded as predominantly the prerogative of Congress, which according to the Constitution was the only branch empowered to declare war. Madison argued further that the express vesting in Congress of the power to determine when conditions warrant the declaration of war necessarily implies that Congress is empowered to judge when circumstances demand the observation of neutrality. Rejecting Hamilton's arguments to the effect that there can be concurrent authority on particular subjects that is shared by both Congress and President, Madison argued that such a distribution of powers "would be as awkward in practice, as it is unnatural in theory."[49] He observed: "If the legislature and executive have both a right to judge of the obligations to make war or not, it must sometimes happen, through not at present, that they will judge differently."[50] He then asked: "In what light would it present to the world a nation thus speaking through two different organs, equally constitutional and authentic, two opposite languages, on the same subject, and under the same existing circumstances?"[51] Madison insisted that Hamilton's arguments in favor of the President's power to determine a condition of peace or neutrality would imply an executive authority to determine that existing conditions between the United States and another nation would also warrant the use of military force. He dismissed this argument, discussing at some length a variety of reasons why military authority of such scope would be too much power to entrust to any single individual:

War is in fact the true nurse of executive aggrandizement. In war, a physical force is to be created; and it is the executive will, which is to direct it. In war, the public treasuries are to be unlocked; and it is the executive hand which is to dispense them. . . . The strongest passions and most dangerous weaknesses of a human beast; ambition, avarice, vanity, the honorable or venerable love of fame, are all in conspiracy against the desire and duty of peace. Hence it has grown into an axiom that the executive is the department of power most distinguished by its propensity to war: Hence it is the practice of all states, in proportion as they are free, to disarm this propensity of its influence.[52]

For Madison, then, the issues raised by the Neutrality Proclamation were profound. And he touched on the basic issue at stake when he argued that the explicit constitutional charge to take care that the laws faithfully be executed did not empower the President to make the laws that shall be executed. Madison insisted that Hamilton could support his argument for executive determinations regarding neutrality only by confusing the royal prerogatives of the British monarch with the intended grant of executive power to a republican President—the scope of the former being a prime reason for the revolution.[53]

The point of reviewing this history is not to demonstrate that either Hamilton or Madison was indisputably correct; the point is that, within four years of the Constitution's ratification, two of its most significant architects and expositors were so thoroughly in public disagreement about the scope of the presidential office they had created. It is implausible in the face of such conflict to argue that the founding generation had reached any legally binding consensus about the scope of the executive power, much less a consensus that measured the President's powers according to the King's.

In practical terms, the Constitution gives Congress and the courts considerably more influence than presidentialists would prefer in delimiting presidential authority. This is the nub of the third view—a *pluralist* view of inherent presidential authority. It was best and most famously expressed in Justice Jackson's concurring opinion in the landmark case of *Youngstown Sheet and Steel v. Sawyer.*[54] *Youngstown* invalidated a 1952 executive order in which President Truman instructed his Secretary of Commerce to take control of most U.S. steel mills, which faced an impending strike, to insure continued steel production during the Korean War. Although the six Justices who made up the majority differed in their rationales, all of the opinions—including the dissent—started from the common premise that the Secretary's power to seize the steel mills under presidential order had to have its source in a grant of power to the President either from the Constitution or from a statute constitutionally enacted by Congress.

The majority Justices agreed—and the dissent did not dispute—that the President's constitutional role as commander-in-chief did not encompass power to seize the steel mills. Writing for the Court, Justice Black, with

Justice Douglas in close agreement, held that the President was simply powerless to act as he did. Absent independent constitutional authority, the President could lawfully seize the steel mills only if authorized, explicitly or by fair implication, by statute. Without legislative authorization, the President, they believed, could not invade individual rights of private property. Because no statute authorized the President to take the action he undertook, these Justices determined the seizure was simply unlawful.

Justices Clark and Burton, also in the majority, took a different tack. Each argued that the President, in an emergency, might in principle have sufficient inherent power to take affirmative steps to protect the public interest in ways not expressly authorized by Congress. Congress, however, had specifically contemplated the possibility that labor disputes would threaten the national interest, including the national defense, and had responded by enacting a number of statutes—none of which conferred the power that the President claimed. Because Congress had provided through legislation for the kind of emergency Truman faced, even though not in the manner he would have preferred, these Justices believed no further claim of inherent power was sustainable. Congress's affirmative steps effectively preempted whatever authority the President might otherwise have had to act on his own initiative.

In the most celebrated opinion in the case, Justice Jackson analyzed the particulars of the dispute against what he called a "somewhat oversimplified" tripartite "grouping of practical situations in which a President may doubt, or others may challenge, his powers."[55] Jackson noted first that Presidents sometimes act pursuant to express or implied statutory authority, where their authority is at its utmost. The President's action would be lawful in these situations if the Constitution vested power either in the President to act as he had or in Congress to authorize the challenged initiative through delegated authority. Such cases would not require a court to determine in any precise way whether Article I or Article II of the Constitution was the main source of presidential power.

Conversely, presidential action could contradict Congress's express or implied policy. In such a circumstance, the President's claim of authority would be most dubious. The action would be lawful only if based on a constitutional grant of exclusive power to the President that was beyond Congress's power to limit or regulate. Justice Jackson clearly regarded such circumstances as quite limited, and he did not regard the President's unilateral invocation of national security concerns as being enough to give him such unregulated authority. In a ringing passage, he declared: "[A] state of war may, in fact, exist without a formal declaration. But no doctrine that the

Court could promulgate would seem to me more sinister and alarming than that a President whose conduct of foreign affairs is so largely uncontrolled, and often even is unknown, can vastly enlarge his mastery over the internal affairs of the country by his own commitment of the Nation's armed forces to some foreign venture."[56] As a former Attorney General, of course, Justice Jackson could hardly have insensitive to the arguments in favor of vigorous presidential initiative. As chief Nuremberg prosecutor, however, he would also have been alert to the dangers of executive overreaching. The ardency of his position is all the more striking because it was uttered by a conservative Justice against the background of a military conflict in which the presidential concerns for national security were hardly trivial.

Finally, Jackson observed, there is a third area in which the President may act "in absence of either a congressional grant or denial of authority." The President in such a case "can only rely upon his own independent powers, but there is a zone of twilight in which he and Congress may have concurrent authority, or in which its distribution is uncertain. Therefore, congressional inertia, indifference or quiescence may sometimes, at least as a practical matter, enable, if not invite, measures on independent presidential responsibility."[57] At first, this may seem a puzzling statement. Congress makes law through a precise process described in the Constitution. There is no doubt that Congress may confer power on the President by making law within its areas of enumerated authority, utilizing the precise procedures of statutory enactment elaborated in the Constitution. But what does it mean to suggest that presidential initiative may be rendered legitimate when the "distribution of power" to the President is uncertain, but Congress has exhibited "inertia, indifference or quiescence?" How can "inertia, indifference or quiescence" create legal authority?

As our constitutional law has developed, there are really two possibilities. In a separate concurrence, Justice Frankfurter pointed to one of them: "[A] systematic, unbroken executive practice, long pursued to the knowledge of the Congress and never before questioned, engaged in by Presidents who have also sworn to uphold the Constitution, making as it were such exercise of power part of the structure of our government, may be treated as a gloss on 'executive Power' vested in the President by § 1 of Art. II."[58] In other words, if Presidents uniformly implement their executive power in a particular fashion that the Constitution does not clearly authorize, but also does not clearly reject, and if Congress, despite its knowledge of such initiatives, never objects, then in such cases, Frankfurter is suggesting, history may "ratify" the inclusion of such authority within the scope of the "executive power" that the Constitution is deemed to vest in the President.

A norm of interbranch interaction, if sufficiently stabilized, could thus establish a constitutional rule. An example of this is the claim of Presidents, since the Jefferson Administration, to have plenary and unilateral discretion to determine whether to recognize foreign governments. Our historical practice is uniform in ratifying the claim of every President to be the sole source of authority for determining who constitutes the lawful government of another nation. It would now take a constitutional amendment to vest this power elsewhere. Not surprisingly, very few categories of unilateral presidential initiative beyond the precise text of the Constitution can be sustained in so uncontroversial a way.

Alternatively, Congress's silence in the face of presidential initiative, especially if succeeded by legislative acts ratifying that initiative, can be interpreted as a kind of implied legislative delegation of power. The leading recent case of this sort involved the presidential settlement in 1981 of certain claims with Iran in order to secure the release of Americans held hostage in the U.S. embassy in Tehran.[59] No statutory language precisely authorized some of the measures undertaken by President Reagan in settling the hostage crisis. The Supreme Court, however, quoting Justice Frankfurter, upheld the President's order on the ground that Congress had so frequently supported executive initiative in the settlement of international claims that it could regarded as having delegated that power to him: "Past practice does not, by itself, create power, but 'long-continued practice, known to and acquiesced in by Congress, would raise a presumption that the [action] had been [taken] in pursuance of its consent. . . .' Such practice is present here and such a presumption is also appropriate. In light of the fact that Congress may be considered to have consented to the President's action in suspending claims, we cannot say that action exceeded the President's powers."[60] The Supreme Court did not assert that congressional acquiescence had ratified a particular interpretation of the constitutional phrase "executive power." Instead, such acquiescence simply manifested Congress's willingness to delegate authority to the President to act as he did. The difference between this position and the former is that, if history actually amends the Constitution—if it gives rise to an operational understanding of the Constitution that actually becomes as binding as if written into the Constitution explicitly—then the imputed meaning of the text cannot be changed to some other interpretation without a formal constitutional amendment or some drastic shift in institutional practice of equal significance and equally long standing. On the other hand, if we interpret Congress's silence to mean only its consent, the prospect remains that, in a different context, Congress may simply enact a statute to express a lack of consent to what the President wishes to do.

Jackson's approach has become the classic pluralist statement of how to analyze unilateral presidential initiatives, even in a national security context. It lacks the neatness or seeming elegance of the presidentialist position. The presidentialist view embraces a bright line, namely, the President may do anything the king could do, except as the Constitution specifically modifies or limits the executive power. Moreover, the Jackson approach seems to raise hard metaphysical questions, such as, "How often must a President get away with doing something over congressional silence before Congress's consent may be legitimately inferred?" But the ambiguities inherent in Jackson's opinion are actually truer to the ambiguity in the thinking of the founding generation about the meaning of executive power—as was clear in the debate between Madison and Hamilton. And, although his methodology in principle may seem to pose some difficult metaphysical questions of legal history, Jackson's three-part approach is quite a straightforward framework to apply in practice. It has the decided virtue of allowing not only an incumbent President, but also Congress and the courts to have an important voice in delimiting the reach of executive power.

The pluralist version of presidential authority is also plainly more consistent with the specific enumeration of legislative and executive constitutional powers in national security and military and foreign affairs. It is true that the President is expressly authorized to make treaties (with the advice and consent of two-thirds of the Senate), to appoint ambassadors, and to receive the public ministers of other nations. He is also explicitly made commander-in-chief of the armed forces. Building on these express assignments, historical practice, and the resulting norms, as I have mentioned, have ratified presidential claims for certain additional discrete inherent powers that are implicit in Article II. These include the unique power to communicate U.S. foreign policy authoritatively to other nations, the authority to recognize and establish diplomatic relations with other governments, the duty to repel invasions or sudden attacks upon the United States, and the power to gather foreign intelligence aimed at protecting the safety and security of the nation and of its people. None of these points is at issue.

But Congress, after all, has its own impressive constitutional menu of national security powers. Article I, Section 8 empowers Congress to provide "for the common defense," "to regulate commerce with foreign nations," "to establish a uniform rule of naturalization," "to define and punish piracies and felonies committed on the high seas, and offenses against the Law of Nations," "to declare war, grant letters of marque and reprisal, and make rules concerning captures on land and water," "to raise and support armies," and "to provide and maintain a Navy." Each of these powers is of fundamental importance to our foreign affairs and military policy making. Moreover, the Constitution expressly authorizes Congress to make all laws "necessary and proper for carrying into Execution . . . all . . . powers vested by the Constitution in the Government of the United States, or in any Department or Officer thereof." This would seem, at the very least, to articulate a strong constitutional presumption that, even where the Constitution vests authority in the President, he is still not immune from congressional regulation. It is thus perhaps unsurprising that an exhaustive 2008 study by law professors David S. Barron and Martin S. Lederman uncovered numerous examples throughout history of congressional legislation, accepted by Presidents as binding, that constrained the President's operational decision making in wartime and generally regulated the conduct and composition of the armed forces and militia more generally.[61]

Given the impressive menu of Congress's military and foreign affairs powers, and Justice Jackson's sound analytic framework for measuring the legality of presidential initiative against a backdrop of congressional authority, prohibition, or acquiescence, the important point is this: the presidentialist case for a near-monarchical President in foreign and military affairs fails. It is no more persuasive than the presidentialist version of the unitary presidency. Neither is based on a sound reading of constitutional text or history. The document written and ratified in 1787 does not compel us to have an imperial presidency. The Constitution we inherited from the Framers provides profound roles for both Congress and the judiciary in setting the appropriate bounds of executive power.

There are two reasons, however, why this conclusion does not end the matter—one reason, a matter of constitutional theory, and the other, a matter of political reality. The constitutional theory point is that we are not actually compelled either by law or logic to interpret the Constitution as our Framers did. On matters such as racial segregation and gender equality, we have given the text a more modernist meaning. Indeed, before the Reagan Administration, the most assertive claims for executive power were modernist, and not "originalist." When the State Department argued in the 1960s for the breadth of President Johnson's war powers, it explicitly acknowledged its nonoriginalist approach.[62] It did not purport to justify Johnson's powers by reference to an interpretation of the Constitution that the Framers would themselves have intended or anticipated. On the contrary, the argument was that we should update our reading of the literal provisions of the Constitution in order to achieve the Framers' larger purpose—assuring the United States the capacity to maintain its national security—in a world of exigencies that the Framers could not have envisioned.

The political reality point is one I have already made. Justice Jackson's legal analysis, which potentially imposes significant formal limits on the President's unilateral powers, still leaves Congress the political discretion to defer very substantially to the pleas of the executive for highly centralized and relatively unchecked power. The particular claims of the Bush 43 Administration for unilateral presidential authority were breathtaking, and the Administration's seeming contempt for the law as enacted by Congress, outrageous. But, if Congress became persuaded *as a matter of policy* that a President ought to have the kinds of authority President Bush claimed, Congress could make sure he got them.

Reflecting on these two points, it becomes clear that they really amount to more or less the same thing—a debate over whether the presidentialist vision of executive power is good for the United States, regardless of what the 1789 drafters had in mind. That is why it is important to go beyond the question whether the founding generation commanded or even anticipated a unilateral presidency. They did not. But we must also face the presidentialist case for the imperial presidency on its policy merits. Does a presidency unfettered by congressional accountability and judicial oversight actually serve the public interest better than a concededly robust presidency that is nevertheless subject to meaningful checks and balances? If so, that would be a frequent argument for Congress cutting the President a wide berth and perhaps even updating our reading of the Constitution to improve on the Framers' original design. The next four chapters provide a compelling negative answer to the question whether presidential unilateralism generally serves the public interest.

3

Iraq and the (Unlearned) Lessons of Vietnam: Presidentialism and the Pathologies of Unilateral Policy Making

Americans like to regard themselves as more practical than theoretical in thinking about public affairs. Although the Constitution does not require us to have a unilateral presidency as a matter of law, many Americans will pragmatically hold that whether we ought to have a unilateral presidency depends mostly on how the presidency actually operates. Whether presidentialism or pluralism actually works better as a framework for action in terms of positive presidential leadership is a real-world empirical question and a rather different matter than pure constitutional interpretation. Even if pluralists are legally correct that Congress and the courts are entitled to play a substantial checking role with regard to executive authority, the legislative and judicial branches would still have the discretion to allow the President very great delegated power. So, the question needs to be faced: Is presidential decision making likely to be better or worse if the other branches treat the President as presumptively autonomous and substantially immune from accountability to the other branches?

Foreign affairs and especially military policy have been realms in which Congress and the courts have historically delegated considerable power to presidents. At least since the Korean War, war making has been a national policy making arena in which presidentialism has held great sway. In the foreign deployment of military force, presidents have urged with considerable success that they ought to be treated as having extensive powers that are largely immune to the other branches' oversight and input. Following the Vietnam War, Congress tried to reclaim some power of policy initiative through the enactment, over President Nixon's veto, of the War Powers Resolution of 1973.[1] Yet, for a variety of institutional reasons, the influence Congress wields in war making is still largely up to the President. Military policy thus serves as a kind of natural laboratory in which to explore the question whether presidentialism is pragmatically a good thing.

The rhetoric of presidentialism generally applied to military decision making and foreign policy portrays the executive branch—left to its own devices—as a lean, mean policy making machine. The President, as one person, can supposedly coordinate decisional processes and insure policy coherence in ways that a 535-member legislature cannot. Presidents have access to confidential information and presumably know how to keep a secret. Presidents can make decisions quickly. They can marshal expertise. These functional advantages of the unitary presidency are routinely trumpeted as bolstering the case for a unilateral presidency in military and foreign affairs.[2]

There is, however, a subtle non sequitur at work in stepping from these venerable observations to presidentialism as a guide to government practice. The President's functional advantages may well provide reasons for vesting final authority over at least certain kinds of foreign affairs or military operations in a single individual. Within any large organization, even a highly pluralistic decision making environment may require a single presiding "magistrate" to bring decision making to a definitive close. But this does not say much about the institutional context in which that individual is likely to make the best decisions. Presidentialism and pluralism can shape that context in two ways. First, as approaches to institutional design, they may lead to different decision making structures and practices. But, second, equally as important, as ideologies—as premises against which institutional practices unfold—they may shape behavior differently almost without regard to the formalities of decision making process because of the expectations they create regarding the nature of legitimate decision making and likely expectations for external review. To reiterate, then, the key question in the pragmatic debate between presidentialism and pluralism is whether the President is likely to make better decisions against a background understanding that the executive branch is constitutionally entitled to policy making autonomy that is substantially beyond the power of Congress to regulate or the authority of the courts to review. Or is the President likely to make better decisions if we posit the reverse—that Presidents are substantially susceptible to congressional regulation in foreign and military affairs, and at least presumptively accountable to oversight by the other branches of government?

The argument for pluralism as the better context for presidential decision making is rooted in the realities of individual and group psychology. Presidents who believe they are constitutionally entitled to preserve all decision making power in their own hands and in the hands of their closest political associates—without external accountability—are likely to involve a group of actors in evaluating events and deciding how to respond that will be too small and too homogeneous for best results. It has long been known that, among small groups, whether in business or other organizations, the erosion of pluralism can readily result in bad decision making. Conversely, operating against a pluralist understanding of the presidency would mean functioning in an environment where presidents would want to take advantage of open discussion, the presentation of various perspectives, and the conscientious weighing of even dramatically diverse options both within and beyond the bureaucracy they oversee. The reason is straightforward: People who think their decisions can be held externally accountable to sources of authority with multiple points of view are more likely to attend to those points of view when they make decisions in the first place.

For a variety of reasons, courts are likely to serve only marginally as a source of accountability in foreign and military affairs. They have no merely consultative or planning role to play, and their role in litigation is limited by rules regarding discovery and standing to sue that will place out of bounds a great many lawsuits that might otherwise be hypothesized regarding the conduct of our foreign and military policy.

On the other hand, the elected branches of government, Congress and the executive, can promote pluralism within presidential decision making routines in a variety of ways. Pluralism may be operationalized by actual legislation that forces presidents to hew to congressionally specified requirements in making foreign affairs and military decisions. It may be operationalized by legislative requirements that the executive branch consult widely with members of Congress in the course of making decisions. It may be operationalized within the executive branch by giving great weight to the views of career professionals—people whose political allegiances transcend particular Administrations and whose contributions are evaluated chiefly under criteria of accuracy and reliability rather than loyalty. What all these techniques have in common is the attempt to force presidential accountability to something other than the President's personal or partisan ideology and political agenda. The most striking episodes of presidentialism in action that we have seen since the end of the Korean War have, correspondingly, sought to fend off each of these possibilities.

To make the pragmatic case for pluralism, I will review briefly some of what we know about small group psychology and the pathologies of decision making by groups that are excessively homogeneous and insulated from accountability. I then want to show the striking consistency between social psychologists' concerns for bad decision making in certain kinds of groups and two sets of accounts available to us regarding policy making on Vietnam and Iraq. These case studies are appropriate for three reasons. First, they represent the United States' two most intense, sustained, and costly military engagements over the last fifty years. Second, in each case, the relevant Administrations behaved as if presidentialist assumptions regarding executive authority were, in actuality, the law. Third, these are case studies from different times and involving both the Democratic and Republican parties. To the extent we can observe similarities between the Johnson Administration, the most liberal in recent history, and the much-later George W. Bush Administration, the most conservative, such findings may buttress our confidence that the dangers of presidentialism transcend specific eras and the political ideologies of the particular Presidents involved. The accounts on which I rely may ultimately prove to be too partial or preliminary to count as definitive, comprehensive histories of the policy making in each period, but their consistency with the predictions of pathological decision making can so readily be linked with the logic of presidentialism in action that we ought to reject outright the presidentialists' confident argument that, as a practical matter, unilateralism produces better decision making.

Presidentialism and the Psychology of Group Decision Making

Implicit in *The Federalist* and, in particular, Madison's theory of faction are the ideas that government decisions may be assessed objectively as being more or less congruent with the public interest and that human psychology can interfere with our capacity to make the best decisions. The sources of bad decision making, according to Madison, include inadequate information, the elevation of self-interest over collective interest, and the capacity of momentary passion to subvert our powers of judgment. Since the 1970s, however, cognitive psychologists have elaborated a model of human judgment and decision making that systematizes these concerns somewhat differently. Modern cognitive psychology starts from the premises that the human brain is limited in its capacity to process information and that this limitation causes human beings to make decisions through certain forms of mental shortcuts. These shortcuts, while frequently useful, systematically cause a variety of judgment errors—errors that, to some extent, can be combated or exacerbated by the group environment in which decisions are made.[3]

In a famous 1972 book using the same name, social psychologist Irving Janis popularized the idea of "groupthink" to capture an especially important way in which group interaction can degrade the quality of decision making.[4] When a group responsible for evaluating the environment, coming up with options, and suggesting a policy resists and even rejects alternative viewpoints and becomes fixated on one interpretation and one implication for policy, it is suffering from groupthink. As John Levine and Richard Moreland have summarized the Janis hypothesis: "According to Janis, the antecedents of groupthink include high group cohesion, structural faults (e.g., directive leadership), and a provocative emotional context (e.g., external; threats). These factors produce overestimation of the group, closed-mindedness, and pressures toward uniformity, which in turn lead to defective decision making, including an incomplete survey of available options, a failure to assess the risks of the preferred option, and a selective bias in processing information. As a result, the group is less likely to make a good decision and more likely to become psychologically entrapped in a poor decision."[5] Imagine, then, a set of presidential advisers united in their personal and political commitments to the President, a President who is highly directive in specifying to the group the range of decisions that would be acceptable, and the emotionally charged atmosphere of war. Janis would predict a tendency among the advisory group to exaggerate the quality of its own decision making, to limit its willingness to consider proposals or analyses that would make it harder to give the President what the President is perceived to want, and to accept too easily evidence that confirms the President's preferences, while discounting contrary evidence. To the extent any member of the group experiences doubt, the group's social dynamics are likely to induce silence.

Such a process, despite the obstacles, might still yield a good decision. As Philip Tetlock has pointed out, Winston Churchill's suppression of dissent in cabinet meetings in 1940–1941, when some members of the British government favored a negotiated pace with Hitler, may have induced groupthink—but to good effect.[6] Nor does a well-designed decision making process guarantee success, as President Carter's 1980 Iranian hostage rescue attempt may remind us.[7] Still, all things being equal, a more open and inclusive decision making process seems likelier to counter the predictable dysfunctionalities of expert group decisionmaking than the converse. A pragmatically oriented public should want to operationalize a set of understandings concerning the prerogatives of the presidency that is most likely to correct for those dysfunctionalities.

This is perhaps the most important reason why pluralism, as a baseline understanding of the presidency, is of such great pragmatic importance in military and foreign policy making. Both groups and individual decision makers, including the President, who have internalized the notion of "accountability"—the idea that arguments, premises, and conclusions may all have to be justified to others whose agreement cannot be taken for granted—will simply work harder in analyzing the options before them.[8] Accountability can offset the tendency of experts to be overconfident about their decisions and the tendency of cohesive groups to exclude options from consideration and sift evidence in a biased fashion.

McNamara's War: The Failures of Executive Policy Making under Kennedy and Johnson

When Irving Janis wrote his 1972 account of groupthink, his analysis was very much shaped by his understanding of how the United States escalated its involvement in the Vietnam War—surely one of the more tragic examples of presidentialism at work. It may thus seem entirely unsurprising that the decision making history on which Janis relied is consistent with his theory. Striking confirmatory evidence, however, appeared in the mid-1990s, with the intimate look at executive branch decision making made available through Robert S. McNamara's 1995 memoir of his life as Secretary of Defense.[9]

It was in the early to mid-1960s that the U.S. presence in Vietnam escalated from a small cadre of military advisers to a substantial armed force. The pattern of decision making that produced that escalation was shallow, ill informed, hostile to genuine debate, unwilling to confront uncertainties about basic issues, and driven more by wishful thinking and by perceived political momentum than by sound interpretations of fact. McNamara's account shows how the process was slow, sloppy, and in some respects incoherent. Because the executive was never seriously tested as to its underlying assumptions about the nature of the conflict and the soundness of alternative strategies, the imperative governing the decision making process was never to admit error. Those responsible for giving the President sound factual analysis on which to predicate decisions generally fed to the White House only the spin it wanted to hear. A more vigorous assertion of influence by Congress—where prominent antiwar voices could be heard—could not possibly have made things worse, and might well have made things better.

Much of McNamara's rhetoric harkens wistfully—and more than a lit-tle ironically—to the ideal of lean and mean executive policy making that presidentialists hold dear. He seems to measure his failures by the imagined distance he and his colleagues fell short of a heady brand of self-confident, hard-nosed, expert decision making by brilliant men (and I do not here use that last noun generically). But this is an ideal of decision making that, by McNamara's account, was nowhere realized during the Vietnam years. Every key decision that McNamara recounts belies the ideal's implicit ar-rogance. Indeed, conceit among key decision makers, perhaps McNamara most of all, contributed mightily to the tragic sequence of events they helped sustain.

The pattern of poor decision making was forged early in the Kennedy Administration. Throughout fall 1961, meetings were held among President Kennedy, McNamara, and Secretary of State Dean Rusk to discuss how to respond to increasing guerilla infiltration from North into South Vietnam. Though positioned to exert potentially strong influence, McNamara waf-fled in trying to decide whether to support sending more advisers, equip-ment, and even combat troops to Vietnam. He first suggested his endorse-ment and then, in combination with Rusk, withdrew it. "Looking back," he writes, "at the record of those [1961] meetings, it is clear our analysis was nowhere near adequate. We failed to ask the . . . most basic questions."[10] In explanation, McNamara cites his inexperience, naïveté, the sheer number of problems clamoring for attention, and an unwillingness to confront in a deep way "problems for which there were no ready, or good, answers."[11] None of the deficiencies were to change over an eight-year period—not-withstanding an increase in experience.

The President's access to confidential information availed key decision makers little in the quest for sound decision making. According to Mc-Namara, "None of us—not me, not the president, not Mac [Bundy], nor Dean, nor Max [Taylor]—was ever satisfied with the information we got from Vietnam."[12] The inadequacy of written reports from both the military and from the American embassy in Vietnam led the Kennedy Administra-tion to stage special consultative meetings in Hawaii at the headquarters of the U.S. military commander of the Pacific. There, McNamara and others "would listen to a long series of briefings."[13] But the results were not much better: "The crowded atmosphere and agenda often made it hard to focus on the issues at hand and ensure we were receiving candid reports and thoughtful recommendations."[14]

The problem of misinformation was multidimensional. The South Viet-namese tended to relay to the United States only information that they perceived the Americans wanted to hear.[15] Then, American military commanders tended to put their own spin on that information, affected both by wishful thinking and by misjudgment as to the complexity of evaluating military success in a guerilla war.[16]

The pace of decision making was also a problem. Key decisions were often delayed because of persistent disagreements within the Administration over central issues. Once momentum for a decision developed, reluctant participants could find themselves going along without ever forcing real debate on the unresolved points of doubt. This was tragically evident in the Kennedy Administration's handling of the unraveling Diem government in South Vietnam. Given Kennedy's premise that the war could not be won except by the South Vietnamese themselves, the destabilization of the Diem regime by Buddhist protests and Diem's violent retaliation might well have counseled an immediate withdrawal. No such decision was made, however, because key advisers within the Administration could not bring themselves to consensus.[17]

Instead, what ensued was a chaotic, even bizarre decisional process about whether to support a military coup to overthrow Diem. According to McNamara, setting in process the decision to support the coup was a draft cable from Under Secretary of State for Far Eastern Affairs Roger Hilsman, Jr., to the new U.S. ambassador in Saigon, Henry Cabot Lodge, Jr.[18] The draft cable was sent to President Kennedy in Hyannis. The President said he would agree to transmitting the cable "if his senior advisers concurred."[19] Somehow, and rather strangely, this conditional statement, one that practically opened the issue to debate, was apparently interpreted as Kennedy favoring the coup. In a perverse version of the telephone game, as various advisers communicated with each other, the perception that Kennedy had already given approval was only reinforced. Thus even though high-level advisers were either unenthusiastic or even reluctant to agree, they "went along because the President had already done so" or so they believed.[20]

After Kennedy's assassination, it was left to Lyndon Johnson to decide what course to take in Vietnam and, especially, to decide whether to introduce significant numbers of U.S. combat troops. Notwithstanding the importance of military advice on the topic, Johnson allowed the Joint Chiefs of Staff to avoid answering key questions about the advisability of military involvement: "We never carefully debated what U.S. force would ultimately be required, what our chances of success would be, or what the political, military, financial, and human costs would be if we provided [the direct application of U.S. military force]."[21] During 1964, LBJ refrained from a major buildup, but he ordered the development of military plans and asked that a resolution be drafted to give "congressional validation of expanded U.S. military action in Indochina."[22]

Executive decision making again failed to distinguish itself in 1965 when the Administration initiated the definitive escalation of American involvement in the war. Johnson accepted the decision to bomb North Vietnam because the weakening government in Saigon looked too fragile to pursue any effective course of action without the United States, and no obvious alternative to bombing existed.[23] Once bombing began, however, protecting U.S. airbases from the Vietcong became a bootstrap argument for escalating the introduction of ground troops.[24] LBJ convened a working group to review the key options, but it was rife with disagreement: "(Their) presentation to the President was full of holes."[25] The group again "failed to confront . . . basic questions."[26]

As debates persisted over the proper course of action, Johnson "brought to Washington a bipartisan group of elder statesmen who became known as the Wise Men [sic] . . . an impressive group with knowledge, experience, and prestige."[27] Unfortunately, of course, their knowledge was even less complete than that of official policy makers. Their military advice to Johnson was keyed more to ideological predisposition than analysis of fact, and LBJ altogether ignored their political advice to be far more candid with the American public.[28] Two years later, when LBJ reconvened the group for further advice, he even went so far as to disinvite those "wise men" who had decided they disagreed with his policy.[29]

In retrospect, McNamara judges harshly the results of so much inward-looking deliberation. Policies were shaped by "loose assumptions, unasked questions, and thin analyses" he wrote in his memoirs.[30] Contrary to the unitary executive myth, the hierarchical structure of executive authority did not promote well-coordinated policy making or implementation. Proper coordination on whether to support the coup against Diem was lacking, and that decision was limited to a few top advisers; as policy involved more actors and agencies, coordination deteriorated further. McNamara sums up the executive's performance as follows: "Underlying many . . . errors lay our failure to organize the top echelons of the executive branch to deal effectively with the extraordinarily complex range of political and military issues, involving the great risks and costs—including, above all else, loss of life—associated with the application of military force under substantial constraints over a long period of time."[31] As McNamara noted, there was a general failure to pose the most basic questions, including the fundamental issues of whether the United States should have stayed in Vietnam and what the implications would be if it withdrew. Johnson was, however, exposed to such arguments, and it is an indictment of the unitary presidency that he denied to his advisers key information, such as a report from the so-called Navy Vietnam Appraisal Group that military victory was impossible, and an analysis by former CIA director Richard Helms concluding that the dangers posed by unilateral disengagement from Vietnam for U.S. national security and foreign policy would be limited.[32]

In retrospect, McNamara seems clear as to the key process failure that led to such disastrous decision making: "We failed to draw Congress and the American people into a full and frank discussion and debate of the pros and cons of a large-scale military involvement in Southeast Asia before we initiated the action."[33] As a result, it was not only the case that fundamental issues went unexamined, but also that no firm basis of public support was ever created to sustain the Administration's policy:[34] "There is no 'right' moment to obtain popular consent for military action through a vote of Congress. Debate will always arise over how and when to do so. The fact is it *must* be done—even if a divisive vote risks given aid and comfort to our adversary. We did not do it, and we would learn the hard way that a government must accept that risk in order to lead a united country into war and maintain support. Instead of working toward unity, we chose to sweep the debate under the Oval Office carpet."[35] The decision making that McNamara describes misjudged the "geopolitical intentions" of America's adversaries, misperceived the motivations of the leaders of South Vietnam, underestimated the importance of nationalism as a force driving the Viet Cong effort, and exaggerated the likely benefits to be realized from our superior equipment and fire power.[36] This picture hardly provides evidence of the pragmatic benefits of presidentialism, either in terms of institutional design or the underlying theory of the prerogatives of the unilateral presidency.

Nixon's War: Presidentialism and the Cambodia Disaster

The ascendancy of Richard Nixon to the presidency exacerbated the penchant for tightly controlled executive branch decision making and the affinity for secrecy and deception in connection with Vietnam policy as Nixon intensified the President's relative isolation in reaching critical judgments. The results were disastrous, especially with regard to Cambodia.[37]

Nixon began during the 1968 transitional period to design a system of national security policy making that would largely insulate the President from the influence of the State Department. In a personification of presidentialism, Nixon thought that he could best achieve goals based on "[s]ecrecy, aloofness, an aura of mystery, limiting personal statements and achieving maximum surprise and effect with those he did make, [and] frequent dissimulation of his true purposes in order to keep criticism at bay."[38] He chose as his chief agent in this project Henry Kissinger, whom he named Special Assistant to the President for National Security Affairs (popularly known as the National Security Adviser). Kissinger was responsible for chairing "panels" comprising deputies from the State and Defense Departments, in effect creating a parallel reporting structure and bypassing the Cabinet-level secretaries. As a result, "[t]he system permitted the President to intervene all the way, through Kissinger, while making it difficult for the Secretaries of State and Defense to get hold of an issue until it had virtually been decided in one of the panels. It was a palace coup."[39]

Nixon followed the same pattern in orchestrating diplomatic communications. He told Soviet ambassador Anatoly Dobrynin to deal with Kissinger, not the State Department, on any truly consequential matter.[40] His common resort to back-channel communications kept the Departments of State and of Defense away from critical diplomatic meetings and left key officials frequently ignorant even that important communications had taken place relative to their areas of responsibility. Nixon's isolation was all the more intense because he "shunned serious one-on-one talks with his Cabinet members or any kind of searching exchanges with members of Congress alone or in groups."[41]

The extreme insularity of Nixon's decision making style had three profound operational consequences. First, it left unconstrained his tendency to view the communist world in monolithic terms. State Department professionals, largely ignored by Nixon, had a keener understanding of how local and regional factors could create frictions among communist regimes and of the role of nationalism in influencing communist policies. Second, it left room for military leaders to have stronger influence than other high-level policy makers in key debates. For example, while both Secretary of State Rogers and Secretary of Defense Laird advocated U.S. support for a neutral Cambodia, military leaders, volubly represented by Kissinger's deputy, Alexander Haig, championed intervention to prevent North Vietnam's access to Cambodia for supply and operations coordination.[42] Third, it left his support in Congress increasingly vulnerable to erosion through distrust and a lack of genuine participation in critical policy making.

These shortcomings helped to provoke all-but-unimaginable calamity in Cambodia. As recounted by presidential historian William Bundy:

Cambodia was the site for bad decisions on no fewer than five occasions: the 1969–70 secret bombing of the border areas; the incursion of May 1970, with its devastating effect on key sectors of American opinion and negligible offsetting military gains; the decision in the fall of 1970 to provide continuing military and economic aid to Cambodia (leading Congress to ban American military advisors in both Laos and Cambodia, which in turn hamstrung the disastrous Laos offensive of early 1971); and (less noted in most accounts) the failure to understand that North Vietnam by the summer of 1972 no longer controlled the Communist side in Cambodia—that the Khmer Rouge had taken over. This led directly to the fifth grave error, the inhumane and ineffectual bombing of Cambodia in the spring of 1973, which finally persuaded Congress to ban all future American military action in Southeast Asia.

The policy behind these five decisions produced extraordinarily tragic consequences in human terms, with no remotely offsetting strategic benefits. If the United States had stayed out, the alternative outcome—most likely a North Vietnamese takeover of Cambodia, or a struggle for control between China and North Vietnam, with a puppet regime set up by either—could never have been as devastating as what happened.[43]

"What happened" included the dropping of 108,823 tons of bombs in nearly 3,900 secret bombing raids between March 1969 and May 1970,[44] plus the dropping of another 80,000 tons of bombs between February and June 1973.[45] Bundy shares the judgment that the resumption and intensification of bombing in 1973 accelerated the military efforts of the Khmer Rouge and left them less susceptible to influence by any of their less extreme supporters, thus helping to set the stage for nightmarish regime of Pol Pot.[46]

Nixon neglected to involve Congress in any serious way in the development of a Cambodia policy. He lied about the 1969–1970 campaign: "[H]e had the military devise a system of double bookkeeping under which strikes on targets within Cambodia were reported as having taken place in South Vietnam."[47] The State Department, the Secretary of the Air Force, and the Air Force Chief of Staff were all kept ignorant of the bombing, as were the relevant congressional committees. The bombing was not formally revealed to Congress until confirmation hearings for a new Air Force Chief of Staff in 1973.[48]

It would be hard to overstate the negative institutional consequences of Nixon's aggressively presidentialist view of his military authorities. Given the weakness of the American bargaining position in 1973—after all, ground troops were being withdrawn from Vietnam—Nixon pinned his hopes for the durability of any peace accord chiefly on two factors. First, as he secretly promised South Vietnam's President Thieu, Nixon was prepared to retaliate through furious air power should North Vietnam renege on any negotiated truce.[49] Second, Nixon envisioned offering North Vietnam a substantial postwar aid package as a "carrot" for keeping the peace.[50] Again, however, he never consulted Congress on the formulation of either of these commitments.

By 1973, Nixon's arrogance and deception in conducting the war led to bipartisan congressional distrust of his willingness genuinely to end American military involvement in Southeast Asia. Congress, led by a bipartisan coalition in the Senate, forced Nixon to accept a legislatively imposed cutoff of funding for any military activity in Indochina as of August 15, 1973—thus eviscerating his secret promise to Thieu.[51] In April 1973, the Senate voted, 88–3, that Nixon could not provide any funds to Vietnam for reconstruction aid without Congress's specific approval.[52] The clear implication was that none would be forthcoming.

The picture that emerges from Nixon's version of presidentialist decision making is not one of sound, coherent, efficient, and accountable decision making. Nixon's Cambodia policy was often informed by poor intelligence and a flawed perspective on Cambodian politics. The 1973 bombing seemed to implement no strategic objective at all, much less a coherent one. Nixon had asserted that securing the return of POWs was the sole justification for continued U.S. military action in Indochina; yet, the bombing continued even after the POWs returned. Any expediency Nixon achieved in making policy without congressional consensus building has to be judged against the fatal blow he dealt to his own capacity to secure any legislative support whatever for his enforcement of the Paris peace accords. And one can hardly praise for accountability a decision making process that Nixon strained to keep secret and that ultimately provided grounds for a proposed impeachment article. In short, it is hard to imagine a policy process that could have been worse. And yet . . .

Iraq and the Dysfunctions of the Unilateral Presidency

Prior to the March 2003 American invasion of Iraq, popular and academic commentators debated vigorously whether our anticipated incursion boded for the United States a military and political quagmire akin to Vietnam.[53] In the wake of the invasion, debate brews about the geopolitical analogy—arguably, Iraq is a worse disaster for American interests than was Vietnam—but, in one respect, we are truly replaying an earlier script. In defining American objectives and elaborating our strategies, the executive branch under George W. Bush allowed ideological commitment to override debate, followed flawed intelligence, and made policy by wishful thinking. Worst-case scenarios about Iraq's nuclear and unconventional weapons programs were proffered as the basis for the invasion, while best-case scenarios of how American troops would be received and the ease of creating a new government were used to justify the invasion plan. Intelligence was over- or underplayed depending on whether it tended to support or call into question the decision to invade. Decision makers suppressed personal doubts in the face of what they believed to be conclusions already determined by higher authorities. In all of this, the Bush Administration's penchant for executive unilateralism—its largely successful attempt to fend off any genuine engagement with or oversight by anyone not precommitted to the Administration's position—consistently undermined sound decision making, all but identically to earlier Administrations.

America's role in Iraq has been largely defined by four colossal blunders:

1. Basing the invasion on suspicions that Saddam possessed weapons of mass destruction, notwithstanding contrary evidence, the contrary opinion of at least some weapons inspectors, doubts as to the reliability of the key intelligence sources on which we were relying, and Saddam's last-minute willingness to allow UN inspectors comprehensive and unconditional access to look for WMD;
2. Invading Iraq with insufficient forces to secure the country after the toppling of Saddam;
3. Toppling Saddam without any plan to rebuild the civilian or military infrastructure of Iraq; and
4. Toppling Saddam without regard to unleashing potential sectarian violence in Iraq, the radicalization of the Muslim populace in other nations, and the inevitable enhancement of the geopolitical position of Iran.[54]

In the run-up to invasion, the Administration sought to persuade the American people that Saddam was allied with al Qaeda, that overthrowing Saddam would eliminate an existing and imminent threat to the United States, that the invasion would essentially pay for itself because of the availability of Iraqi oil money to finance reconstruction, that Iraqis would unite in their support of the invasion and in welcoming an end to the Baathist regime, and that the eventual Iraqi example of a genuine multiparty democracy would sustain forces of democratic reform through the Mideast. As it turns out, there was no Saddam–al Qaeda connection. Iraq posed no imminent threat to the United States. The cost to Americans of the war and reconstruction was projected as of spring 2008 to be $845 billion in 2007 dollars and growing.[55] The U.S. invasion unleashed a period of deadly instability and sectarian violence in Iraq, and the Mideast forces strengthened by our intervention have so far been the forces of radical Islam, most notably as embodied in the Iranian government of Mahmoud Ahmadinejad and the Lebanese Hezbollah.

Nothing has more bedeviled our Iraqi adventure than the failure of intelligence. In their meticulous study of the invasion and occupation of Iraq, journalists Michael R. Gordon and Bernard E. Trainor, the latter a retired Marine Corps lieutenant general, quote the view of Paul Pillar, the CIA's national intelligence officer for the Near East and South Asia in 2002: "It was certainly fairly clear early in 2002 to just about anyone working in intelligence on Iraq issues that we were going to war, that the decision had essentially been made. For any analyst, favorable attention to policymakers is a benchmark of success. There was a natural bias in favor of intelligence production that supported, rather than undermined, policies already set."[56] Among the views most dangerously suppressed was the strong belief of CIA counterterrorism officials that invading Iraq would distract from the fight against al Qaeda at a critical time. *New York Times* national security reporter James Risen quotes a former aide to CIA Director George Tenet, explaining that Tenet, in essence, told the CIA that the White House was already committed to the invasion. As summarized by Risen: "Agency officials who appeared to be unenthusiastic about Iraq soon mysteriously found themselves sidelined, while their more eager and ambitious colleagues began to rise, both within the Directorate of Operations and in the Directorate of Intelligence, the analytical arm."[57] In this context, presidential unilateralism imposed a kind of ideological discipline that disabled sound analysis.

The fundamental issue that our intelligence community got wrong, of course, was the question whether Saddam possessed weapons of mass destruction. In fall 2002, pressed by Senator Bob Graham of Florida—before an anticipated congressional vote on a resolution authorizing military force in Iraq—the CIA produced a "National Intelligence Estimate" (NIE), which claimed Iraq was producing poison and possible chemical and biological weapons.[58] It expressed these conclusions with less tentativeness than a similar report two years earlier, despite evidence undermining these conclusions. It also asserted that Iraq was moving to restart its nuclear weapons program. President Bush had famously asserted in his 2002 State of the Union Address that Iraq had sought to buy uranium in Niger to support that program.

The NIE actually papered over profound uncertainties within lower echelons of the Administration concerning the state of Iraq's WMD program. When Secretary of State Colin Powell was preparing his intelligence briefing for the United Nations Security Council, the State Department's intelligence bureau asserted thirty-eight of the claims being made were "'weak' or 'unsubstantiated.'"[59] Some of these claims actually remained in the text Powell delivered. The underlying source of U.S. intelligence on Iraqi germ warfare intentions was a defector code-named Curve Ball, a source deemed so unreliable by the Defense Department official who interviewed him that he e-mailed the CIA not to rely on Curve Ball's statements as a basis for Secretary Powell's presentation on germ warfare.[60] Powell also cited reports by an al Qaeda detainee that Iraqis were training the terrorists in how to make chemical and biological weapons.[61] A year earlier, the Defense Intelligence Agency had warned that the man was probably lying.

With regard to Iraq's nuclear program, Mohammed Al-Baradei, director general of the International Atomic Energy Commission, had expressed doubts about Iraq's nuclear intentions and capabilities. The report on Iraq's interest in uranium in Niger had been substantially discredited. Most telling of all, the CIA had recruited at least thirty relatives of Iraqi nuclear scientists to travel to Iraq and glean from those scientists the state of Iraqi nuclear research. All thirty returned with the same report, that the program had been dead since 1991, that Iraq lacked parts and materials adequate to a program, and that they did not have the capacity to restart the program without being detected. CIA officials ignored and refused to share this information with the White House.[62]

Administration defenders—including the President—have countered that the intelligence services of numerous allies had also reached a mistaken conclusion about Saddam and WMD.[63] In retrospect, it seems clear that what looked to the West as Saddam's evasiveness about his weapons programs was intended chiefly to befuddle Iran; Saddam doubted the United States would actually invade, given that it made no sense to him that the United States would prefer a Shiite-dominated regime in Iraq to his own.[64] Even though, in January 2003, he offered the United Nations unlimited access for its weapons inspectors, the United States acted as if determined to read every ambiguity in Saddam's behavior as evidence of his WMD ambitions.

As harmful as executive branch insularity proved with regard to intelligence analysis, executive unilateralism had equally devastating results for the planning of the invasion. Specifically, the dangers of tightly hierarchicalized, insular policy making are dramatically illustrated by the Bush

Administration's decision to invade and attempt to secure Iraq with only 170,000 troops. Secretary of Defense Donald Rumsfeld was determined to make Iraq an example of his hoped-for transformative approach to the American military. He was committed to weaning the military from the Powell doctrine of using overwhelming ground force and to pursuing American military objectives instead with smaller, more flexible units, supplemented by superior American weapons and technology.[65] The theory of military transformation to which Rumsfeld was wedded anticipated that reliable battlefield intelligence plus robust communications capacity would change the nature of warfare and make it possible to win decisive victories with small numbers of U.S. troops. None of these assumptions held true in Iraq.

The aim of Rumsfeld's desired transformation was not to improve military performance per se, but to embolden the United States in its use of the military to accomplish foreign policy objectives. As summarized by prominent military correspondents Gordon and Trainor: "[C]onservatives had seen the Powell doctrine of overwhelming force as an impediment to action and an inhibition against the exercise of American power . . . Rumsfeld and his deputies had argued that there was military utility in getting into the fight quickly and avoiding the sort of massive logistical buildup that Powell had overseen in the Persian Gulf War."[66] Because of this commitment, Rumsfeld dismissed out of hand an early proposal to invade Iraq with half a million troops.[67]

To make sure that the evolving invasion plan conformed to his preconceptions, Rumsfeld further arranged for his aides and himself to vet repeated early iterations of the plan, fending off, at every opportunity, any call for large troop deployments. His deputy Douglas Feith assigned staffers to attend CENTCOM military planning meetings. The generals later excluded them after it appeared they were acting more as "moles" than collaborators.[68]

Anthony Zinni, the Marine general who until 2000 led CENTCOM—the U.S. Central Command, which is responsible for planning and conducting U.S. military activity in twenty-seven countries in Northeast Africa and Southwest and Central Asia—had developed a contingency plan before his retirement for invading Iraq with 380,000–400,000 troops.[69] Army General Tommy Franks, who succeeded Zinni, trimmed Zinni's estimate, hoping to satisfy Rumsfeld—but likewise found his first plan dismissed out of hand. Rumsfeld, who was committed to smaller forces and more rapid deployment, pushed Franks to compress his planned deployment from sixty to thirty days, which would allow for fewer troops.[70] At the time, former

GOP House Speaker Newt Gingrich, still influential in Pentagon circles, was insisting that the U.S. Army could defeat Baghdad within two weeks with fifty thousand troops.[71]

From the outset, the Joint Chiefs of Staff were leery of Rumsfeld's approach. Hugh Shelton, the chair of the JCS, thought Rumsfeld was predisposed against the Army because the Army held main responsibility for Balkan peacekeeping operations under Clinton—operations that the Bush Administration was determined to use as an example of what not to do in terms of prolonged entanglements and "nation building."[72] Eric Shinseki, the Army Chief of Staff, likewise expressed repeated doubts about the commitment to a lean invasion force.[73] When Shelton's JCS term ended, Rumsfeld deliberately chose a successor on whom he could count for *not* expressing independent opinions, General Richard B. Myers.[74]

When war preparations began in earnest between Rumsfeld and CENTCOM, plans developed for invading Iraq with force sizes ranging from 4,000 to 275,000.[75] General Franks had turned command over land forces to Lt. Gen. David McKiernan, a trusted officer under Shinseki, who was dubious of the commitment to invade with a lean attack force. He thought reduced combat power up front could prolong the ground war and render operations needlessly complex. Key to the debate were estimates not only of the troops needed to overthrow the government, but also the forces necessary to secure the country and to maintain logistical support adequate to the American mission. In order to be sure that necessary elements were not overlooked, conventional preparations would have included an exercise called a TPFDL—that is, the compilation of a so-called Time-Phased Force and Deployment List—that would spell out all units necessary for the operation. Rumsfeld decided not to do a TPFDL because he did not trust his commanders to keep their demands for units to a minimum. In order to avoid troop commitments exceeding his "transformative" objectives, Rumsfeld wanted to arbitrate personally which units would be sent.[76]

Shinseki objected to proceeding without a TPFDL, along with Rumsfeld's decision not to activate reservists until after Christmas 2002, a move that delayed the establishment of the Theater Support Command, which would be necessary to manage logistics. Shinseki's staff estimated that a proper deployment would require 350,000 coalition forces, and he told Congress in February 2003 that securing Iraq would require the use of several hundred thousand American troops.[77]

With nothing but wishful thinking to support his logic, Rumsfeld dismissed the idea as ludicrous that it would take more troops to secure Iraq than to topple Saddam. His own stance, of course, was truly ridiculous if

Rumsfeld actually believed in Saddam's possession of WMD, all of which would have had to be secured at an unspecified number of sites. Had we been right in insisting that Saddam held WMD, our decision to invade with a relatively small force would have placed our troops at extraordinary risk and raised a realistic specter of WMD being moved out of Iraq and into the hands of terrorists.[78] Nonetheless, Franks acceded to Rumsfeld's insistence that troops would be withdrawn as resistance crumbled. He and McKiernan based their numbers on the assumption that the invasion would leave the Iraqi military not only physically intact, but also willing and able to help secure the nation after Saddam.[79]

In order to avoid getting unwelcome news on the troop strength needed to stabilize Iraq after the fall of Saddam, Rumsfeld and Franks tried to keep the Joint Chiefs and their staff out of direct war planning. A JCS "war game" pointed to the need to create a new military headquarters to take care of Iraq after the invasion. The advice was essentially ignored.[80]

Sound planning for postwar Iraq was disabled by more than wishful thinking about Iraqi reaction to the invasion. The neoconservatives based in the Pentagon and the office of the Vice President were ideologically committed to regarding peacekeeping efforts by the Clinton Administration in the Balkans as misconceived. Thus, almost by definition, any strategy adopted by the Clinton Administration was to be dismissed as necessarily incorrect. For example, because the State Department led American postwar efforts in the Balkans, this alone was taken up by Rumsfeld as an argument for Pentagon primacy in running Iraq after the war.[81] Rumsfeld's plans were largely conceived as being the antithesis of Clinton's. As described by Douglas Feith, Rumsfeld's undersecretary of defense for policy, the Pentagon plan was not "nation-building." Instead, the key concept was "enabling" Iraqis to govern themselves.[82] The United States would topple Saddam, but leave Iraqi institutions intact and get out.

Serious postwar planning did not start in earnest at the Pentagon until nearly Christmas 2002—hardly three months before the invasion.[83] The initial assignment to formulate a military organization plan went to Brig. Gen. Steven Hawkins, who was given no budget, but a fifty-eight-member staff, many of whom had never worked together before. At CENTCOM, however, General McKiernan had already put his own officer in charge of a planning effort, and insisted that Hawkins' task force be under his jurisdiction. That officer, Maj. Gen. Alfred Whitley, produced a plan based on best-case assumptions: Iraqi institutions would remain intact, and other U.S. organizations would finance and facilitate reconstruction of Iraqi infrastructure. No one prepared a fallback plan in the event that Iraqis could not maintain their own postwar security. It is not that no one noticed this problem, but rather, given Rumsfeld's insistence on such a lean invasion force, there were no troops capable of being diverted from fighting to security. Jay Garner, a retired general recruited by Rumsfeld and Feith to head a civilian postwar planning office, was told both by Justice Department official Dick Mayer, head of the International Criminal Investigative Training Assistance Program, and by security expert David Kay, who served as the U.S. chief weapons inspector in Iraq, that the United States was courting disaster if the need for policing postwar Iraq was ignored. Their warnings were echoed in late February 2003, by Robert Perito, a peacekeeping expert from the U.S. Institute for Peace. Yet, no plans for securing Iraq without the help of Iraqi military and police forces were put into place.

Despite the internal pressures toward consensus within the Administration, planners failed, as they had in McNamara's time, to resolve some critical underlying differences in perspective. Among the most important was the need for so-called de-Baathification and the undoing of Iraqi institutions led by Saddam's former partisans. The White House wanted de-Baathification, but Feith warned of dire consequences should the Iraqi military be entirely disbanded.[84] For his part, Jay Garner, whose Office for Reconstruction and Humanitarian Assistance to Iraq represented our first postwar reconstruction effort, had hoped to rebuild the Iraqi military. But, when U.S. oversight was transferred to L. Paul Bremer, Bremer announced a strict de-Baathification policy aimed at every level of the government's infrastructure. He completely abolished the old army. Lt. Gen. John Abizaid, Franks's deputy and later successor, and General McKiernan both objected to the decision. The reaction in Iraq was "incendiary," as the country erupted in demonstrations and the United States found its security problems compounded.[85]

As the American death toll in Iraq increases and ever more Iraqis die, we can see the price exacted by the Administration's ideological rigidity and seeming analytic incompetence. The root of these failures surely lies in part in the quality of the particular decision making team in office. But that is not the full story. The impacts of personal arrogance, political zealotry, and individual fecklessness at play in the Bush Administration were magnified by a decision making context in which the key players felt themselves free of accountability to anyone with a different perspective—free of accountability in fact and free of accountability as a matter of right. Rather than forcing analysts within the Administration to address their differences dispassionately and inviting the scrutiny of experienced Senators and House members, the Administration sought to disclose as little of its thinking as possible and to mislead Congress and the American public as to weaknesses in the case for war. It was their theory of the Constitution that they were entitled to do so. It hardly seems a coincidence that the one person most aggressively leading the charge for an Iraqi invasion and for the unlimited reach of executive constitutional authority over foreign and military affairs was the same person, Vice President Dick Cheney.

Why Presidentialism Promotes Bad Military Decision Making

The Bush Administration's understanding of the constitutional presidency fueled the dysfunctionality of the Bush presidency in operation. Just as in the Johnson and Nixon Administrations, decision making was guided, above all, by the President's ideological commitments, not careful and thorough debate. Subordinates failed to challenge key assumptions made by higher level officials. Decisions proceeded on the basis of poor intelligence because the gatherers of intelligence were aware that no one wished to hear bad news. An executive branch that thought itself routinely susceptible to the effective oversight of other branches would have felt some counterweight to each of these impulses. Administrations believing themselves both entitled to and capable of resistance to any such oversight reacted just as the groupthink model would have imagined.

The sobering lessons of this country's military policy making during the Iraq and Vietnam Wars would be chiefly of historical interest if the decision making flaws thus revealed could be dismissed as mere idiosyncrasies of particular people and unique circumstances. There is good reason, however, to be pessimistic on this score. Robert McNamara's autobiography identifies at least six obstacles to sound executive branch policy making process that were of key significance at various points throughout the Vietnam debacle, and they are similar to the features of groupthink:

1. An agenda overloaded with crises and difficult problems;
2. An unwillingness to confront key assumptions;
3. Reliance upon inaccurate information from non-U.S. sources;
4. An unwillingness to confront profound disagreements among key policy makers;
5. Peer pressure to "clear" controversial decisions; and
6. Hostility to dissent.

It is easy enough to imagine routine circumstances that would unleash these identical forces in future episodes of military decision making. The most serious of them, moreover, are likely to occur or to be costliest when one or both of the following circumstances is present: the U.S. engagement in a military action is of long duration, and the executive feels compelled to insulate itself from potential congressional criticism with regard to the President's handling of a military initiative.

"Agenda overload" will be a fact of life for any Administration and is likely by itself to help create the sort of internal atmosphere of pressure that pushes groups to premature consensus. It is most likely to be a problem for military decision making when a military deployment extends for a significant period of time. With respect to what Professor Peter Spiro calls "strike operations," short-term engagements lasting a few days at most,[86] the crisis that precipitates potential military deployment is likely to be the agenda item that briefly drives everything else off the President's screen. Such sustained focus, however, cannot be indulged for more than a matter of weeks, if that long. After that, as other matters clamor for a Secretary's or for a President's attention, there will be a profoundly felt need to shrink the range of facts or issues under debate, to treat decisions already made as beyond rethinking, and, in general, to economize in one's concentration on any particular item. It should not be surprising, therefore, that, as an operation drags out, important decisions will often be made on the basis of decision makers' shallow analyses.

This dynamic, of course, will reinforce another bureaucratic behavior that will always exist—an unwillingness to revisit key assumptions. Precisely because the presidency is so singular and visible a political target, there will be a built-in tendency not to rethink key commitments, lest the President, as an individual, appear to be weak, indecisive, irresolute, or unprincipled.[87] It would have been politically very difficult for President Johnson to have said something like, "We have reviewed our initial assumption that the imperial ambitions of the Chinese Communists make it imperative to restrain North Vietnamese aggression, and we have changed our mind." As for President Bush, he could reformulate over and over the American rationale for invading and occupying Iraq, but was never willing to reconsider the legitimacy of the course he chose. Of course, the longer a President becomes invested in any foreign policy objective, the harder any such rethinking will become.

Note, moreover, how much harder it would likely be to revisit key assumptions when Congress has never become fully engaged in the deliberative process. In the event that a President should seek to revisit the basis for action that both elected branches had genuinely supported, his capacity to persuade Congress of their joint initial error would diffuse the political costs of changing course. When, however, the President chooses to "go it alone" with respect to the fundamental choices underlying a foreign or military policy initiative, Congress can provide him no equivalent political cover. The lack of shared responsibility makes it harder to undo initial errors, all the more so if those errors were serious.

Decision makers rarely, if ever, can count on information that is completely reliable. Even reliable information demands interpretation, which can be contested. And the problem again will be intensified if Congress is not part of the policy making process. If non-U.S. sources understand that the executive, but not Congress, is committed to an initiative on which foreign parties are relying, the temptation will loom large to skew the information presented to U.S. intelligence agencies—and Congress will not be afforded the capacity to provide an independent check on the reliability of that information. Moreover, the executive will want to believe information presented to it that confirms the rationality of decisions already made. There will be too much political cost associated with being wrong.

If Congress and the executive do not share in a policy commitment, Congress's skepticism may also contribute to a siege mentality within the executive that will make it hard for administrators to confront profound disagreements among key executive policy makers, no matter how persistent those disagreements. Largely, it seems, to avoid paralyzing the President through indecision, key actors in the Vietnam saga managed for years to paper over their differences or to make compromises that ultimately rendered our policy incoherent. The national security team LBJ inherited from the Kennedy Administration was "deeply split over Vietnam."[88] As of fall 1964, there was a "substantial split" among LBJ's military advisers as to whether or not to launch immediate air strikes against North Vietnam. Although all the armed services endorsed the air war by February 1965, the Army and Navy were far more pessimistic than were the Marines and Air Force about what air strikes could likely accomplish.[89] Similar disagreements later surfaced concerning the number of ground troops who ought to be committed to the war effort.[90] None of these conflicts was ever allowed to crystallize genuine public debate over the fundamental underlying issues. The same is true with regard to disagreements in the Bush Administration over WMD, troop levels, plans for postwar security, and the relationship between Iraq and the war on terror.

The pressure to go forward, to leave doubts unexpressed and differences unresolved, intensifies another decision making trait that is to some extent a universal characteristic of executive branch policy making—a desire in each decision maker not to be the "hold-out" in making a decision to which others appear committed. Life is easily made uncomfortable for the person perceived as an obstructionist in the path of accomplishing a presidential objective, especially an objective as seemingly unambiguous as prevailing over a clear adversary. The momentum behind the cable that precipitated Diem's overthrow dramatically illustrates the tendency. McNamara characterizes most of the decision makers as signing on reluctantly to a decision that each assumed had, for all intents and purposes, already been made, and none was sufficiently adventurous to delay.[91]

The inclination toward groupthink, exacerbated by the other factors just outlined, is also likely to manifest itself in a hostility to the expression of dissent within the executive. Dissent not only casts doubt on early decisional commitments, but it takes up everyone's time and calls into question advice earlier rendered—and the advisors who rendered it. McNamara details in his memoir how unresponsively key decision makers reacted to George Ball's arguments in 1964 and in 1965, first, that the Administration should pursue more aggressively a political resolution to the Vietnam impasse, and, second, that it should seriously limit its further deployment of ground troops to Vietnam.[92] McNamara's own deepening conviction in 1967 that the United States should withdraw from Vietnam rendered his continued leadership of the Pentagon untenable. Similarly, both Defense Secretary Rumsfeld and CIA Director George Tenet made clear that dissent was unwelcome in preinvasion discussions about Iraq. James Risen quotes Tyler Drumheller, the chief of the European Division in the CIA Directorate of Operations, as saying: "Why didn't anybody say anything before the war [about how weak the intelligence was]? I did. And I can tell you it was hard, because nobody wanted to hear it, and they made it very clear that they didn't want to hear it."

Had there been more genuine and open debate about Iraq, within both Congress and the executive in fall 2002, it is at least plausible that Congress would not have authorized going forward. In the same way, it is not only possible, but likely that the tragedies of Vietnam, both for that country and for ours, could have been drastically curtailed had the executive branch undertaken a more genuine policy making partnership with Congress. LBJ was determined, instead, to prevent well-informed public debate about his Vietnam objectives and plans. He never publicly stated the singularity of his goal to win the war, or, as McNamara puts it, the absence of any plan in 1964 to accomplish that objective.[93] He withheld public information about the degree to which the United States escalated the air war in 1965. He failed to keep his 1964 promise to consult Congress closely in the wake of the Gulf of Tonkin resolution. He made no public statement regarding the extraordinary fiscal implications of the intensified war effort. Nixon, of course, only intensified the practices of secrecy and deception. His concealment from Congress of our military activities in Cambodia not only undermined Congress's legitimate consultative role; it also put Cambodia on a path to civil war whose human costs were as epic as they were unnecessary.

Had the executive branch been amenable to more serious congressional involvement in the development of Vietnam or Iraq policy, it would have been able to take advantage of the foreign policy experience of senior members of Congress. Members of Congress would have felt freer than the President's subordinates to test the key assumptions underlying U.S. policy and to challenge the quality of information used to inform U.S. decision making. Disagreements among policy makers would have been aired earlier, and greater caution would have been exercised in making controversial decisions.

As to Vietnam, a more open process would have clearly been more receptive to the views of those within Congress who would have counseled restraint. As early as December 1963, Senate Majority Leader Mike Mansfield urged LBJ to pursue the neutralization of Vietnam as a politically acceptable result.[94] Senator Wayne Morse was an early and persistent critic of the war, whose views could have helped catalyze a deeper debate within Congress had the relevant facts not been concealed by the Johnson Administration. Senator Mansfield opposed the buildup of troops in 1965, as did Senator Richard Russell, who urged the President to withdraw in light of the deeply divided public view of the wisdom of a troop buildup.[95] LBJ never cooperated in fashioning an interbranch dialogue that would have had to grapple seriously with these views held by powerful Senators.

The potential significance of congressional involvement is evident if we look back to an earlier stage of the Vietnam conflict. In the spring of 1954, President Eisenhower faced the decision whether to intervene in Indochina on behalf of the French. Advocates for intervention included such powerful figures as Joint Chiefs Chairman Admiral Radford and Secretary of State John Foster Dulles.[96] Their view was sustained, in part, by cold war ideas about the communist menace and the fear of damage to U.S. interests should the nations of Southeast Asia fall to communist control. Eisenhower, however, was ambivalent and demanded consultation with leaders of Congress. In Congress, it became evident that the Joint Chiefs were not unanimous in supporting intervention. Significant risks appeared that a U.S. air strike could not accomplish its objectives and that American intervention would start down a potential slippery slope toward major armed conflict in Asia. Within the Administration, the leading voice forcing a realistic cost-benefit analysis of intervention was Gen. Matthew Ridgway, Chief of Staff of the Army. He sent army specialists to Indochina to make a firsthand assessment of the challenges U.S. intervention would have to overcome; he reported to Eisenhower that the potential cost in terms of both money and manpower could exceed that of the Korean War. As political scientist Alexander George wrote of this episode: "Given the strength of [the anticommunist] decisional premise and the initial definition of the situation, intervention could be avoided only because the *process* of policy making worked in such a way as to force decision makers to face up to the sobering question of the costs and risks of intervention."[97] That process was entirely pluralist in its orientation.

The contest between pluralist and presidentialist visions of government is sometimes reduced to debates over whether, and in what form, Congress is required to authorize military engagements formally before they begin. These debates, while important, do not fully capture, however, what is at stake. After all, aside from the Cambodia catastrophe, Congress provided sufficient authorization for virtually every aspect of the Vietnam War to address all constitutional requirements, and Congress likewise enacted resolutions authorizing the use of military force in Afghanistan and Iraq. The formality of congressional authorization to deploy military force is not enough to insure that available information is freely shared and that underlying premises as well as projected costs and benefits are fully and conscientiously assessed. In order that the prospect of interbranch accountability truly discipline the executive in terms of assuring full and open debate, Congress must be prepared to pose a consistent counterweight to the pressures within the executive to avoid asking hard questions, to cover up differences, to leave convenient information unexamined and conceal inconvenient information, and to leave ambiguous, even inconsistent objectives untested by analysis. We had none of this in Vietnam, and none of it regarding Iraq from at least 2002 to 2006. The human costs, as well as the costs to our international standing and national security position, are well nigh incalculable and can be laid, in some significant measure, to the defects of the unilateral presidency in operation.

4

Presidentialism, National Security, and the Breakdown of Government Lawyering

Presidentialism is bad constitutional theory and bad government practice. The executive branch's excessive belief in its entitlement to unilateral action sets up a decision making dynamic that produces irresponsible, sometimes catastrophic, results. The military and foreign policy disasters generated by unilateralism may seem quite sufficient by themselves to demonstrate the importance of maintaining a pluralist view of checks and balances. Equally troubling, however, presidentialism also risks our national commitment to the rule of law. It exhibits a seemingly irresistible tendency to undermine America's claim for itself, that ours is a "government of laws, not of men."

At one level, this seems true by definition. Presidentialists assert that, to an extraordinary extent, the President, as a matter of constitutional entitlement, is simply not subject to legal regulation by either of the other two branches of government. It follows from this theory that the President is relatively free from the rule of law to the extent that there are simply fewer laws that effectively bind him.

But the story runs deeper than this. Political officials are not simply rational actors who respond with dispassionate calculation to evidence and circumstance—they are human, after all. Facts and options are always filtered through officials' ideological prisms, prisms that shape how facts are weighed and options comprehended. Pluralism works to offset that filtering. Pluralism guards against too much distortion by seeking to maximize the number of meaningful institutional voices in the policy making process. Every perspective offers a potential check on the partiality of the others.

By contrast, the ideological prism of presidentialism bends the light of the law so that nothing is seen other than the prerogatives of the sitting chief executive. What is distorted is not only the scope of law's application, but the very processes through which government attorneys in virtually every agency determine and render advice on law's meaning—the enterprise commonly called "government lawyering." The quality of this enterprise is essential because, for the overwhelming majority of administrative decisions, government lawyering represents the exclusive avenue through which the law is actually brought to bear on decision making. As noted earlier, most government decisions are simply too low in visibility or too diffuse in impact to elicit judicial review or congressional oversight as ways of monitoring legal compliance.

For this reason, it is also essential that government lawyers understand their unique roles as both advisers and advocates. In adversarial proceedings before courts of law, it may be fine for each of two contesting sides, including the government, to have a zealous, and not wholly impartial, defense, while the judge acts as a neutral decision maker. But government lawyers, in their advisory function, must themselves play a more objective, even quasi-adjudicative role. They must give the law their most conscientious interpretation. If they do not, there will frequently be no one else effectively situated to do the job of assuring diligence in legal compliance. Government lawyers imbued with the ideology of presidentialism too easily abandon their professional obligations as advisers and too readily become ethically blinkered advocates for unchecked executive power. Especially in their advisory role, government lawyers must remember that their "client" is the American people, and not the ephemeral roster of incumbent federal officer holders. The threatened subversion of the government lawyer's special advisory function is a large part of the danger embodied by what chapter 1 described as the presidentialist culture of governance.

We can see this phenomenon dangerously at work in the lawyering under the George W. Bush Administration that accompanied the civilian side of national security policy making—that is, policy making regarding the protection of the United States through nonmilitary means from both internal and external threats. As in its deployment of military power, the Bush 43 Administration, in the making of national security policy, tried to the maximum extent to insulate itself from legislative or judicial accountability. The results, since September 11, 2001, were calamitous in terms of Americans' civil liberties at home and the image of America abroad. Millions of Americans were potentially subject to the electronic surveillance of their telephone calls and e-mails without any sort of judicial warrant.[1] For the first time in U.S. history, our government publicly approved cruel and degrading interrogation techniques for enemy detainees, quibbling chiefly as to whether the exploitation of fear, the imposition of stress positions, the exposure to extreme variations in temperature, the deprivation of light and auditory stimuli, and even waterboarding amount to "torture." For much of the world's population, the best known image of American power abroad is now a picture of U.S. prisoners at the Abu Ghraib prison being subjected to sexual humiliation.

To be clear, I am not suggesting that Bush Administration lawyers—or, indeed, the government lawyers of any Administration—ignore the law routinely. Most legal matters that arise in the day-to-day life of government have no political bite to them, and, in every Administration, you can find committed lawyers wrestling conscientiously and professionally with many high-pressure legal questions that politicians care about intensely. The fact remains, however, that, with notable exceptions, government lawyers were deeply complicit in the worst human and civil rights travesties of the Bush 43 Administration. Given the ideological atmosphere in which lawyers were asked to operate, the exceptions—lawyers doing their jobs in the face of intense political pressure—appear heroic. That conscientious fidelity to one's conventional professional role should count as heroism is itself a measure of how deeply presidentialism under Bush 43 weakened the rule of law. In this chapter and the next, I wish to explore presidentialism's two major blows to the rule of law. The first is fostering an atmosphere hostile to balanced and conscientious legal debate, thus producing a series of irresponsible legal opinions ranging from the dubious to the outright unethical. The second is the replacement of a healthy and self-aware institutional conception of the rule of law by a highly formal, mechanistic conception that is antagonistic to genuine democratic accountability.

Warrantless Electronic Surveillance

Under a secret order signed in early 2002, President George W. Bush authorized the National Security Agency "to monitor and eavesdrop on large volumes of telephone calls, e-mail messages, and other Internet traffic inside the United States to search for potential evidence of terrorist activity."[2] He did this, notwithstanding thirty years of Supreme Court decision making, legislative enactments, and executive branch administrative policy making aimed at taking NSA out of the business of spying on Americans.

The legal reforms repudiated by the Bush Administration are rooted in intelligence scandals of the mid-1970s that revealed extensive violation of the rights of Americans and illegal activities by the CIA, FBI, and other intelligence-gathering units within the executive branch.[3] Government officials were found to have violated the law on a breathtaking scale. The revelations were sparked chiefly because a series of *New York Times* articles disclosed massive, illegal domestic intelligence operations aimed at antiwar and dissident groups by the Nixon Administration. The newspaper's startling disclosures followed close upon the heels of alleged CIA links to the Watergate scandal and allegations of CIA efforts to "destabilize" the government of deposed Chilean President Salvador Allende, episodes that had likewise spurred calls for deeper scrutiny of executive branch intelligence and law enforcement agencies.

Reports of CIA abuse provoked responses from both the President and Congress. On January 5, 1975, following the resignation of James Angleton, the CIA counterintelligence chief, President Ford named an eight-member commission (including future President Reagan) under Vice President Rockefeller to investigate alleged CIA violations of statutes banning domestic intelligence gathering. The Rockefeller Commission reported that, although most CIA intelligence operations were within statutory bounds, some were "plainly unlawful and constituted improper invasions upon the rights of Americans." Among its revelations was the existence from 1962–1972 of a special group within the CIA called Operation CHAOS, charged with collecting information on dissident groups within the United States. CHAOS developed a computerized index with the names of more than 300,000 persons and organizations, and compiled files on 7,200 Americans.

The revelations of the Rockefeller Commission were but a hint, however, of the more comprehensive findings to be reported by an eleven-member Senate Select Committee chaired by Idaho Senator Frank Church to investigate the activities of the CIA, FBI, and other law enforcement and intelligence agencies to determine if they had engaged in any illegal or unethical intelligence activities during the Vietnam period. (A parallel study was undertaken in the House of Representatives, under Rep. Otis G. Pike, of New York.) The Church Committee revealed the existence of a twenty-year mail surveillance program undertaken by the CIA even though the Agency knew it to be illegal and regarded it as of little value. The mail included correspondence of several prominent figures including Richard Nixon, Senators Edward Kennedy and Hubert Humphrey, Martin Luther King, Jr., Federal Reserve Board Chairman Arthur Burns, and even Senator Church. Between 1970 and 1972 alone, the CIA examined about 2 million pieces of mail a year. Apparently, in the highly secretive worlds of intelligence and law enforcement, the Nixon belief that presidential acts were beyond legal control had deep roots. The Church Committee specifically reported widespread use of the FBI by past Presidents for personal political ends. The Committee concluded that Presidents Roosevelt, Truman, Eisenhower, Kennedy, Johnson, and Nixon had all received reports from the FBI on journalists, political opponents, and critics of Administration policy. Although the practice began in the Roosevelt Administration, the committee reported that it "grew to unprecedented" dimensions during the Johnson and Nixon eras.

According to the Church Committee, the lack of congressional oversight was a basic reason for the intelligence community's failures and misdeeds: "Congress, which has the authority to place restraints on domestic intelligence activities through legislation, appropriations, and oversight committees has not effectively asserted its responsibilities until recently. It has failed to define the scope of domestic intelligence activities or intelligence collection techniques, to uncover excesses, or to propose legislative solutions. . . . If Congress had addressed the issues of domestic intelligence and passed regulatory legislation, and if it had probed into activities of intelligence agencies and required them to account for their deeds, many of the excesses in this Report might not have occurred."[4] In short, the Church Committee found a significant cause of executive branch abuse to be the lack of pluralism in both setting and monitoring the implementation of national security policy. The absence of external checks and balances enabled an executive branch atmosphere in which systems of accountability and control either broke down or were nonexistent. This was presidentialism at work.

The early 1970s also witnessed the Supreme Court's most important opinion on the constitutional regulation of foreign intelligence investigations. In 1967, the Court had held for the first time that electronic surveillance of telephone communications amounted to a "search" under the Fourth Amendment, for which law enforcement authorities would need a warrant in any case in which the target speaker had a "reasonable expectation of privacy."[5] That decision, *Katz v. United States,* applied, however, only to ordinary law enforcement surveillance—that is, wiretaps to obtain evidence for the prosecution of crimes that had already been committed. A year later, Congress enacted the Omnibus Crime Control and Safe Streets Act of 1968,[6] which authorized a procedure for federal law enforcement authorities to obtain wiretap warrants.[7] That statute limited its reach to law enforcement wiretaps and expressly did not apply to electronic surveillance in connection with national security investigations.[8] The central aim of national security investigations is often not to prosecute crime, but primarily to uncover information about espionage and other threats to national security before they occur. Presidents and Attorneys General had long asserted, both to Congress and within the executive branch itself, the inherent authority of the federal executive to conduct national security surveillance without going through any warrant application process.

In 1972, in *United States v. U.S. District Court*[9]—commonly known as the *Keith* case because the trial judge involved was Hon. Damon Keith—the Supreme Court put a stop to warrantless national security wiretaps, at least in domestic national security investigations. Contrary to longstanding executive branch arguments, the Court held that the Fourth Amendment did protect Americans against warrantless search and seizure even in the national security investigation context. The particular case that reached the Court involved an alleged national security threat arising exclusively from American defendants who were not asserted to have any significant connection to a foreign nation or to a nonstate organization based outside the United States. The Court thus passed "no judgment on the scope of the President's surveillance power with regard to the activities of foreign powers, within or without this country."[10]

Although insisting on the applicability of the Fourth Amendment's warrant requirement to national security cases, the Court recognized also that the conventional warrant procedure might not be well tailored to the national security context. Law enforcement warrants require a government officer to establish to an ordinary trial court judge that probable cause exists to believe that surveillance will yield evidence of a crime. The scope of a national security wiretap typically cannot be delimited in terms of evidence of a crime already committed. The Court explicitly acknowledged that Congress might tailor a distinct new form of judicial warrant procedure to take account of the unusual demands of national security investigations.[11]

In response to *Keith,* and with the findings of the Church Committee fresh in recent memory, Congress enacted the Foreign Intelligence Surveillance Act of 1978. The statutory text was hammered out through lengthy and intensely detailed negotiations with the Carter Administration.[12] Its intricate provisions defy easy summary, but the basic framework of the statute is clear. FISA authorizes the President to engage in electronic surveillance for up to one year without a judicial warrant if the surveillance is directed only at communications between or among foreign powers, wherever located, and "there is no substantial likelihood that the surveillance will acquire the contents of any communication to which a United States person is a party."[13] For surveillance directed at what the statute calls "United States persons," the President may authorize the Attorney General to seek a warrant from a special Foreign Intelligence Surveillance Court that is set up just for this purpose.[14]

In contrast to rules regulating searches for ordinary law enforcement, the Attorney General, on behalf of the executive branch, need not allege probable cause that the surveillance will yield evidence of a crime. Instead, two key elements must be documented. The first is that the target of the surveillance is a foreign power or "the agent of a foreign power."[15] A "group engaged in international terrorism or activities in preparation therefor" is a "foreign power" under FISA, and any American is an "agent of a foreign power" if he or she "knowingly engages in sabotage or international terrorism, or activities that are in preparation therefor, for or on behalf of a foreign power," or "knowingly aids or abets any person . . . or knowingly conspires with any person to engage in" such activity.[16] In other words, if you are an American aiding international terrorism, you are a legitimate FISA warrant target.

Second, the Attorney General must certify that the information sought is "foreign intelligence information,"[17] which includes "information that . . . is necessary to, the ability of the United States to protect against . . . actual or potential attack or other grave hostile acts of a foreign power or an agent of a foreign power [or] . . . international terrorism . . . by a foreign power or an agent of a foreign power."[18] In conducting such surveillance, the Attorney General is required to follow what are called "minimization procedures,"[19] in order to protect against the unnecessary acquisition, retention, and dissemination of information about "United States persons."[20] For example, the FBI may set up a log to verify that no information acquired through surveillance is distributed in a way that identifies any "United States person" without his or her consent, unless the identity is needed "to understand foreign intelligence information or assess its importance."[21]

Two other provisions of FISA are critical to the interbranch bargain it embodies. First, Congress gave the President authority to conduct warrantless national security surveillance for fifteen days upon a congressional declaration of war.[22] This provision would give Congress time to amend the FISA procedures as might be appropriate to take account of wartime conditions. Second, FISA provides that the federal government may conduct electronic surveillance only as permitted by Title III of the Omnibus Crime Control and Safe Streets Act for ordinary law enforcement or as authorized by FISA itself for national security investigations. In other words, Congress, by law, has defined all electronic surveillance as falling within one of two categories—law enforcement and foreign intelligence—and, for each category, it has furnished a single statutory procedure as the one and only federal procedure for conducting such surveillance lawfully, To make this point clear, Congress has even made it a felony for government authorities to conduct electronic surveillance except by following one of these exclusive procedures.[23] As a result, there is simply no other source of general statutory authority on which the President may rely for conducting electronic surveillance. A President who does not follow these procedures for conducting electronic surveillance, including surveillance against potential terrorists, is not following the law.

Notwithstanding this painstakingly constructed process, Americans learned in December 2005 that the Bush Administration had been ignoring FISA for three years.[24] Amazingly, the Administration had embarked on this course even though Congress, in the wake of September 11, had actually followed Bush Administration recommendations to amend FISA to make legal compliance easier—for example, creating "roving wiretap" authority, which allows the interception of any communications made to or by an intelligence target without specifying the particular telephone line, computer, or other facility to be monitored.[25] Since 2002, the National Security Agency had been given access by presidential order to an enormous volume of international telephone communications involving Americans.[26]

The NSA's so-called Terrorist Surveillance Program (TSP) proceeded without judicial warrant. Telecommunications companies provided the NSA with direct access to the electronic switches that carry America's phone calls. The NSA was given "the ability to conduct surveillance on the e-mail of virtually any American it chooses to target."[27] The NSA, and President Bush, claimed that the TSP targeted only communications in which one party is connected to international terrorism, but this claim is triply troublesome. First, Attorney General Alberto Gonzales stated that the TSP may target any person who "is a member of al Qaeda, affiliated with al Qaeda, or a member of an organization affiliated with al Qaeda or working in support of al Qaeda."[28] Without any specification, however, of what it means to be "affiliated with" or work "in support of al Qaeda"—might this include, for example, news organizations publishing stories sympathetic to radical Islam?—the net cast by this targeting could plainly include a substantial number of Americans with no palpable connection to terrorism. Second, the Administration claimed that it needed only "reasonable grounds to believe" that one party to any intercepted communication fits within its targeting.[29] This falls far short of probable cause to believe that any American on U.S. soil, whose communications are intercepted through the TSP, is him- or herself a foreign power or the agent of a foreign power. Without judicial approval, the interception of communications from such U.S. persons would be unconstitutional.

Finally, and deeply troubling, there is no believable way of squaring the Administration's claims of narrow targeting and the massive volume of phone call data apparently being sifted through agency technology. Two scenarios seem most probable. Under the first, the Administration started by listening in on phone calls to or from persons with respect to whom it did have a warrant. Then, with or without regard to the content of any of those calls, it began surveillance of every other party with whom the warranted target had any conversation. This surveillance could then be extended, just as a tree grows its branches, to everyone who had ever talked to anyone who had ever spoken to the original target, and then to anyone who had ever talked to anyone who had every talked to anyone who had ever spoken to the original target, and so on. It is easy to see how such networked surveillance could easily reach large numbers of persons about whom no real suspicion exists with regard to the possession of foreign intelligence information. Indeed, if such suspicions could be specified, there would be no reason to avoid a warrant application to the FISA court.

The other possibility is that the TSP intercepted data about millions of phone calls and then used a technique called "pattern recognition" to try to isolate phone calls that might be suspicious. Using computers to sift through these data—things like call length, points of origin and reception, and so on—as well as word sampling from the conversations themselves, the NSA could develop algorithms for patterns that are plausibly characteristic of al Qaeda–related phone calls. Of course, if this were so, then the Administration could accurately say that it limited its "listening" to al Qaeda–related phone calls if we don't count any automated word sampling of the contents of phone calls as "listening." In other words, even if the Administration took electronic note of selected words in your phone call, it could purport not to be "listening" to your call if no human being was actually hearing the words when spoken or electronically replayed. Moreover, the information that led to the identification of certain phone calls as al Qaeda related would have to exclude any information specific to the actual parties to the phone call. The information would only constitute a neutral "pattern," which, judging by press reports, was typically not well designed to yield fruitful "hits."[30]

That the Bush Administration hid the TSP from the American people by failing to disclose it was bad enough. That it intentionally misrepresented the processes by which it conducted antiterrorism surveillance demonstrated an equally troubling disdain for the American people. In an April 20, 2004 public "conversation" in Buffalo, New York, President Bush insisted: "Now, by the way, any time you hear the United States government talking about wiretap, it requires—a wiretap requires a court order. Nothing has changed, by the way. When we're talking about chasing down terrorists, we're talking about getting a court order before we do so."[31] This was not true, and the President, who personally authorized the TSP program, presumably knew it.

The obvious legal question was how the Administration could justify the TSP in the face of explicit language in the Foreign Intelligence Surveillance Act precluding the warrantless electronic surveillance of Americans. In contrast to the Administration's decision making with regard to enemy combatants, few details have been publicly disclosed about the internal lawyering that accompanied the initial decision to authorize the TSP. We do know that Berkeley law professor John Yoo, while at the Justice Department's Office of Legal Counsel, authored an opinion within days after the September 11 attacks, arguing that, by virtue of the attacks, the government might possess enhanced authority to conduct warrantless surveillance to protect the United States against al Qaeda.[32] We also know that pressure to maintain an ambitious stance regarding inherent executive authority emanated from the Office of the Vice President, most emphatically from a lawyer named David Addington, who was first Counsel, then Chief of Staff to Vice President Cheney.[33] As a context for government decision making, covert surveillance perfectly illustrates what I said earlier about the unique capacity and obligation of government lawyers, playing an advisory role, to help assure diligence in legal compliance. Without conscientious government lawyering, accountability to law simply may not exist where decisions are made behind closed doors, and there is little prospect for timely (if any) judicial review. Yet, in the words of Harvard law professor Jack Goldsmith, who headed the Office of Legal Counsel for a little less than ten months in 2003–2004: "After 9/11 [Cheney, Addington] and other top officials in the Administration dealt with FISA the way they dealt with other laws they didn't like: they blew through them in secret based on flimsy legal opinions that they guarded closely so no one could question the legal basis for their operations."[34] Goldsmith quotes Addington's view of the tribunal Congress created to oversee foreign intelligence surveillance warrants: "We're one bomb away from getting rid of that obnoxious court."[35]

After the program's disclosure in the *New York Times,* the Administration prepared two public full presentations of its legal position. The more extensive of these is a January 19, 2006 Justice Department memorandum of unattributed authorship, entitled, "Legal Authorities Supporting the Activities of the National Security Agency Described by the President."[36] In this memorandum, as in an earlier letter from Assistant Attorney General William Moscella to the leadership of the House and Senate Select Committees on Intelligence,[37] the Administration's legal stance can be boiled down to two essential propositions. The first is that warrantless electronic surveillance directed at al Qaeda and its supporters falls within the President's inherent war powers, as confirmed by the Authorization to Use Military Force in Afghanistan, or the AUMF,[38] enacted by Congress on September 12, 2001.[39] In other words, the President has inherent constitutional power to conduct the TSP and, even if it were necessary for Congress to ratify his commander-in-chief powers in this respect, the AUMF effectively did so. The second is that the President has inherent constitutional power to conduct the TSP no matter what the AUMF says and, if FISA is read to preclude this particular program of foreign intelligence surveillance, then FISA is unconstitutional.[40] That is, notwithstanding FISA being mandated by Congress and notwithstanding its acceptance since having been enacted in 1978, the Bush Administration was arguing that, once the President finds FISA impracticable, applying it to the President violates the separation of powers.

As it happens, the AUMF does not say anything about electronic surveillance. The Administration argued, however, that power to launch the TSP is implicitly encompassed by the general grant of authority to the President to "use all necessary and appropriate force against those nations, organizations, or persons he determines planned, authorized, committed, or aided the terrorist attacks that occurred on September 11, 2001, or harbored such organizations or persons, in order to prevent any future acts of international terrorism against the United States by such nations, organizations or persons."[41] In 2004, the Supreme Court held, with regard to the AUMF, that the explicit authorization for the use of "appropriate force" implicitly authorizes also what are taken to be "fundamental and accepted incident[s] of war,"[42] such as the capture of enemy combatants. Because foreign intelligence surveillance is, according to the Administration, a "fundamental" and "accepted" incident of war making, the AUMF must be read to permit it.

In light of the Foreign Intelligence Surveillance Act, however, this argument is quite plainly wrong. FISA clearly states that no statute other than FISA or Title III—the law that applies to ordinary federal criminal prosecutions—provides authority for electronic surveillance by the federal government.[43] The AUMF could supersede FISA only by implicitly repealing it, but courts rarely infer in any context that Congress has repealed prior law, unless Congress makes the repeal explicit. Clearly this was not the case in the AUMF.[44] Moreover, any compelling argument for implicit repeal would have to be based on the proposition that the AUMF, as the more recent piece of legislation, deals with an extraordinary circumstance that an earlier Congress could not have envisioned and should therefore not be regarded as having dealt with. But no such argument could withstand scrutiny. FISA not only anticipated that foreign intelligence surveillance needs may differ during wartime, but it expressly provided for how that difference is to be taken account of. Specifically, FISA provides that, upon a declaration of war, the President shall have fifteen days to conduct foreign intelligence surveillance without recourse to the judicial process otherwise applicable.[45]

The Administration's argument was implausible and convoluted. Bear in mind that the AUMF was precisely as it stated a statutory authorization to use military force for a particular purpose, not a formal declaration of war that would entail, as a matter of both international and domestic constitutional law, a complex array of legal consequences for the warring states and their citizens. In effect, the Bush Administration argued that, in enacting the AUMF, which thus stopped short of a declaration of war and which does not say a word about expanding executive wiretapping, Congress implicitly authorized the President to conduct warrantless surveillance potentially for all time. This would be so even though Congress, when it explicitly considered the sensitive issue of wartime surveillance in 1978, limited the President's authority to conduct warrantless surveillance to a period "not to exceed fifteen calendar days" following a formal declaration of war. Such an argument is logically and legally absurd.

The Administration's fallback provision was that FISA is an unconstitutional intrusion into the President's constitutionally vested commander-in-chief powers,[46] insofar as it might operate to preclude the President from engaging in warrantless electronic surveillance to gather foreign intelligence, albeit from "United States persons." This argument makes a typical presidentialist leap from two uncontested propositions to a wholly unfounded conclusion. The first is that the President is the constitutionally designated commander-in-chief of the armed forces. The second is that the Framers of 1789 presumably expected the President to have intelligence-gathering powers with regard to foreign powers and that gathering signal intelligence against enemies in wartime has been routine executive branch activity.

Neither of these truths, however, leads to the conclusion that the President is constitutionally authorized to ignore a warrant process that Congress has enacted for foreign intelligence surveillance directed at Americans. Prior to 1972, it was not a matter of settled law that warrants were required for national security surveillance at all. Indeed, prior to 1967, it might have been argued that, constitutionally speaking, electronic surveillance did not count as a form of search.[47] FISA was thus not enacted to *prevent* the President from engaging in foreign intelligence gathering. Congress created FISA precisely to *enable* the President to include Americans, as appropriate, within the range of foreign intelligence surveillance targets by affording him a constitutionally adequate warrant procedure, following the Supreme Court's decision in 1972.

FISA prescribes the terms under which the President may discharge his authority in wartime—accepting, for the sake of argument, that the campaign against al Qaeda counts as "war" for constitutional purposes. As a bipartisan group of legal scholars wrote in their critique of the Justice Department's memorandum, "Congress has routinely enacted statutes regulating the Commander-in-Chief's 'means and methods of engaging the enemy.'"[48] On the rare occasion that the Supreme Court has been presented with a case in which the executive acted contrary to statute in the prosecution of war, the Court has each time upheld the statute and required the President to conform to it. This is hardly surprising given that the Constitution expressly authorizes Congress to enact laws necessary and proper for implementing not just its own authorities, but also the constitutionally vested authorities of the executive branch. Congress crafted FISA carefully to be supportive of legitimate executive initiative. If the President finds it necessary to commence surveillance before a warrant can be obtained, FISA provides emergency authority to act while the application for a warrant is prepared and pending. In cases of declared war, as noted earlier, Congress has recognized that the FISA scheme may need to be reconsidered and has given the President fifteen days of blank check authority to proceed without warrant while Congress considers how to handle the exigencies of war.

Given that the arguments against the Administration's position are so powerful, why would the Administration take the position it took? One answer might be that Justice Department lawyers are institutionally expected to advocate for the President's powers and simply adopt the most ambitious arguments consistent with appropriate standards of professional competence in legal research and analysis. There are two problems, however, with this view. First, it is not the responsibility of Justice Department lawyers to advocate for every contemplated assertion of presidential authority, no matter how far-fetched. Even in my brief period at Justice, I witnessed multiple and significant examples of Department lawyers refusing to provide analytic support for legally ill-conceived proposals for executive action. Second, it is difficult to make a case for the professional competence of the FISA memorandum. Although the Justice Department manages to elaborate its views in over forty pages of single-spaced and highly technical verbiage, its memorandum never confronts the enormity of the initiative it is endorsing or the power of alternative arguments. Instead, it proffers distinctions from contrary precedent that are often, in a word, silly. Even if the authors felt institutionally constrained to reach a particular bottom line, the failure to assert any principle limiting the claims being made and the too frequent lack of rhetorical judgment in structuring their argument suggest something other than diligent lawyering was at play. This is all the more troubling if one discounts, as I do, the possibility that the lawyers in question were simply deficient in legal skill or analytic capacity.

What accounted for the bad arguments was political and professional pressure. When I worked at Justice, the refusal to take positions that could not be defended by respectable standards did not result in the lawyer suffering. As anyone who has ever worked in an organization knows, however, informal pressure can be an extraordinarily effective method of stifling disagreement and guiding decisions in the way top management desires. We know that supervision of the process of executive branch lawyering on the NSA memorandum was significantly taken over by the Office of the Vice President. David Addington, the Vice President's Counsel, and John Yoo, then a staff attorney in the Justice Department's Office of Legal Counsel, worked together to craft a series of arguments for unprecedented claims of executive power to pursue the campaign against terrorism.[49] Addington was a central figure in conveying to Justice Department attorneys the Administration's intolerance toward legal dissent; Jack Goldsmith reports that Addington blackballed from future advancement in the executive branch any lawyer who dared cross swords with him.[50]

The consequences of this intolerance were played out in 2004. The Bush memo creating the surveillance program provided that the Attorney General had to reapprove the program every forty-five days. In March 2004, the program came up for review while Attorney General John Ashcroft was hospitalized. The Justice Department's review of the program fell to Deputy Attorney General James Comey and to Goldsmith, then the new head of the Office of Legal Counsel. Comey and Goldsmith entertained serious doubts about the TSP and told the White House they were not prepared to reauthorize. Addington was furious, and then White House Counsel Alberto Gonzales and White House Chief of Staff Andrew Card made a middle-of-the-night pilgrimage to Ashcroft's hospital bedside in the hope he would overrule Comey, who was also present for the meeting.[51] Ashcroft refused and stood behind Comey's judgment. Nonetheless, through a process of which we do not have the details, Justice agreed to some form of compromise that left the NSA free to proceed without warrants, but under putatively tougher (albeit still secret) legal standards. Goldsmith was gone from the Justice Department by summer.

The likeliest explanation for the Administration's legal position lies in two factors: first, the probable predetermination by any lawyer asked to consult on the matter that they had *no choice* but to approve the President's sought-after wiretapping initiative and, second, an atmosphere that signaled scorn for any lawyer's reluctance to express, on behalf of executive initiative, any argument that could be articulated with even minimal rhetorical plausibility. These conditions are the entirely foreseeable outcome of presidentialism at work as an ideology of governance. Presidentialism is insensitive, as a matter of principle, to nuance in arguments about the constitutional distribution of government power. It is committed, as a matter of principle, to discounting sources of legal authority beyond the executive that would seek to hold the President accountable. Especially in times of crisis, both real and perceived, these attitudes will inevitably subvert good legal analysis. This is not to say that the lawyers making the arguments will be cynical or insincere. Rather, irrespective of the lawyers' personal character, the social dynamics in a presidentialist milieu are likely, especially in crises, to impede the production of legal analysis that persuasively balances the factors arguing for and against any politically charged presidential initiative.

The American public might well suspect that the distortion of legal analysis will always occur, regardless of the constitutional ideology of Justice Department lawyers. Executive branch lawyers will always be predisposed, and appropriately so, to advocate for the President, and the structure of professional rewards will always encourage creativity on behalf of presidential initiative. But—and this point is critical to the rule of law as government practice—there are critical differences between *predisposition* and *predetermination,* between *encouragement* and *intimidation.* Predisposition and encouragement at least leave room for a measure of independent judgment that is essential to the ethical discharge of a government lawyer's responsibilities.

The government's position in defense of warrantless surveillance in violation of FISA strongly suggests that the scope for independent judgment was dangerously narrowed. What we know about the NSA lawyering process, plus the deeply nonsensical positions that the Administration's legal memorandum includes, cannot help but suggest that the lawyers felt constrained to deliver a predetermined outcome and to defend that outcome with pretty much any argument they could conjure, no matter how implausible.

The Treatment of Enemy Combatants

If the government's defense on behalf of warrantless electronic surveillance implies the possibility of distorted lawyering, the Administration's lawyering process with regard to the treatment of persons captured in Afghanistan or otherwise suspected of aiding and abetting terrorism confirms it. It is a history that cleared the path to horrors at the Abu Ghraib prison and Guantanamo, crimes whose stain upon our national honor is likely to remain, for decades at least, firmly embedded in the world's collective memory, deeply undermining our image and influence abroad.

After the attacks of September 11 and our deployment of military force in Afghanistan, the Bush Administration faced a significant range of critical legal questions regarding our national response to al Qaeda and to the Taliban who sheltered them. Among the most pressing were what do with persons detained in the course of battle. Were they prisoners of war? Did they have rights under the Geneva Conventions? Could they test the conditions of their detention in American courts? Could they be tried for war crimes and, if so, how and by whom? What rights did they have with regard to their conditions of confinement and interrogation?

On all of these questions, the Justice Department, through its Office of Legal Counsel (OLC), produced legal opinions stating, in effect, that anyone captured in the Afghanistan campaign had few, if any rights under U.S. or international law and certainly no rights susceptible to vindication in American courts.[52] The goal of Bush Administration policy makers was manifestly to place the detainees beyond the reach of our judiciary and to absolve anyone involved with their interrogation or confinement from any legal liability. Hence, the function of these legal opinions—indeed, their obvious purpose—was to ratify a scheme of maximum license to do with the detainees whatever the military, the CIA, or any other American authority might choose to do with them.

The substance of these opinions is worrisome on multiple counts. They are worrisome, of course, as a matter of policy. It was understandable, to be sure, that the Administration would want some flexibility in dealing with a threat they rightly regarded as in some ways unprecedented and of very grave magnitude. And yet, the instinct to move the detainees so completely beyond the realm of normal legal process was itself a plainly risky strategy in terms of compromising international support, exposing U.S. military personnel to mistreatment, compromising the honor of U.S. military culture, and weakening the fabric of international law generally as it protects both combatants and civilians during wartime. The desire for flexibility was understandable, but not at the cost of all other values.

Some of the opinions are worrisome from the point of view of morality—the memoranda on detainee interrogation particularly so, because it is unsettling to think that our government was actually parsing which admittedly cruel, inhuman, and degrading acts are sufficiently extreme to amount to unlawful torture. Merely wading this far into the waters of willful brutality would surely seem to many Americans to risk compromising our national character, as well as our standing in the world community—all for possibly little gain even in terms of short-term intelligence gathering.

The opinions might also seem worrisome because of their technical legal conclusions. On a number of the most important points discussed in the lawyers' memoranda, the courts subsequently held them to be wrong. Contrary to OLC, the Supreme Court held that foreign detainees at Guantanamo who challenged their classification as enemy combatants were entitled to judicial review of the legality of their detention.[53] Contrary to OLC, the Court held that the Geneva Conventions protected the detainees, whether or not they strictly qualified as prisoners of war.[54] Contrary to OLC, the Court held that the military commissions as originally constituted were not sufficiently protective of the detainees' rights to permit their use for war crimes trials.[55]

But the point I want to make actually goes beyond these, because on all of these questions, whether of morality, policy, or law, there were at least serious arguments to be entertained on both sides. The fact that the Administration reached incorrect conclusions is, in itself, only a limited indictment of its lawyering. Even good lawyers make mistakes, and the fact that executive branch lawyers would consistently make mistakes erring on the side of executive authority is not in itself damning.

What is damning, however, is that, on critical questions—questions going to the core of our national honor and identity—executive branch lawyering was not just wrong, misguided, or ethically insensitive. It was incompetent. It was so sloppy, so one-sided, and at times so laughably un-persuasive that it cannot be defended as ethical lawyering in any context. Tax advice this bad would be malpractice. Government lawyering this bad should be grounds for discharge.

The legal opinions on three critical issues are illustrative. The first set went to a question about the implications of a potential presidential decision that the Taliban would be, as a matter of law, protected by the Geneva Convention Relative to the Treatment of Prisoners of War, sometimes called Geneva III. Geneva III includes a so-called Common Article 3, which imposes a set of minimum requirements regarding the treatment of all wartime detainees, plus a more demanding Article 4, which applies exclusively to those detainees entitled to "prisoner of war" status. Thus, even if the President decided that captured Taliban were entitled to the general protection of Geneva III, he would still have had to face significant issues regarding standards for how to treat the Taliban; specifically, would the Taliban be entitled to the special Geneva III protections reserved for prisoners of war or only to its more general protections?

OLC wrote two legal opinions to the effect that—even if Geneva III did apply generally to the Taliban—the President might still consider the Taliban to be categorically excludable from POW status under Article 4 of that Treaty.[56] Article 4 confers POW status only on certain limited categories of armed combatants, such as "members of militia or volunteer corps who are commanded by an individual responsible to his subordinates." Depending on the facts about the Taliban that might be disclosed through further investigation, it is plausible that the Taliban would not fit within Article 4's precise categories. OLC had to take note, however, of a provision of Article 5 of Geneva III, stating: "Should any doubt arise to whether persons. . . . belong to any of the categories enumerated in Article 4, such persons shall enjoy the protection of the present Convention until such time as their status has been determined by a competent tribunal,"[57] presumably some sort of adjudicatory body. In other words, the President might well have believed he had persuasive reasons to justify excluding the Taliban from POW treatment, but, until those reasons were adjudicated, the Taliban still had to be treated as POWs. To this problem, OLC gave a resounding, "Not so!" In OLC's view, the Article V provision would not protect the Taliban because (1) the President has constitutional authority to interpret American treaty obligations, and (2) once he interprets Article 4 to exclude the Taliban from POW status, there would no longer be any doubt as to whether they belong to the POW category.[58] As if by magic, OLC simply obliterated the obvious purpose of Article 5, which was to make sure that a detaining authority could not, without an impartial arbiter looking individually at each case, simply deny POW status to persons captured in battle by categorically defining them as non-POWs. It was breathtaking; Article 5 was written to preserve a right of adjudication by "a competent tribunal" in cases of factual doubt about captured combatants, and the President's lawyers were permitting him to remove doubt regarding the facts by simply asserting that he personally had none.

The second legal issue that the Administration addressed with what Jack Goldsmith has called an "unusual lack of care and sobriety"[59] deals with whether the President may vest in civilian or military employees of the United States authority to interrogate persons detained in Afghanistan or Iraq in a manner inconsistent with federal statutes. Two federal statutes enacted in 1994, 18 U.S.C. § 2340 and 2340A, implement the U.S. obligation to enforce the Convention against Torture and Other Cruel, Inhuman and Degrading Treatment or Punishment. The OLC opinion states, flat out, that the President may simply ignore the law. Without any authority, the opinion announces ex cathedra: "Any effort by Congress to regulate the interrogation of battlefield combatants would violate the Constitution's sole vesting of the Commander-in-Chief clause of the President."[60] That is a stunning proposition, and one that no worthy legal adviser would advance without due examination of counterarguments. For example, a competent legal memorandum on this particular point would proffer such a startling conclusion only after considering the implications of constitutional text pointing conspicuously in the other direction: the sole vesting in Congress of the power to define offenses against international law, the sole vesting in Congress of the power to make laws necessary and proper to carrying executive authorities into effect, and the vesting in the President of the obligation to take care that the laws be faithfully executed, which, at its historic core, is a bar against the executive suspension of statutes. The OLC memorandum did not even bother to go through the motions of sound lawyering nor cite any legal authority supporting its position, instead saying in effect that the President may effectively suspend a statute that directly implements express constitutional authority vested in Congress. To use Jack Goldsmith's words once again, the opinions seem "more an exercise of sheer power than reasoned analysis."[61] The conclusion is indefensible, but, worse, there is not even a remotely plausible effort actually to defend it. This represents the extremes of presidentialism, a tendency to express disregard, even disdain, for other opinions, and to argue by fiat in the belief that the rightness of a largely unprecedented position is self-evident, beyond dispute, and to be taken on faith.

The third issue on which OLC lawyering utterly failed involves the office's infamous opinion on the definition of physical torture. Federal statutory law prohibits any person acting under color of law—that is, clothed in the authority of government—to inflict on any other person within his or her custody or physical control "severe physical or mental pain or suffering."[62] OLC interpreted "severe physical . . . pain or suffering" to be pain or suffering at "the level that would ordinarily be associated with a sufficiently serious physical injury such as death, organ failure, or serious impairment of body functions."[63] This raises such questions as whether waterboarding or, for that matter, the ripping out of fingernails, would count as "torture."

How did OLC determine that torture is limited to physical pain of only the most unendurable, excruciating sort? At least gesturing toward lawyerly argument, OLC relied on the idea that other statutes with similar phrasing may shed light on the textual meaning in question through analogy. Specifically, OLC turned to other statutes that refer to "severe pain." Not finding any such statutes that apply to a military context, however, they cited statutes that define emergency medical conditions that would entitle their victims to federally funded health benefits. As OLC notes:

These statutes define an emergency condition as one "manifesting itself by acute symptoms of sufficient severity (including severe pain) such that a prudent lay person, who possesses an average knowledge of health and medicine, could reasonably expect the absence of immediate medical attention to result in—placing the health of the individual . . . (i) in serious jeopardy, (ii) serious impairment to bodily functions, or (iii) serious dysfunction of any bodily organ or part." Although these statutes address a substantially different subject from [the statutory prohibition on torture], they are nonetheless helpful for understanding what constitutes severe physical pain.[64]

In other words, to count as "torture," physical pain would have to be of comparable severity to the pain that would entitle its sufferer to government-provided health insurance![65]

This is an amazing performance for two reasons. First, I think we can safely assume that, whatever policy considerations underlay the structuring of our Medicare statutes, they probably have nothing to do with the policies underlying the Convention against Torture. In defining "severe pain" for emergency health insurance purposes, Congress was presumably creating a very narrow entitlement to fill a hole in a much more comprehensive scheme of health insurance. This has nothing to do with levels of brutality appropriate to military detainees. Looking at health insurance statutes to determine the meaning of torture is a little like defining the rules in a "court" of law by looking up the rules that apply to a basketball "court." It is more of a play on words than serious lawyering.

OLC's argument is also implausible, however, because, as it happens, the phrase "severe physical pain or suffering" actually does appears elsewhere in the U.S. Code. It appears in 18 U.S.C. § 2340 itself. Federal law also bans the infliction of severe mental pain, and Section 2340 defines "severe *mental* pain or suffering," in part, as "the prolonged mental harm caused by or resulting from—. . . the intentional infliction or threatened infliction of severe *physical* pain or suffering."[66] In other words, Congress perceived a direct connection between the severe mental pain it intended to prevent and the separate category of pain, "severe physical pain," that was also not to be inflicted. OLC's argument that "severe physical pain" includes only pain at "the level that would ordinarily be associated with a sufficiently serious physical injury such as death, organ failure, or serious impairment of body functions" makes the connection Congress drew between physical and mental pain bizarre. It suggests, if we do a word substitution, that Congress intended to outlaw only "the prolonged mental harm caused by or resulting from—. . . the intentional infliction or threatened infliction of death, organ failure, or serious impairment of body functions." But this does not make sense. There is no logical reason why Congress would limit its concern for mental harm in this way.

The obvious inference from the mental pain portion of the statute is that Congress intended to protect against the prolonged mental harm caused by or resulting from the actual or threatened infliction of *any* physical pain or suffering so severe that, in a reasonable person, it could be expected to result in lasting mental or emotional damage. The degree of mental pain that the infliction of physical pain might elicit would thus become a measure of what physical pain counts as severe. The most sensible reading of the statute requires us to interpret "severe physical pain or suffering" as that level of physical pain or suffering that, upon its actual or threatened infliction, poses a reasonable threat of severe and prolonged mental harm. Certainly, one can imagine forms of physical pain short of the pain associated with death or organ failure, the threat of which could induce lasting mental or emotional trauma—but if threats of those forms of physical pain qualify as inducing mental pain that counts as "severe," then these forms of physical pain should also count as "severe," and thus, unlawful. This reading may not reconcile the torture statute with the Medicaid statute, but it reconciles the torture statute with itself. None of this is mentioned in the OLC opinion.

Even a careful legal analysis of the permissibility of torture might seem barbarous. If you think any kind of cruel and degrading brutal treatment of human beings is immoral, what difference does it make whether the legal opinion excusing such treatment is well or badly reasoned? But the fact that OLC omitted the most elementary analytic steps in defending executive prerogative with regard to interrogation speaks volumes as to the nature of government lawyering in an Administration where presidentialism is a matter of constitutional faith. Presidentialism operates not just as a constitutional philosophy, but also as an ethos, a fundamental element of the spirit with which the government conducts business. The Bush 43 Administration not only insisted, in theory, on a robust constitutional entitlement to operate free of legislative or judicial accountability, but it largely got away with this stance. And that success—the Administration's unusual capacity to resist answering to Congress and the courts—fed, in turn, its sense of principled entitlement—its theory that the Constitution envisions a Presidency answerable, in large measure, to no one. Its lawyering was distorted to insure adherence to that theory.

Pluralism is also an ethos. When operationalized by the executive branch, it emphasizes the importance of listening to multiple voices in determining how policy should get made and how law should be interpreted. These "voices" take the form of statutes and judicial opinions—the handiwork of other branches—as well as opinions by Attorneys General from earlier Administrations, including Administrations of a different party and with a different policy orientation. Pluralism also invites robust contemporary debate within the executive. This is, in fact, the historic role of OLC. The Office of Legal Counsel exists as an office outside the White House precisely to insure that the President's legal advice has some measure of independence to it. OLC includes both political appointees and "career employees," the latter often long-time members of the office whose institutional memory spans more than a single presidency. However predisposed it may be to uphold plausible assertions of executive power, OLC is traditionally mindful of its quasi-adjudicative role. It is supposed to be a conscientious adviser to the President and to the Attorney General, not their blind advocate.[67] The location of OLC outside the White House, its reliance on career lawyers as well as political appointees, and the quasi-adjudicative norms that traditionally shape OLC legal advice are intended to mitigate the gravitational pull of politics. Especially in contexts where the executive branch works in secrecy and largely free of either judicial review or close congressional oversight, the dedication to a balanced, dispassionate, multivocal approach to legal interpretation is indispensable to any meaningful adherence to the rule of law. Under the Bush 43 Administration, OLC too frequently abandoned this role in the name of executive prerogative.

Thanks to Jack Goldsmith, the conservative Republican lawyer who took over OLC briefly in 2002 and "withdrew" OLC opinions he found to be "legally flawed, tendentious in substance and tone, and overbroad and thus largely unnecessary,"[68] as well as a handful of journalists—Tim Golden, Daniel Klaidman, Jane Mayer, Stuart Taylor, Jr., and Evan Thomas—we know that the process of securing legal analysis of the difficult national security questions arising after September 11 was anything but balanced, dispassionate, and multivocal. Genuine influence was deliberately limited to a group of lawyers united by ideology, not only in terms of amenability to claims of executive power, but also in hostility to international law, a likely source of constraint on that power. Members of the group wanted to distinguish themselves by the risks they were willing to advocate in order to maximize the President's flexibility. Many of the key younger lawyers were members of the right-wing Federalist Society for Law and Public Policy Studies. Some had clerked for the Supreme Court's most aggressively right-wing justices, Clarence Thomas and Antonin Scalia, and many for Lawrence H. Silberman of the U.S. Court of Appeals for the District of Columbia Circuit, a judge known for his cultivation and promotion of young conservative lawyers.[69]

Perhaps most oddly, despite the number of immediate legal questions that would affect military personnel, military lawyers were largely excluded from the key legal deliberations following September 11. Then–White House Counsel Alberto Gonzales, with little national security experience, was exposed chiefly to the views of the Vice President's Counsel, David Addington, an extreme presidentialist, and Deputy White House Counsel Timothy Flanigan, an alumnus of the Office of Legal Counsel during its aggressively presidentialist days under President George H. W. Bush. While these people led the effort to organize a legal team to rationalize maximum flexibility for presidential authority after September 11, other key figures, like John Bellinger, the National Security Council's top lawyer, were not even told of their plans. It was Bellinger's apparent sin that he was too involved in a bipartisan Washington, D.C. elite, being a friend of President Clinton's White House Counsel Lloyd Cutler.[70]

Addington brought into the circle John Yoo, then an OLC lawyer who, as an academic, had written an article indicating that Congress's constitutional power to declare war had no bearing on the President's unilateral authority to deploy American military force wherever and whenever he likes. Yoo was ultimately lead author of the infamous torture memo, but his thinking was foreshadowed in an earlier memo he wrote shortly after September 11, which declared that Congress may not "place any limits on the President's determinations as to any terrorist threat, the amount of military force to be used in response, or the method, timing, and nature of the response."[71]

Little more than a week after September 11, Gonzales convened an interagency group, led by State Department official Pierre-Richard Prosper to draw up options for prosecuting terrorists. They came together with high expectations.[72] By the end of October, however, the White House Counsel's office became impatient with the group's deliberations, and especially with its seeming lack of receptivity to the use of military commissions, instead of civilian courts or military courts-martial, for the purpose of trying enemy combatants. The White House evidently believed—in what turned out to be a huge political miscalculation—that the legal apparatus of the armed services could be used to mete out a kind of rough justice to terrorism suspects, unencumbered by some of the procedural protections that they would enjoy in more conventional judicial settings, including either civilian courts or military courts-martial. Flanigan took personal responsibility for researching the prospect of using military commissions for this task, turning significantly to work that had been done under Bush 41 Attorney General William P. Barr, who had also been the Assistant Attorney General in charge of the Office of Legal Counsel, when Flanigan was at Justice. Flanigan took the lead in drafting what turned into President Bush's November 13, 2001 "Notice" on the "Detention, Treatment and Trial of Certain Non-Citizens in the War against Terrorism."[73] That Order purported to allow the executive unilaterally to detain suspected al Qaeda members and other terrorists without judicial recourse to test the legality of their incarceration, to try them by military commission under flexible rules of evidence and procedure, and even, conceivably, to impose capital punishment following a majority, but not necessarily unanimous vote of commission members. Although the Flanigan team did consult then–Attorney General John Ashcroft and his deputy, Larry D. Thomson, other key figures—such as Michael Chertoff, then Assistant Attorney General in charge of the Justice Department's Criminal Division—were left "out of the loop." Chertoff had argued earlier for trying suspected terrorists in federal court. The military's lawyers, working on their own input, were not even aware that a White House order was already being fine-tuned for mid-November release.[74]

As time went on, efforts intensified to exclude senior State Department officials and National Security Council staff from key discussions of the policy. *New York Times* reporter Tim Golden said he spoke to two people involved in the drafting of the November 2001 Bush order, who stated that Vice President Cheney advocated withholding the draft from National Security Adviser Condoleezza Rice, as well as Secretary of State Colin Powell.[75]

Even as attention turned in 2002 to a daunting set of legal questions concerning U.S. treaty obligations with regard to the detention and trial of detainees, the State Department continued to be shut out of the process. The Flanigan group did not trust State Department legal adviser William H. Taft IV to toe the line on extreme presidentialism, even though he had served in the Reagan Administration.[76]

Perhaps the most celebrated of the attorneys who sought to slow the Administration's embrace of unlimited discretion with regard to the treatment of detainees is Albert J. Mora, who served from 2001 to 2006 as General Counsel to the Navy.[77] Alerted in late 2002 to the possible abuse of detainees at Guantanamo, Mora brought his concerns about both policy and legality to senior Pentagon officials. His efforts were recounted in an unclassified 2004 memorandum that he prepared in connection with the investigation by Vice Admiral Albert Church into allegations of Guantanamo abuse. As succinctly stated by reporter Jane Mayer, the memo shows "Mora tried to halt what he saw as a disastrous and unlawful policy of authorizing cruelty toward terror suspects. . . . Mora's criticisms of Administration policy were unequivocal, wide-ranging, and persistent."[78] Mora had taken his concerns originally to Gordon England, then Secretary of the Navy, who became Deputy Secretary of Defense. With England's approval, Mora then approached William Haynes, the Pentagon's General Counsel, who was a protégé of Addington's. Mora's efforts went nowhere. He continued to press his concerns with Haynes throughout 2002. Although Haynes told him in January 2003 that Secretary Rumsfeld was suspending harsh interrogation techniques and convening a working group to develop interrogation guidelines, Haynes did not reveal that the working group would be following the August 2002, OLC "torture memo" authored by John Yoo. The Working Group produced a report evaluating thirty-five possible interrogation techniques, nine of which were concededly "more aggressive."[79] Mora did not get to see the working group report or learn that Rumsfeld had approved a set of interrogation guidelines based on the report until the Abu Ghraib pictures became public in April 2004, and news of Rumsfeld's approval of harsh interrogation techniques was revealed in Senate hearings. Meanwhile, Haynes, for his steadfastness, had been nominated for a judgeship on the U.S. Court of Appeals for the Fourth Circuit—a nomination that the Abu Ghraib pictures effectively derailed.

Another dramatic case of how the Administration responded to any internal dissent involves Jack Goldsmith.[80] He succeeded Jay Bybee, the head of OLC who signed off on the Yoo torture memo and who received a successful nomination to the U.S. Court of Appeals for the Tenth Circuit. It is widely supposed that David Addington wanted John Yoo to get the job, but that the promotion was vetoed by Attorney General Ashcroft, who resented Yoo's status as a direct White House conduit to the Justice Department.[81] As an academic, Goldsmith was well known for his doubts about the capacity of international law to constrain executive action. He did not, however, embrace Yoo's broad view of the President's entitlement to ignore statutory law, and, in December 2003, Goldsmith informed the Defense Department that the torture memo was "under review" and should no longer be treated as reliable legal authority for aggressive interrogation techniques. Addington repeatedly attacked Goldsmith in frequent face-to-face confrontations. He demanded that Goldsmith review all relevant OLC opinions and identify those that he would stand by.

Goldsmith's review led ultimately to a revised opinion on the applicability of the torture statutes, issued on December 30, 2004.[82] Although the opinion is far from a human rights manifesto, it is significantly less expansive in tone than the Yoo memo. Its issuance, after prolonged in-fighting with the White House, was a victory of sorts, but those involved with it suffered ostracism or worse career damage as a result. James Comey, the Deputy Attorney General, who strongly supported the review (and who had raised questions about the Administration's approach to NSA surveillance), left the Department. A key deputy, Patrick Philbin, in line to become a Deputy Solicitor General, found his promotion blocked by Addington, who had the Vice President's support. Daniel Levin, the senior OLC lawyer who was principal author of the revised memo on torture, left for private practice, and, by summer 2005, Jack Goldsmith was back in academics.

This pattern of behavior, in which legal analysis is treated merely as executive branch advocacy and in which dissent is not merely discouraged, but punished, shows an utter disregard for the norms of Justice Department behavior that had been shaped over decades to help promote sound decision making. Perhaps the most important thrust of these norms, embodied in the very structure of the post–World War II National Security Council, is the importance of interagency debate. The voices that were suppressed—such as those of Secretary of State Colin Powell or even Navy General Counsel Alberto Mora—could hardly be regarded as voices of disloyalty, inexperience, or national security naïveté. Powell, with successful leadership of the first Persian Gulf War and a term as Chairman of the Joint Chiefs behind him, agreed that al Qaeda did not qualify for protection under the Geneva Conventions, but worried, as our nation's chief diplomat, about the consequences of construing the Taliban as somehow beyond the reach of our treaty obligations. Mora, whose family fled Cuba after the

Castro revolution and who was physically present in the Pentagon during the attacks of September 11, could hardly be viewed as indifferent to military necessity. But legal strategy was formed within a tight circle, inspired if not directed by Cheney as cheerleader-in-chief for executive power. His Counsel, Addington, was in de facto charge of the Administration's legal strategy after September 11; Addington's long-time protégé, Haynes, sat in the Pentagon's General Counsel's office; and a newer protégé, John Yoo, served up from the Justice Department the most expansive interpretations imaginable of executive power under the Constitution.

This team put a higher priority on pioneering their theories of executive power than honoring long-standing norms of both legal and military behavior. A story related by Jane Mayer concerning a meeting in late 2005 captures the spirit.[83] Gordon England, the Deputy Defense Secretary with whom Mora had shared his initial concerns, convened the meeting—including the civilian Secretaries and highest ranking officers of each armed service, along with half a dozen military lawyers—to discuss a proposed new directive on military detentions. Deputy Assistant Secretary of Defense Matthew Waxman proposed a formal Pentagon policy that would have extended the protections of Common Article 3 of the Geneva Conventions to all detainees, barring not only "torture," but also other forms of cruel, inhuman, and degrading treatment.

Although all military officers present urged a return to this policy, Haynes opposed it, along with Stephen Cambone, the Undersecretary of Defense for intelligence; they thought it would expose the Administration to too much legal liability. Not only did their opposition end the proposal, but Addington summoned Waxman to the White House, where he berated Waxman for his position.

The topics of interrogation technique, trial, and conditions of confinement do not exhaust the range of issues the Bush Administration confronted with regard to the war on terror. Another operation resulting in significant embarrassment to the United States is the practice of so-called extraordinary rendition, delivering detainees to third countries—not to the United States or where they were seized—in order to facilitate their interrogation.[84] Secretary of State Condoleezza Rice has correctly stated that earlier Administrations also engaged in "rendition," moving persons from one jurisdiction to another without engaging in the formalities of extradition.[85] In all previous Administrations, however, as far as we know, the United States "rendered" persons only to countries where they would face trial and imprisonment for their alleged crimes.[86] The practice of rendition for the purpose of interrogation—presumably, for interrogation pursuant to techniques that U.S. officials are barred from using—was new.

The history of legal opinions supporting extraordinary rendition is not public. In 2005, however, stories began to leak that U.S. personnel were seizing suspected terrorists and delivering them to third countries, notorious for the brutal treatment of political prisoners. The *New York Times* reported on a network of CIA-operated prisons, linked to the rendition practice.[87] As of spring 2007, Italian and American intelligence agents implicated in the 2003 extraordinary rendition from Milan of Egyptian cleric Hassan Mustafa Osama Nasr were facing possible indictment for kidnapping.[88]

If one needs a mnemonic device to recall the miscarriages of justice likely to be entailed when law is abandoned, the name "Maher Arar" should suffice. Arar, then a twenty-nine-year-old Syrian-born Canadian citizen and wireless telecommunications consultant, was detained by U.S. officials on September 26, 2002, while in transit through New York's JFK airport. Arar, returning from a vacation, was interrogated about alleged al Qaeda links. Twelve days later, he was flown in chains to Syria, where was he was detained under draconian conditions, beaten, tortured, and forced to make a false confession. Under public pressure, he was returned to Canada in October 2003, and, in January 2004, the Government of Canada launched a Commission of Inquiry into the Actions of Canadian Officials in Relation to Maher Arar. That inquiry not only cleared Arar of terrorism charges, but found no evidence at all suggesting he was a security threat. The Commission's report was accompanied by an official letter of apology from the Prime Minister, and a settlement award of $10.5 million in damages and another roughly $1 million in legal costs.[89]

Because we do not have a complete public record of the legal opinions sustaining the Bush Administration's rendition practices, we cannot assess them as they would could the opinions on torture or on the applicability of the Geneva Conventions. One memo that became public—a draft March 19, 2004 OLC opinion—purports to explain only why the temporary removal from Iraq, for interrogation purposes, of persons concededly protected by the Geneva Convention on the protection of civilians is consistent with the terms of that treaty.[90] Judging by the way the Administration handled other issues regarding detainee confinement, interrogation, and trial, it would surely be surprising if the legal analysis supporting rendition followed a balanced, open, and dispassionately reasoned process. The Convention against Torture, to which the United States is a party, expressly prohibits the removal of any person to a country where there are "substantial grounds" for believing that there is a danger of torture.[91] Given the jurisdictions to which rendition occurs, and the treatment of such persons as Maher Arar, it seems doubtful that the Bush Administration has generated a legal framework adequate to guarantee the rights of suspects, the immunity of U.S. personnel, or the American reputation for fidelity to the rule of law.

Such is presidentialism at work. The theory that the President is accountable to no one invites a style of decision making in which any dissent from the expansion of executive power is regarded not merely as wrong, but disloyal. Dissenters do not just lose arguments; they are punished. The Supreme Court has since vindicated the legal positions of the dissenters, holding that Guantanamo detainees do have habeas corpus rights, that the Geneva Conventions protect all detainees, and that the military tribunals as originally constituted were legally insufficient to try detainees lawfully for war crimes. But the Administration's error was not just in failing to predict correctly how the Supreme Court would construe the law; it was in its hostility toward, and contempt for, processes of open and balanced legal deliberation that would have strengthened the Administration's position. The tension between presidentialism and the rule of law is not just a matter of principle. Presidentialism licenses a style of executive policy making that, in utterly foreseeable ways, makes certain types of violations of law more likely.

Nor has aggressive presidentialism produced superior decisions in terms of their wisdom or attractiveness as public policy. Instead, the pattern we saw with regard to war powers persisted throughout the Bush Administration—constricted debate among the like-minded and unaccountable produced decisions at odds with even the Administration's professed vision of the national interest. Prisoners in the war on terror began arriving at Guantanamo on January 11, 2002. In part because of the rush to dubious legal judgment after September 11, the first five years of their detention produced not a single concluded war crimes trial. Five years in, half the eight hundred men and boys imprisoned remained in prison, with questions about their rights and status still largely unresolved.[92] The Bush Administration announced in the summer of 2005 that 70 percent of the prisoners were slated for release because they posed no threat to Americans and that most of the remainder would be transferred to a less spartan facility. None of this happened; as of at least early 2007, most of those imprisoned in 2005 remained in limbo in Guantanamo.[93]

As for the Administration's decision making on aggressive interrogation, there is a direct link between the efforts to legitimate cruel and inhuman treatment at Guantanamo and the application of extreme procedures to alleged terrorists and other prisoners in Iraq. The damage to our national honor and influence is incalculable. In words penned jointly by attorney Joseph Margulies, who successfully established the right of Guantanamo prisoners to habeas corpus, and Lawrence Wilkerson, who served from 2002 to 2005 as Secretary of State Powell's Chief of Staff: "Guantanamo has become a word that inspires rage for millions of Muslims."[94] They say: "Of all the images that symbolize this country—the Statue of Liberty, the Bill of Rights, the Declaration of Independence—the fact is that to a growing, and increasingly radical, fraction of the Muslim world, the two indelible symbols of America are Abu Ghraib prison and Guantanamo Bay, a monster with two heads."[95]

As with the episodes of military policy making recounted in chapter 3, the decisions analyzed in this chapter occurred in a policy making context—national security policy—in which Presidents have not only promoted presidentialism in theory, but in which they have very substantially succeeded, especially in the Bush 43 Administration, in making policy under conditions of secrecy and unaccountability that embody presidentialist assumptions. Guantanamo, Abu Ghraib, Maher Arar—these are the real-world fruits of presidentialism. The link between ideology and practice is plain. The threat to sound legal judgment and to the check on official abuse that legal analysis is supposed to represent could hardly be more evident.

5

Form over Accountability: Executive Privilege, Signing Statements, and the Illusion of Law

Critics of presidentialism not infrequently charge that unilateralism is antagonistic to the rule of law. After all, the ideal of a "government of laws, not of men" seems on its face to contradict expansive claims of plenary authority. We have already seen how presidentialism in action distorts the processes of legal analysis that are supposed to serve as a protection against the abuse of power. Presidentialism's threat to rule of law ideals appears all too transparent.

No sane President claims to be above the law, however, and even George W. Bush took pains to defend his controversial actions as legal. These initiatives included the widespread warrantless electronic surveillance of Americans[1] and the aggressive interrogation of detainees in the war on terror. His defense of the program of extraordinary rendition is typical: "In addition to the terrorists held at Guantanamo, a small number of suspected terrorist leaders and operatives captured during the war have been held and questioned outside the United States, in a separate program operated by the Central Intelligence Agency.... This program has been subject to multiple legal reviews by the Department of Justice and CIA lawyers; they've determined it complied with our laws."[2] It is highly doubtful that President Bush consciously thought himself antagonistic to the rule of law.

What seems quite apparent, though, is that President Bush and his legal advocates presumably had a specific idea of what the rule of law consists of; what they seemed to believe in is a version of the "rule of law" as *formalism*. It is a rule of law that claims to be no more and no less than "law as rule." In the formalist view, Americans enjoy a "government of laws" so long as executive officials can point, literally, to some formal source of law—typically, a constitutional provision, a statute, a judicial opinion, or an executive branch regulation—as authority for their acts. They would presumably count this as the rule of law even if no institution outside the executive were entitled to test the consistency of those acts with the source of legal authority cited.

To take an example I explore in greater detail below, White House lawyers defending claims of executive privilege against Congress would presumably assert they were acting in a manner consistent with the rule of law because the Supreme Court expressly sanctioned claims of executive privilege in the famous Watergate tapes case involving President Nixon.[3] (Technically, the *Nixon* case did not involve a claim against Congress, but its analytic framework for claims levied in a judicial forum could easily be extended to claims against the legislative branch, as well.) Lawyers could thus formally cite the *Nixon* decision as a source of authority for the President's refusal to disclose information. Yet the President would be in compliance with the *Nixon* decision only if each claim of privilege reflected the principled balancing process that the *Nixon* decision calls for. That is, *Nixon* allows the President to withhold documents based on his or her generalized interest in confidentiality only if the executive branch interest in confidentiality in a particular context is weightier than the interests of the coequal branch of government—in this case, Congress—seeking disclosure of the President's information. The Reagan and George W. Bush Administrations both asserted that the executive branch is entitled to do that weighing unilaterally; that is, these Administrations believed that the executive branch has unreviewable discretion to come to its own decision whether or not its asserted interest in confidentiality was entitled to be upheld. Their version of the rule of law, in this instance, would call for formal acknowledgment of the *Nixon* decision as controlling legal authority, but would not call for the President to subject his or her legal judgment to the review of either Congress or the courts.

In our checks and balances system, the formalist version of the rule of law runs into two more or less immediate problems. The first is that the Constitution, the document that vests the President with whatever core powers he has, is notoriously vague. Executive branch formalists extract from such delphic text the constitutional license for virtually unlimited executive power by converting every acknowledged grant of *some* executive power into the most expansive and rigid category of power consistent with that grant. To convert vague implications into hard and fast rules, extreme presidentialism takes all conceded kernels of presidential power under the Constitution to their furthest analytically plausible limit.

Consider, for example, the implications of the Framers' textually explicit decision to make the President chief executive. Everyone agrees, presidentialists and pluralists alike, that the President's position as chief executive implies some scope of constitutionally vested supervisory authority regarding the rest of the executive branch. But, once that core is conceded, the devotees of presidentialism argue that this authority must, as a matter of analytic logic, encompass the power to direct the exercise of any and all discretionary authority vested in any subordinate executive official. As chapter 6 explains, once acknowledged to be the general overseer of the executive branch, the President, according to presidentialists, must automatically be regarded as "the Decider,"[4] that is, as constitutionally entitled to dictate how every member of the executive branch discharges his or her functions. According to the formalist mind-set, the chief executive power must be extended categorically—it must pertain to every member of the executive branch—or the grant of executive power does not really amount to a rule. The emphasis on rule of law formalism thus seems, at least superficially, to favor analytically expansive interpretation. (We will see later what is wrong with this logic.)

The second problem is that, as legal formalists, the President's lawyers want to have some piece of paper—parchment might be preferable—to hold up as authoritative legal support for any claim of executive authority. Constitutional text, statutes, and judicial opinions are the pieces of paper that usually serve this kind of function. Unfortunately for the presidentialists, the Constitution is ambiguous, at best, on the nature of executive power. Congress enacts very few statutes that embody anything like congressional ratification for the executive branch's most prodigious ambitions. There are few judicial opinions supporting the presidentialist view of the presidency because separation of powers disputes are rarely litigated, and the courts have not been receptive to extreme presidentialist claims of executive authority. There are no cases to cite with anything like strong support for many of the President's most frequently asserted claims, and there is frequently strong contrary authority. There is thus a pressing need for the executive branch to manufacture its own legitimating documents, formal pieces of paper that seem to sanction the President's expansive assertions of unilateral power.

The Bush 43 Administration exhibited both of these behaviors—a tendency toward conceptually rigid interpretations of executive power and a penchant for minting its own currency of formal legal legitimacy. The audacity—even bizarreness—of these behaviors paints a clear and unattractive picture of the thin, ideologically driven conception of the rule of law that is a hallmark of modern-day presidentialism. But to understand fully what is stake, it is critical also to contrast rule of law formalism with a more compelling alternative, a version of the rule of law that fits comfortably with checks and balances and respect for constitutional pluralism. I call this alternative the "institutionalist" conception because it emphasizes the informal norms and processes of official self-restraint that are part of day-to-day government in a checks and balances system. What we count on as the rule of law, under this more attractive conception, depends at least as much on the informal ordering of the three branches' political behavior as it does on the formal rules that purport to delimit each branch's authority.

Thinking Hard about the Familiar: What Does the Rule of Law Mean?

"Rule of law" is one of those concepts that can seem hopelessly nuanced to academics, but commonsensical to most citizens.[5] Imagine a survey that asks people the meaning of "the rule of law," or of its close cousin, "a government of laws, not of men." It seems a safe wager that the most common answer would be some variant of the following: "The 'rule of law' means that those in power cannot do what they want just because they want to do it, or because they have force on their side. The 'rule of law' means they can do only what the law permits." Despite the intellectual puzzles that philosophers might extract from that answer—for example, what counts as "law?"—my brief experience of government suggests that something like this formulation is deeply ingrained in how most people who work for the government actually think of themselves and of the jobs they do.[6]

Yet, to count as something like plausible common sense, the conventional notion of the "rule of law" I have just described has to take account of two other equally commonsensical facts. One is that public officials, even if conscientiously attentive to law, will often find the written law applicable to their particular problems or opportunities to be genuinely vague. A Federal Communications Commissioner knows, for example, that she cannot impose broadcast licensing conditions that do not serve the "public interest, convenience, and necessity."[7] But what does that actually mean as a limitation on her decision making?

The second fact is that, with regard to a great deal—perhaps most—government activity, the chances are remote that law can and will be enforced against nonconforming behavior. Thus, for example, the officials who review Freedom of Information Act requests know that the law imposes a specific obligation to respond within twenty business days.[8] They also know, if they dally for an extra day or two—and probably, much longer than that—nothing adverse will happen to them. They will not be imprisoned, fined, or even reprimanded. Yet, as citizens, we still want and expect them to obey the law. We expect the rule of law to operate even when the prospects of sanction are remote.

The kind of government we have will clearly depend, to a significant degree, on how government officials respond to the inevitability of legal uncertainty and lax enforcement. Government officials might profess allegiance to the rule of law but still interpret every legal ambiguity to favor their personal political preferences. They may indulge their preferences as much as possible even in the implementation of clear rules, so long as they can do so with impunity. As citizens, however, we can safely dismiss this as an illegitimate view of the rule of law for one simple reason: It is unimaginable that any government official would be willing to declare in public, "This is actually how I am behaving." What government officials want us to believe, even when law is vague and enforcement is uncertain, is that they are behaving in a legally accountable fashion. They want to appear to be guided by reasons they would be willing to declare publicly, and these reasons must be consistent with the law they are charged with implementing. They are thus mindful not only of what makes them personally better off, but also of the needs and interests of the public more generally and of all the critical institutions of government. For this account of legal accountability to be plausible, however, the written documents of law have to be buttressed by a set of norms, conventional expectations, and routine behaviors that lead officials to behave as if they are accountable to the public interest and to legitimate sources of legal and political authority even when the written rules are ambiguous and even when they could probably get away with merely self-serving behavior.

What I am describing is a version of the rule of law that is not formalistic, but institutional. Checks and balances, in operation, depend on an assemblage of norms, cooperative arrangements, and informal coordination activities that actually fit the political science definition of an "unstructured institution." James March and Johan Olsen have usefully defined an "institution" as "a relatively enduring collection of rules and organized practices, embedded in structures of meaning and resources that are relatively invariant in the face of turnover of individuals and relatively resilient to the idiosyncratic preferences and expectations of individuals and changing external circumstances."[9] Sometimes the relevant "rules and organized practices" are exceedingly clear and documented, like the rules inside the cover of a board game. But sometimes, as political scientist Kenneth Shepsle has pointed out, these rules and practices "are more amorphous and implicit rather than formalized."[10] We still recognize them as institutions because they "may be described as practices and recognized by the patterns they induce,"[11] but compared to, say, a game of golf, they are, relatively speaking, "unstructured institutions."[12] Understanding the rule of law as an unstructured institution provides a far more attractive account of what citizens expect from a "government of laws" and a far more plausible account of why they might just get it; it provides an account of government behavior that rests on observable patterns of actual human behavior, not just the formal specification of legal rules in the form of written documents.

An excellent example of what I have in mind is provided by the traditional stance of Attorneys General in assessing the constitutionality of congressionally enacted statutes. For many decades, Attorneys General have advised their executive branch clients that, outside the separation of powers context, they will not call into question the constitutionality of any federal statute unless the law is so patently unconstitutional that no defense of it could be mounted in good conscience.[13] In other words, should the constitutionality of a statute be called into question by either a private citizen or an implementing agency, the Attorney General will defend the statute or order its implementation so long as the Attorney General can formulate a constitutional rationale for the statute—even if that rationale is not airtight and might be overturned in court in light of a more compelling argument against the statute. Unless and until a court order determines that the statute is unconstitutional, the Attorney General will thus give Congress the benefit of the doubt on most questions of constitutionality.

From a formalist perspective, this practice might well seem problematic. Specifically, such deference to Congress might be regarded as formally in conflict with the President's constitutionally prescribed oath to protect and defend the Constitution[14]—a promise that might be thought to entail the duty to engage in and to implement a more searching independent judgment. Because the President has sworn to protect and defend the Constitution, it is arguable that the President should refuse to enforce any statute that he is persuaded is unconstitutional, even if he accepts that Congress might responsibly disagree and could write its own reasonable brief in defense of the disputed law.

Despite the formalist argument, Attorneys General have realized that, in balancing the independent obligation of the executive to protect the Constitution with another constitutional charge, namely, the duty imposed on the President to take care that the laws be faithfully executed,[15] government works better, in the ordinary case, if issues of constitutionality are left for the resolution of a disinterested judicial branch. It is thus that Attorneys General have established an informal norm of deferring to Congress (and, if a question is ultimately presented to a court, to judicial decision making) as the best way to achieve legal accountability in a system of checks and balances.

Professor Jack Goldsmith, the conservative head of OLC from 2003 to 2004, wrote in 2007 about the critical role of institutional norms in preserving the rule of law within the executive branch. He explained that, in order to prevent itself from simply interpreting the law opportunistically to serve the political ends of the executive branch, OLC "has developed powerful cultural norms about the importance of providing the President with detached, apolitical legal advice, as if OLC were an independent court inside the executive branch."[16] His statement echoes the observations of a group of former OLC attorneys, led by former Assistant Attorney General Walter Dellinger, who were deeply upset by the national security opinions discussed in the last chapter—most notably, the so-called John Yoo torture memo[17] later withdrawn by Jack Goldsmith—and felt compelled in 2004 to distill their criticisms into a set of recommended prescriptions to guide future OLC attorneys in the process of legal analysis on behalf of the executive branch.[18] Their ten recommendations are all loose norms, not highly specified commands, such as: "OLC's obligation to counsel compliance with the law, and the insufficiency of the advocacy model, pertain with special force in circumstances where OLC's advice is unlikely to be subject to review by the Courts,"[19] or, "Whenever time and circumstances permit, OLC should seek the views of all affected agencies and components of the Department of Justice before rendering final advice."[20] But the lawyers' statement does not merely assert these recommendations as future-oriented prescriptions. They purport to be descriptive, "based in large part on the longstanding practices of the Attorney General and the office of Legal Counsel, across time and administrations."[21] What they are describing is part of the rule of law as an unstructured institution—a "rule of law culture."

Because paper limits on the exercise of power are never self-enforcing and, in any event, can never be sufficiently detailed to address every conceivable context in which legal accountability is important, the institutionalist version of the rule of law is critical to democratic governance in a society as complex as ours. Understanding the institutionalist version also helps clarify why that view was especially unattractive to many of the right-wing lawyers who have served in recent Administrations. To the Reaganites and their ideological successors, the norms prevailing in American government as of 1980 were ineluctably associated with a public policy regime that they considered too liberal, too egalitarian, too regulatory, too internationalist in outlook, too oriented toward civil and human rights at home and abroad. Anything based in pre-Reagan institutional norms of governance was thus automatically suspect by virtue of its guilt by historical association with the governing philosophy of the New Deal. This, I think, is a necessary part of the explanation behind the right-wing norm-breaking initiatives recounted in chapter 1—the Iran-Contra affair, the threat of government shutdown, the impeachment of Bill Clinton, and *Bush v. Gore*. If the Reaganites and their ideological successors were constrained to follow ideas of the rule of law that bound them to pre-1981 governance norms, they might have been locked in (or feared they would have been locked in) to a set of public policies they wanted to overthrow. One can add to the list of conservative norm-breaching behaviors the imprisonment of Americans as enemy combatants, the GOP upending of traditional congressional procedures between 2003 and 2006, and much more. Whether consciously or not, the Right placed no value on norms of governance that evolved between 1945 and 1981, and often earlier, to make interbranch friction manageable. Put bluntly, the Right wanted to jar the national government rightward and largely assumed that pre-1981 norms were antagonistic to that aim. Where long-standing norms of institutional behavior—including rule of law norms—appeared to obstruct immediate accomplishment of the right-wing agenda, the norms were rolled back or even abandoned.

A hallmark of the Bush Administration's aggressive presidentialism was thus a seeming indifference to the informal ordering mechanisms that give life to the rule of law. Its vision of the rule of law implicitly rested instead only on two premises: first, that any official action must find sanction in a formal source of law, whether the Constitution, a judicial opinion, a statute, or a regulation, and second, such sources of law must be interpreted to yield, insofar as possible, bright-line rules rather than open-ended, contestable standards. The insistence on categorical rules appears clearly in the presidentialists' preferred theory of constitutional interpretation—the categorical formalism that reads every constitutional kernel of executive power, such as the Vesting Clause or the Commander-in-Chief Clause, as a signal of broad and unregulable presidential authority. To a formalist, Justice Jackson's view of presidential power under which the President's authority varies somewhat unpredictably with evidence of congressional acquiescence in or rejection of presidential initiative is simply too uncertain a legal prescription to be favored as law.

The presidentialists' expansive approach to interpreting Article II, however, is open to an exceedingly obvious objection as a method of reading the Constitution. That is, there is no reason evident from either constitutional text or constitutional history why we should read the concededly delphic provisions of Article II, which creates the presidency, any more or less generously than we should read the general provisions of Article I, which vests the authorities of Congress. If we read the President's grants of authority rigidly and expansively, we should presumably read the powers of Congress just as liberally. If the Commander-in-Chief Clause implies a vast category of implicit power, Congress's authority to declare war should be read just the same way. If we infer from the structure of the Constitution an unspoken, but exceedingly broad scope of implicit presidential authority to protect executive branch information, then Congress has equivalent interpretive grounds to have us find similar breadth in its unspoken, but implicit authority to demand executive branch information and to investigate government operations. Of course, if we read both articles this way, the powers of Congress and the President will come frequently into conflict. The constitutional text seems to specify clearly who is supposed to win such battles. It expressly authorizes Congress to make all laws necessary and proper for carrying into execution the authorities vested by the Constitution in any officer of the United States.[22] Given this express congressional power over Presidents, it would seem that a constitutional formalist should always favor congressional power over executive. Yet, presidentialism conspicuously ignores this obvious problem.

A candid presidentialist response to this would require an acknowledgment that pure formalism cannot work as a complete theory of what the rule of law entails. Recent Republican Administrations have been hostile to the prevailing norms of checks and balances governance, and they seem to disregard informal norms generally as a critical element in their thinking about the rule of law. Yet, to explain their preference for reading Article II more expansively than Article I, presidentialists have to rely on their own implicit normative understanding of the Constitution. They have to have some kind of informal understanding of how to read the Constitution that is not actually contained in its text, but that justifies always coming down on the side of the presidency. If we read the academic work of the presidentialists, this informal understanding becomes clear: Presidentialists feel justified in elevating Article II over Article I because they regard the executive branch as a *better* institution than Congress. They think it better at making decisions because it is more centralized and hierarchical.[23] They may think it is better at handling sensitive information because of the same structural features. And, most notably, they think it more reliable in pursuing the national interest because the President, unlike his legislative colleagues, is accountable to a national constituency, thus supposedly fostering an accountability to the general interest that is less parochial, less factional, than the perspectives of individual members of Congress.[24]

These normative claims are important to evaluate, especially because—as discussed in chapter 6—the last does not hold water and the others are easily overstated. In considering the implications of presidentialism for the rule of law, it is important that the Framers did not share this sense of executive branch superiority for making policy decisions. On the contrary, they designed an elaborate and pluralistic legislative process out of the conviction that Congress's structural characteristics—its size and bicameral design—were superior for resolving issues of public policy because they would insure due discussion and thorough deliberation. State legislative abuses during the 1780s had undoubtedly prompted a rethinking of the importance of executive power and of reliable checks against legislative excess. But this rethinking did not entail any rethinking of the basic legislative role and its primacy. Whether privileging executive power in the making of public policy makes contemporary sense may be debatable, but it would not have made sense to the founding generation. To the extent presidentialism embraces informal norms of governance or legal interpretation that disrespect the role and perspective of Congress, presidentialism is at odds with constitutional originalism.

My strategy, however, in painting the dangers of presidentialism is to rely ultimately not on theory, but on experience. The performance of the Bush 43 Administration gave Americans a kind of natural experiment in how the presidentialists' rule of law attitude plays out in practice, and it is the record of that Administration that indicts the presidentialist vision of the rule of law most effectively. The excesses of presidentialism in this regard are notably easy to spot in two contexts—the Administration's efforts to expand government secrecy and the use of presidential signing statements to object to new laws.

The Expansion of Executive Privilege Theory

The formalist tendency toward conceptually rigid interpretations of executive power is beautifully illustrated by the stance of Bush 43 Administration regarding executive branch prerogatives to withhold government information. The period of 2001–2006 was marked by a much-noted increase in federal government secrecy. In the year following the September 11 attacks, the government classified 11.3 million documents, which jumped to 14.2 million the following year and 15.6 million the year thereafter.[25] At the same time, the increase in pages classified was accompanied by a substantial drop, since Fiscal Year 2001, in the number of pages of previously classified information that the government declassified.[26] Yet, there was no change in the statutory law enacted by Congress with regard to the President's classification authority.

Likewise, agencies removed government documents from Web sites and publicly available databases, severely limiting the public's ability to assess environmental and other risks.[27] The government became less willing to turn over records requested by members of the public under the Freedom of Information Act, or FOIA. According to a study of twenty-two agencies by the Coalition of Journalists for Open Government, the use of FOIA exemptions to deny requests jumped by 21 percent between 2000 and 2004, even though the total number of FOIA requests processed by these agencies, the largest-volume handlers of FOIA requests, dropped by 13 percent.[28] Most surprisingly, the increase in denials had no apparent connection to national security. FOIA explicitly exempts classified information from mandatory disclosure, and agencies withholding documents because they are classified may cite this statutory exemption as the reason for keeping documents out of the public eye. Yet, agency citations to the FOIA exemption that protects classified information from mandatory disclosure actually dropped during the time period when denials of FOIA requests were increasing.[29]

The fact is that the Bush Administration's pursuit of increased secrecy was well in development prior to the September 11 attacks. It revealed itself in litigation to fend off public disclosure of who in the oil industry had met with the Vice President's task force to develop the Administration's legislative proposals on energy.[30] The bizarre scope of the Administration's asserted entitlement to secrecy appeared dramatically in a November 1, 2001 executive order, also presumably in development well before September 11, concerning the government's handling of presidential records from prior Administrations.[31] The Bush Administration's treatment of executive privilege illustrates beautifully the impoverished presidentialist version of the rule of law.

Executive privilege is understood most easily as an umbrella term covering a variety of legal claims regarding sensitive government information. At the core of the concept is the so-called state secrets privilege, which shields the executive from demands to disclose information whose release would work serious harm to our national security.[32] The Administration's efforts to bolster executive privilege focused chiefly, however, on the forms of executive privilege that are the most general and furthest reaching—the presidential communications privilege[33] and the so-called deliberative privilege.[34] The first covers documents prepared by or for the President, and the second supposedly shields from mandatory disclosure any documents that would shed light on the internal deliberations of the executive branch preliminary to deciding any final matter of policy. The "deliberative privilege" operates on communications at every level of the executive branch and, according to its defenders, whether or not the particular records at issue are actually sensitive in any respect.

In its 1974 *United States v. Nixon* decision, the Supreme Court interpreted the Constitution as giving the President a qualified privilege to withhold from the public his private communications while in office. The Court underscored the importance of confidentiality in securing full and frank advice.[35] Although the Constitution does not make any presidential privilege explicit—unlike the right of Congress to maintain some secret proceedings, which the Constitution creates expressly[36]—the Court plausibly reasoned that the President could not effectively oversee a coequal branch of government without the ability to assure people counseling him that he could maintain the confidentiality of politically sensitive discussions.[37]

The Court held, however, that this privilege is not absolute but instead qualified to the extent other institutions of government might demand the disclosure of privileged information to fulfill their functions—as did the Watergate prosecutor in the *Nixon* case. When the President or his representatives seek to invoke executive privilege in a judicial proceeding, a court is entitled to weigh the urgency of the demanding institution's need against any harm that would result to the executive from a particular disclosure.[38] In *Nixon*, the Supreme Court held that the trial court's need for certain tapes of presidential conversations outweighed the executive's interest in confidentiality.[39] In its executive privilege disputes with Congress in the early 1980s, even the Reagan Administration acknowledged the need for constitutional balancing.[40] They added, however, a critical innovation. Attorney General William French Smith insisted that the balancing could be determined unilaterally by the President in the absence of a court order.[41] In other words, if the President, weighing what he takes to be Congress's interest in certain information against his own need for confidentiality, happens to find that his own needs are weightier, that supposedly concludes the matter. This was apparently the view also of the George W. Bush Administration.[42]

The breadth of the Bush 43 Administration's professed legal entitlement to secrecy was spelled out in two episodes early in the first term. The first involved a so-called National Energy Policy Development Group

(NEPDG) that President Bush created during his second week in office. He designated Vice President Cheney to chair the group, which comprised a number of agency heads and assistants.[43] Both Congress and a number of public interest groups, the latter resting their demands on "open government" statutes, sought to discover the names of oil industry executives and private lobbyists who met and participated with the group, allegedly to a degree tantamount to actual membership. The Administration resisted all such efforts.

The public interest groups—Sierra Club and Judicial Watch—sought access to information about the NEPDG through the Federal Advisory Committee Act (FACA), which Congress enacted in 1972.[44] FACA imposes on groups that are constituted to provide advice to the President and federal agencies a set of open meeting and disclosure requirements that apply only if those groups include members who are not federal employees.[45] The Administration insisted that no private parties were actually members of the NEPDG, but the district court gave the groups a right to "discovery," that is, a chance to demand documents that could contain evidence to confirm or refute the plaintiff groups' claim that the NEPDG was failing to fulfill its openness requirements under FACA.[46] The Vice President, arguing that discovery threatened the President's interest in confidentiality, sought from the D.C. Circuit Court of Appeals a special order—a writ of mandamus—to direct the trial court to vacate its discovery orders. This was denied because the Court of Appeals regarded itself as without authority to issue such a writ while other legal remedies were available to the Administration.[47] For example, the Administration had not yet asserted any formal claim of executive privilege in the trial court, and the Court of Appeals thought itself powerless to entertain the Vice President's petition unless executive privilege were asserted and ruled upon. The Supreme Court reversed the District Court, however, indicating that the Vice President's personal involvement in the suit and the sensitivity of the potential separation of powers issues made early judicial consideration of the mandamus request appropriate.[48] The Court of Appeals was entitled to narrow the discovery orders, if they were overbroad, or even to determine that the threat posed by discovery to the functioning of the executive could not justify the demand for the information sought in this special civil litigation context.

On reconsideration, the Court of Appeals decided to grant the Vice President the relief he had requested.[49] The court reasoned that the private parties would count as members of the NEPDG—thus rendering the NEPDG subject to disclosure requirements—only if they could vote regarding, or exercise a veto over, the decisions of the group.[50] Because Judicial Watch and the Sierra Club had not even alleged either possibility, they could not win their suit, and the discovery orders were unjustified. Thus, without formally uttering the words "executive privilege," the Vice President succeeded in protecting the NEPDG's secrecy based on a balancing argument all but identical to the argument he would have had to have made had he formally claimed executive privilege in the first place. His victory potentially expanded the effective reach of executive privilege, however, by allowing the executive branch to resist disclosure not only when definitive adjudication of a formal claim would uphold the privilege, but even in litigation where a hypothetical executive privilege claim would be plausibly justifiable.

Of course, fending off public interest groups is a different matter from fending off Congress. In spring 2001 the Government Accountability Office (GAO) asked the Vice President to provide information concerning the membership and operations of the NEPDG, based on the request of two Congressmen, John D. Dingell, the ranking Democrat on the House Committee on Energy and Commerce, and Henry A. Waxman, the ranking Democrat on the House Committee on Government Reform.[51] David Addington, the Vice President's Counsel, provided some general information about the task force, but would not disclose "the names of NEPDG staff members, the names of persons in attendance at the NEPDG meetings or at meetings between staff and persons outside of the government, or the dates, locations, and subjects of any meetings with non-federal employees."[52] Addington also questioned the legal basis for the GAO investigation. When the Comptroller General, the head of the GAO, demanded the information not yet provided, Vice President Cheney sent letters to both the House and Senate indicating that the GAO was exceeding its investigative authority and that, if its investigation were carried forth, it would "unconstitutionally interfere with the functioning of the executive branch."[53] As negotiations over some degree of possible disclosure proceeded, the Vice President's office did provide the names of the staff members who were government employees, but not the private parties who had met with the NEPDG.[54]

With Democrats in control of the Senate from 2001 to early 2003, key Democratic Senators wrote the Comptroller General in early 2002 to urge him to press forward.[55] When the Vice President persisted in his nondisclosure, the GAO filed suit in February 2002. The executive branch responded that the investigation was unconstitutional because the NEPDG operated pursuant to two of the President's explicit constitutional authorities, the power to "require the Opinion, in writing, of the principal Officer in each of the executive Departments, upon any Subject relating to the Duties of their respective Offices"[56] and the power to "recommend to [Congress's] Consideration such Measures as he shall judge necessary and expedient."[57] According to Cheney, how a President seeks information in connection with these authorities cannot be overseen by either Congress or the judiciary. Congress could not, according to this argument, legislate how the President fulfills these powers, so it cannot investigate how he does so, either through a congressional committee or through the Government Accountability Office.[58]

Avoiding what it took to be difficult constitutional arguments, the U.S. District Court for the District of Columbia dismissed the case in December 2002 on the ground that the Comptroller General, on these particular facts, could not constitutionally be allowed to sue the executive branch. Employing the highly technical constitutional doctrine of standing, the court held that GAO had no right to sue where the denial of the information sought would not actually inflict an injury on Congress.[59] Given GOP legislative victories in November 2002 and the impending Republican takeover of the Senate, the GAO then declined to pursue an appeal from this ruling, presumably realizing that it would not have the political backing of either the Republican-controlled House or the Republican-controlled Senate.

The district court was arguably too contrived in its argument for dismissing the Comptroller General's case, but the point that needs to be made about this history of litigation is not just a matter of legal technicality. The point is that the Vice President, at significant taxpayer expense, persisted in litigation until 2005 to avoid telling Congress and the public which oil industry lobbyists and executives had advised the President on national energy policy. It is impossible to articulate persuasively a single public interest that was advanced by this insistence on secrecy. The matter at issue had no implications for national security. There was no prospect of politicizing a law enforcement matter. The disclosures did not involve any personal communications of the President. This was not a case of whistle blowing in which revealing the identity of an information source would discourage other people from coming forward on other occasions. Indeed, if the Vice President disclosed the names of those with whom he had met, it would probably have worked to the reputational benefit of the industry representatives involved. After all, who would not want it known that they had direct access to the Vice President of the United States on a matter critical to his or her company? Moreover, in a country truly committed to the rule of law, there are few features of government more important than transparency. The Vice President nonetheless thought the confidentiality of his industry contacts was important enough to justify pushing the courts to narrow the investigative authority of the Government Accountability Office and limiting the reach of the Federal Advisory Committee Act.[60]

While the Vice President's stance on the NEPDG was ambitious, it was modest in its creativity compared to the view of executive privilege encapsulated in a presidential executive order on the implementation of something called the Presidential Records Act (PRA)—an order deeply revealing regarding the presidentialist constitutional vision and its proponents' conception of the rule of law.[61]

The PRA[62] gives an executive branch official, the National Archivist, custody of a former President's records upon the conclusion of the President's term of office. The PRA requires the Archivist, within specific procedural guidelines, to make presidential records "available to the public as rapidly and completely as possible."[63] The key procedural guidelines are twofold. First, a President is entitled to restrict access for up to twelve years to any of his records that fall within six specified categories.[64] These do not include the full scope of the executive's so-called deliberative privilege, but they do include records relating to appointments to federal office and records consisting of "confidential communications requesting or submitting advice between the President and his advisers, or between such advisers."[65] The PRA also protects other files, "the disclosure of which would constitute a clearly unwarranted invasion of personal privacy."[66] Second, whenever a presidential record becomes available for disclosure—either because no President has restricted access or because the time for restricted access has expired—the Archivist is to handle requests to view such records as requests under the Freedom of Information Act, with one difference. The Freedom of Information Act allows the executive branch to withhold from disclosure any document that is covered by the "deliberative privilege" branch of executive privilege.[67] The PRA does not.[68] As a result, the mere fact that a document reflects the substance of presidential deliberations leading to a government decision does not exempt it from public disclosure once the general period for restricted access expires.

This structure, while thoughtful in its conception, leaves certain important questions unanswered. In providing for a staged release of records from past Presidents, Congress expressly left untouched "any constitutionally-based privilege which may be available to an incumbent or former President"[69] because it did not want the PRA to be interpreted as an attempt either to expand or contract whatever privilege the courts would otherwise uphold. To help assure the orderly resolution of any privilege disputes, the PRA provides for consultation between the archivist and a former President before the release of any presidential record that the former President had designated for restricted access.[70] It also requires the Archivist to promulgate rules governing notice to a former President "when the disclosure of particular documents may adversely affect any rights and privileges which the former President may have."[71] The PRA explicitly envisions judicial review to protect presidential privilege, vesting jurisdiction in the U.S. District Court for the District of Columbia "over any action initiated by [a] former President asserting that a determination made by the Archivist violates the former President's rights or privileges."[72] In short, in enacting the PRA, Congress tried to walk a balancing act—creating an orderly process for making presidential records "available to the public as rapidly and completely as possible," while preserving opportunities for former Presidents to assert constitutionally based privileges as grounds for withholding documents from mandatory disclosure.

But the PRA leaves two obvious holes in its procedural scheme. First, it provides no administrative process for handling disagreements between the Archivist and either a former or sitting President—who, it must be remembered, may have his or her own rationale for asserting executive privilege with regard to records of earlier Administrations—with regard to a document's release. In other words, what should happen if the Archivist determines that a document is appropriate for public disclosure, but the past or the sitting President disagrees? Second, Congress provided no process to permit incumbent Presidents to consider whether privilege ought be asserted to prevent the mandatory withholding of a predecessor's records. At any point in time, it is the incumbent President—not a former President—who is constitutionally obligated to defend the Constitution and who thus enjoys the right to assert executive privilege in order to protect the functioning of the executive branch.

Prior National Archivists have tried to address these problems by issuing administrative rules. One rule says that, once a former President is notified about the imminent disclosure of his records, the Archivist will ordinarily not disclose the records for at least thirty calendar days after the former President receives his notice.[73] Implicit, but unsaid, is the corollary that the Archivist will continue to withhold records over which a former President claims privilege if the former President files suit for that purpose within thirty days. To give the sitting President a chance to take a position on disclosure, the rule also provides that "[c]opies of all notices provided to former Presidents under this section shall be provided at the same time to the incumbent President."[74]

President Reagan, while in office, realized that his records would be the first to be managed pursuant to the Act. Thinking that even the Archivist's regulations left some critical matters ambiguous, he issued an executive order at the very end of his second term to specify how he hoped future Administrations would handle those records.[75] First, the Reagan order required that the National Archivist follow guidelines provided by incumbent or former Presidents regarding the identification of records that might raise a substantial question of executive privilege.[76] The order provided that either an incumbent or a former President could extend, by a claim of executive privilege, the thirty-day period otherwise provided between notice and disclosure of a record by the Archivist.[77] Finally, in the event that a former President claimed executive privilege, President Reagan's order would require the Archivist to heed the incumbent President's determination whether or not to respect the former President's claim of privilege.[78]

President Reagan left office in 1989. Hence, for any records he sought to protect from immediate disclosure under the PRA, the twelve-year statutory grace period expired in 2001. It would thus fall to whoever became President in 2001 to implement the elaborate framework for handling President Reagan's records that was erected through the complex interaction of Congress, the National Archivist, and President Reagan. On November 1, 2001, however, President Bush issued a new executive order to govern his own implementation of the PRA with regard to President Reagan's records. The Bush order erects a variety of new rules for the implementation of the Presidential Records Act. Four, to put it mildly, are startling.

The first of these, in Section 10 of the Bush order, allows a former President to "designate a representative (or series or group of alternative representatives, as the former President in his discretion may determine) to act on his behalf" with regard to the handling of his records.[79] With an eye obviously cast on President Reagan, then incapacitated with Alzheimer's disease, Bush determined that, "[u]pon the death or disability of a former President, the former President's designated representative shall act on his behalf . . . , including with respect to the assertion of constitutionally based privileges."[80] In other words, a former President could designate someone—a friend, a family member, a lawyer, anyone—who, upon the President's incapacity, could purport to claim the privileges of the President of the United States with regard to the disclosure of records to which the public would otherwise be legally entitled.

It may take a moment to for the full implications of this provision to sink in. "Executive privilege" is extended to Presidents of the United States in order to enable them, as the duly elected leaders of the executive branch, to keep information secret if its disclosure would disable the executive branch from fulfilling its constitutionally assigned functions. They enjoy the authority to exercise this privilege precisely because they are elected to the presidency. A sitting President, for example, could not specify that, in the event of his incapacity while in office, executive privilege could be asserted by the family lawyer. If the President is incapacitated, the Constitution provides who shall be President in his stead. On the ascent of the Vice President to be Acting President under the Twenty-Fifth Amendment, the exercise of executive privilege would become the prerogative of the Acting President because of his or her constitutionally assigned role. The prerogative goes with the office, and the office can be conferred only by constitutional process. The idea that any President could abdicate this role to a person who is not constitutionally in the presidential role is a completely new invention.

But, for those not already stunned by the notion that a former President could personally elect some other individual to exercise his constitutional privileges, Section 10 goes further. The Bush order provides that, if a former President becomes incapacitated without having designated anyone to implement executive privilege on his behalf, "the family of the former President" may do so. Imagine now that it is 2021. Imagine that George W. Bush has sadly become an incapacitated widower and has chosen no one to determine if his records ought be protected by executive privilege. If the Bush order is still in effect, the Bush twins could designate a person of their choosing to insulate their father's records from what would otherwise be legally mandated disclosure. To paraphrase a schoolyard taunt, "Who died and made them President?"

This might seem harmless enough if the order contemplated that, as President Reagan himself provided, the key judgment would truly be the judgment of the incumbent President. Reagan implicitly recognized that, even if the courts recognize some capacity of a former President to assert privilege, it ultimately falls to each elected incumbent to protect the integrity of the executive branch during his or her tenure. Presumably, that is why President Reagan provided, in the event that a former President would claim executive privilege, the National Archivist should heed the incumbent President's determination whether or not to respect the former President's claim of privilege.

But the Bush order actually abdicates this responsibility. It provides that the National Archivist shall be bound by the decision of the former President, even if the incumbent President disagrees.[81] Going back to our 2021 scenario, this would mean that the National Archivist would be legally bound by the decision of the Bush twins' designee, even if the sitting President of the United States regarded the invocation of privilege as unnecessary or improper.

The fourth exertion of presidentialist imagination in the Bush order comes in Section 11. In brief, that section seeks to preserve whatever authority a former Vice President might have to claim executive privilege, should a court agree that a Vice President has constitutional authority apart from the President to claim privilege over vice presidential records.[82] (In a rare show of legal modesty, the former Vice President could not invoke "any constitutional privilege of a President or former President except as authorized by that President or former President."[83]) Prior to the Bush order, however, there is not a sentence in any statute or judicial opinion suggesting that there is any independent vice presidential privilege to protect vice presidential records. Lest we forget, the first Vice President to be empowered by the Bush executive order would be the President's father, who served as President Reagan's Vice President.

An interested citizen might well ask, what exactly is the point of all this? The executive order seems utterly unnecessary to assure that the Reagan records are handled in a manner that President George W. Bush would approve. He might well find it appropriate, as the incumbent President, to defer to the wishes of his predecessor. He might, within his own authority, consider it prudent to take the counsel of someone President Reagan or his family might have designated to weigh possible privilege claims on Reagan's behalf. He might, within his own authority, consider it prudent to take his own father's counsel on what vice presidential records to protect. He could simply have sent a letter to the National Archivist, stating, in effect: "Just so you know, here are the ground rules I'm going to follow in deciding whether to claim executive privilege for any records of the Reagan Administration that President Reagan designated for twelve years of nondisclosure. Whether to assert executive privilege is my responsibility, but, in exercising my responsibility, this is what I'm going to take into account."

Such an approach seems so obvious and straightforward that it is fair to ask, "What purpose does a far-fetched executive order serve that could not have been served through a much more conventional approach?" The answer cannot be the binding of any future Administration; every President gets to embellish, amend, or even revoke the orders of his predecessors. President Bush's November 11, 2001 order is effectively an order only to himself and his own appointees. Here's the only logical answer: What Executive Order No. 13,233 accomplishes is the embodiment, in a formal document with all the trappings of law, of a series of outlandish claims about the scope and survivability of executive privilege claims. Prior to this order, there was no legal document that suggested an independent basis for vice presidential privilege, the obligation of a National Archivist to honor the orders of a former President instead of the incumbent, or the entitlement of a former President to designate someone without constitutional office to exercise privilege on his behalf. Now there is. To repeat the earlier point about the rule of law as formalism: For an aggressively presidentialist Administration dedicated to constitutional theories of executive power that go well beyond the scope of actual legal authority, there arises a pressing need for the executive branch to develop its own legitimating documents, formal pieces of paper that sanction the President's expansive assertions of unilateral power. Executive Order No. 13,223 purports to be one of those documents.

Signing Statements and the Flowering of Faux Law

The Bush Administration's handling of the Cheney-NEPDG matter and, most especially, its executive order on presidential records reveal the twin impulses of rule of law formalism, presidentialist style. They are the insistence on the expansion of every claim of executive power to the outer limits of analytic logic and the imperative to generate what looks like legal authority for even utterly unprecedented claims. On August 1, 2006, the satirical newspaper the *Onion* captured the phenomenon perfectly with a headline that read, "Bush Grants Self Permission to Grant More Power to Self."[84]

The most audacious display of these impulses came with the Administration's expanded use of presidential "signing statements" to interpose constitutional objections to congressional bills that the President was actually signing into law. As every school child knows (or ought to), the Constitution specifies a process for making law in which bills enacted by both Houses of Congress are then sent to the President for his signature or veto. When the President vetoes a bill, the Constitution directs him to return Congress's bill to the first House that voted on it, along with his "objections."[85] There is no constitutional requirement for the President to make any statement with regard to those bills he actually signs. Presidents, however, have taken various occasions to promulgate "signing statements" for legislation they are approving. These statements often tout the benefits that the legislation is projected to achieve, but may also state the President's policy reservations with respect to aspects of the new law. On occasions that were relatively rare—until the Bush Administration—Presidents had also used signing statements to indicate doubts about the constitutionality of particular provisions of the newly enacted statutes they were signing. In such cases, Presidents typically say that they will implement or interpret the statutory provision in question to minimize the perceived constitutional difficulty.

The propriety of this practice is debatable. After all, each President swears to protect and defend the Constitution. If he thinks part of some bill is unconstitutional, should he not feel duty bound to veto what Congress has enacted? There are good reasons, however, why Presidents may think differently. Most obviously, a great deal of legislation takes the form of a fairly complex package, some of which a President may think is urgently required for the good of the country. Requiring him to veto an entire bill because some narrow feature of the package is arguably unconstitutional may be exacting too high a price in terms of sacrificing the public interest as embodied in those parts of the new law that the President thinks are salutary. Moreover, a President might responsibly take the position that, in the ordinary case, the courts are available to address questions of law. Courts are perhaps better positioned to decide on questions of unconstitutionality. If a provision of an enacted bill is unconstitutional in a way that inflicts harm on particular members of the public, anyone harmed can sue to vindicate their rights. A court most often can effectively excise the offending provision from the law.

On a number of occasions, however, Presidents have stated constitutional objections precisely because the law is arguably objectionable in a way that would be very difficult for a private party to challenge in court. In such cases, the President may object because there would not be an effective judicial alternative to test the constitutionality of the offending legal provision. Prior to the Bush Administration, a fairly common constitutional objection in signing statements involved a legislative practice called the "legislative veto."[86] Congress, from the late 1920s on, started inserting so-called legislative veto provisions into laws that extended some significant administrative authority to the executive branch.[87] Under a legislative veto provision, if Congress delegates administrative authority to an executive agency and then decides it is unhappy with how the executive branch implements that authority, it can nullify what the executive branch has done without enacting a new law. Under a "two-House veto," the executive action would be nullified so long as both the House and Senate disapprove it, even though their disapproval would take the form of a concurrent resolution that would not be sent to the President for *his* signature or veto. Under a "one-House" veto, either the House or the Senate alone could nullify executive action through its own resolution, again without giving the President any further say in the matter.[88]

Legislative vetoes seem obviously problematic under Article I of the Constitution, which prescribes but a single process through which Congress can make law—namely, through a vote of both Houses enacting a particular measure and then, under the Presentment Clauses, by receiving the President's approval or, if he vetoes the measure, by a two-thirds vote of both Houses to overturn the President's veto. Imagine now that Congress enacts a law that originally allows the President to implement any of four options for effecting some public policy, A, B, C, or D. If he does D, and Congress disapproves, Congress—following the Article I legislative process—could always seek to enact a law that amends the first statute, so that, henceforth, only options A, B, and C are authorized. The political difficulty facing Congress, however, would be that the second, amending bill would also get sent to the President for his signature or veto before it could become law. The amendment barring the executive branch from pursuing Option D would become law only if the President signed the second statute, or if Congress enacted the amendment over his veto. It is this opportunity for *presidential* veto that is precisely what the *legislative* veto was trying to avoid. Under a legislative veto provision, Congress would give itself permission to nullify Option D without having to send a new law to the President for his review. Understandably, Presidents reacted adversely to departures from the constitutionally designed legislative process that would undercut their veto power, which is the executive's primary check on the legislative branch. This would seem to be a separation of powers violation of a high order.

But there was another reason for objecting to legislative vetoes. There was a good case to be made that they were not only unconstitutional—a conclusion that the Supreme Court did, in fact, reach when a legislative veto case finally reached the Court in 1983[89]—but that they were genuinely detrimental to the public interest.[90] The existence of a legislative veto in an administrative statute creates legal uncertainty. Agencies effectively do not know the scope of their authority until they determine what will pass muster with the current Congress. The President cannot know fully the scope of the authority he originally signed into law. Giving Congress time to decide whether to veto administrative action adds delay to the regulatory process. In promulgating regulations, the executive branch is ordinarily required to publish a notice of its intentions and to allow the public to comment on the regulations in proposed form. The legislative veto process can make a sham out of this process because an agency knows that, no matter what the public says, the agency has to please the current Congress, not the public. There are other arguments to be made, pro and con, on the policy merits of legislative vetoes, but the fundamental point is this: In objecting to legislative vetoes, Presidents were objecting to a practice that threatened to undermine their own central role in the scheme of checks and balances, and their objections were based on both strong constitutional argument and strong arguments of public policy. It is thus not surprising they would provide the occasion for a number of presidential signing statements asserting their unconstitutionality.

By one count, however, the total number of statutory provisions to which Presidents objected on constitutional grounds between the Administration of James Monroe and the beginning of the first Reagan Administration was 101.[91] The advent of the Reagan Administration, however, marked a significant increase in the frequency of the device, plus a dramatic departure in terms of its intended institutional significance. Attorney General Edwin Meese persuaded the company that publishes new laws also to publish the President's signing statements. The signing statements were intended to become, as one report explained, "a strategic weapon in a campaign to influence the way legislation was interpreted by the courts and Executive agencies."[92]

Over the course of two Administrations, President Reagan, through his signing statements, objected to or unilaterally reinterpreted seventy-one statutory provisions.[93] In a single term, President George H. W. Bush objected to 146.[94] Most of the objections involved the President's asserted foreign policy powers, although many reflected the Administration's full embrace of the unitary executive theory and some of the more expansive claims of presidentialist constitutionalism. President Clinton used the signing statement device also, his objections to 105 statutory provisions[95] exceeding the record of President Reagan, although more modest than the record of President Bush 41. In terms of robust presidentialism, however, none of these three Presidents can compete with the record of the Bush 43 Administration.[96] In his first six years in office, President George W. Bush raised nearly 1,400 constitutional objections to roughly 1,000 statutory provisions, over three times the total of his forty-two predecessors combined.[97] But it is not just the numbers that made the Bush signing statements distinctive. Unlike the long-standing presidential objections to legislative vetoes, the Bush objections were frequently based on no legal authority whatever and had nothing to do with any plausible version of the public interest.

So many examples exist of the bizarreness of this practice that I take, almost at random, the President's signing statement for the 2006 Postal

Accountability and Enhancement Act.[98] That Act amends the law describing an agency called the Postal Regulatory Commission. As amended, this rather undramatic law now reads as follows:

The Postal Regulatory Commission is composed of 5 Commissioners, appointed by the President, by and with the advice and consent of the Senate. The Commissioners shall be chosen solely on the basis of their technical qualifications, professional standing, and demonstrated expertise in economics, accounting, law, or public administration, and may be removed by the President only for cause. Each individual appointed to the Commission shall have the qualifications and expertise necessary to carry out the enhanced responsibilities accorded Commissioners under the Postal Accountability and Enhancement Act. Not more than 3 of the Commissioners may be adherents of the same political party.[99]

In signing the Act, the President objected to this provision as one of two in the Act that "purport to limit the qualifications of the pool of persons from whom the President may select appointees in a manner that rules out a large portion of those persons best qualified by experience and knowledge to fill the positions."[100] He then went on to state that the executive branch would construe these provisions "in a manner consistent with the Appointments Clause of the Constitution."[101] In other words, President Bush wanted to go on record as objecting to this innocuous statute as a violation of his power to nominate and appoint officers of the United States and said he would read the law in some unspecified manner that would be consistent with his authority.

Putting aside constitutional issues for a moment, what exactly could the President be thinking here? The statute invites the President to nominate new commission members "on the basis of their technical qualifications, professional standing, and demonstrated expertise in economics, accounting, law, or public administration." What "large portion of those persons best qualified by experience and knowledge" could possibly be excluded by this requirement? The statute does say the President may not appoint more than three of the five commission members from any one political party. He thus has to find at least two Democrats, two Republicans, two independents, or some combination in addition to any three Commission members who belong to the same party. It boggles the mind to think of this as a substantial limit on the President's capacity to identify the best qualified person for any given opening. For it to be any limit at all, there would have to be fewer than two members of the Democratic or Republican parties whom the President would regard as among his favorite candidates for the Postal Regulatory Commission. Because Congress's specifications are so broad and commonsensical, there is no plausible objection to be made that Congress's new version of the law compromises the public interest in a serious way. The only tenable reason for objecting would be the formalist syllogism: Congress may not constitutionally demand that the President nominate John Smith or Jill Jones, in particular, for any particular office. To the presidential formalist, this implies that Congress may impose no constraints on the President at all regarding his choice of nominee.

The strangeness of the President's insistence is all the more apparent, however, if one considers the institutional context we are discussing. The statutory qualifications for Postal Rate Commissioners are legally unenforceable. If the President fails to nominate someone meeting the statutory standards, no one can sue him. Senators might decline to confirm a nominee they believe falls short of the statutory standard, but Senators are entitled to vote "no" on any nominee for any reason they want, so this hardly leaves the President worse off. To object to a statutory specification of qualifications in this context is really to say to Congress, "I, the President of the United States, am offended, constitutionally speaking, that you think I even have to listen to you with regard to the qualifications of potential office holders. It is irrelevant that this office operates directly to fulfill Congress's constitutionally vested authorities with regard to interstate commerce and the post."

Many of President Bush's constitutional objections fall within areas about which Presidents are typically protective. Of the nearly 1,400 objections lodged in signing statements between 2001 and 2006, 76 mention potential interference with commander-in-chief powers, 147 mention interference with his constitutional authorities regarding diplomacy and foreign affairs, and another 170 point to alleged violations of the President's constitutional authorities to withhold or control access to information to protect foreign relations or national security, sometimes mentioning also his power to protect executive branch deliberative processes or the performance of the executive's constitutional duties.[102]

Even in these traditional contexts, however, the substance of the President's objections is often extreme and hypertechnical. For example, one provision alleged to raise issues regarding executive privilege[103] was a legal requirement in the Intelligence Authorization Act for Fiscal Year 2002 that certain reports to congressional intelligence committees must be in writing and include an executive summary.[104] Similarly, the President found a violation of his foreign affairs powers[105] in provisions of the so-called Syria Accountability and Lebanese Sovereignty Restoration Act of 2003 that required him to take certain actions against Syria unless "the President either determines and certifies to the Congress that the Government of Syria has

taken specific actions, or determines that it is in the national security interest of the United States to waive such requirements and reports the reasons
for that determination to the Congress."[106] In other words, Congress violates the Constitution—according to President Bush—when it requires him
either to perform an act or not perform it, at his sole discretion.

For comic constitutionalism, however, it is hard to beat the following:
A statutory provision allegedly in potential conflict with the President's
commander-in-chief powers would put limits on the number of Defense
Department civilian and military personnel who could be assigned to the
Pentagon's Legislative Affairs Office.[107] According to the President, Congress "cannot constitutionally restrict the authority of the President to
control the activities of members of the armed forces, including whether
and how many members of the Armed Forces assigned to the office of the
Chairman of the Joint Chiefs of Staff, the combatant commands, or any
other element of the Department of Defense shall perform legislative affairs or legislative liaison functions."[108] Apparently, lobbying Congress is an
executive act of war.

Going beyond these somewhat astonishing claims in areas of traditional
presidential concern, there are hundreds in wholly novel areas. For example, the President objected to 212 legally imposed reporting requirements
as interfering with his constitutional authority to recommend measures
to Congress.[109] Apparently, President Bush believes that the President's entitlement to speak his mind to Congress entails a prohibition on Congress
demanding any other reports or recommendations from the executive
branch. This is a historically baseless argument. As our original Secretary of
the Treasury, Alexander Hamilton—the most presidentialist of the Framers—clearly found himself as responsible for filing reports with Congress
as to the President.[110] Any constitutional infirmity in the requirement of
executive reports to Congress is entirely a figment of the contemporary
presidentialist imagination.

In his first six years in office, President George W. Bush lodged 363 objections based on Congress's alleged interference with the President's control
over the "unitary executive."[111] Many of these assertions seem to be merely
"piling on" with regard to other, narrower objections. Thus, when the President objects to a congressional mandate that some executive branch official
do something with regard to foreign affairs, the President may object on
both the foreign affairs ground (i.e., Congress may not make foreign policy)
and the unitary executive ground (i.e., Congress may not tell the President
how to use his subordinates).[112] Likewise, when the President objects to
a congressional requirement that a subordinate member of the executive

branch file a report with Congress, on the ground that this violates the President's "recommendations" power, he may also object on unitary executive grounds, again, that Congress is telling someone subordinate to the President what to do.[113]

Beyond these merely cumulative "unitary executive" objections, some invocations of the unitary executive appear to be distinctively rooted in the Bush Administration's imagined authority to direct personally the discretionary activity of every member of the executive branch on any subject, regardless of what the law prescribes. For example, one statutory provision to which the President objected on "unitary executive grounds" is Section 115 of a 2002 "Act to Provide for Improvement of Federal Education Research, Statistics, Evaluation, Information, and Dissemination and for Other Purposes."[114] The Act creates an Institute of Education Sciences within the Department of Education, to be run by a Director and a Board.[115] Section 115 requires the Director to propose Institute priorities for Board approval.[116] The President of the United States, of course, has no inherent constitutional power over education. Yet, executive branch lawyers seem to imagine that it somehow violates the separation of powers either to allow the Director to recommend priorities or for the Board to decide on those priorities, without presidential intervention.[117] In a similar vein is a "unitary executive" objection to a statutory provision requiring the Secretary of Agriculture to consider, in preparing his annual budget, the recommendations of an advisory committee on specialty crops.[118] Although the law does not require the Secretary actually to implement those recommendations, but merely to take them into account, the President implicitly believes that he has inherent authority to forbid subordinates from giving any weight whatever to public policy input from any source other than the White House.[119]

These examples all demonstrate the expansive interpretive tendency described above with regard to the President's appointment power. The strategy is to insist, in bright-line terms, for the most ambitious and rigid assertions of any conceded executive power. But why have these signing statements proliferated now? The views they embody, even if earlier GOP Presidents pushed them less aggressively, were certainly held also by leading legal thinkers under both Presidents Reagan and Bush 41. As legal formalists, the lawyers in earlier Administrations would surely have appreciated, as much as Bush 43 lawyers, the existence of some formal documents embodying their presidentialist claims that could be cited as a species of legal precedent for their arguments. Moreover, Bush's recent GOP predecessors, facing Congresses controlled by Democrats, actually had less political room to work their will than he had until 2007. One thus might have expected to find them even more strident than Bush 43 in asserting their prerogatives of unilateral action.

As it happens, however, what seems to have tempted Bush 43 to use signing statements so aggressively is not their political necessity, but rather the fact he could get away with them in the face of a largely quiescent Congress. From 2001 to 2006, and especially after Republicans took the Senate in 2002, Congress most often did not stand up to the President on his claims of unilateral power. The President set forth his objections so frequently because Congress was not pushing back. Had Congress been standing up for its own prerogatives with customary institutional vigor, one would have expected ambitious signing statements to be matched with equally robust rhetorical responses—or more—from the House and Senate. That simply did not happen.

The 2006 election, returning congressional control to Democrats, had the potential to alter this dynamic. Consider again the 2006 Postal Accountability and Enhancement Act, which we have already noted for the President's objections to the specification of qualifications for Postal Rate Commissioners. A more newsworthy section of the statute provided for the maintenance of a class of domestic sealed mail, which could not "be opened except under authority of a search warrant authorized by law, or by an officer or employee of the Postal Service for the sole purpose of determining an address at which the letter can be delivered, or pursuant to the authorization of the addressee."[120] With regard to this provision, the President's signing statement responded: "The executive branch shall construe [this] subsection . . . to the maximum extent permissible, with the need to conduct searches in exigent circumstances, such as to protect human life and safety against hazardous materials, and the need for physical searches specifically authorized by law for foreign intelligence collection."[121] In other words, the Bush signing statement asserts that the President retains authority to open first-class mail without a warrant, notwithstanding the plain statutory language. (Of course, part of what makes this statement odd is that, under the *Keith* case discussed in chapter 4, it seems doubtful that the President even in a national security case would have authority under the Fourth Amendment to open first-class mail without a warrant no matter what the statute says.)

The November, 2006 ouster of so many right-wing Republicans from Congress, however, emboldened not only Democrats, but also the few remaining Republican moderates to push back. One such GOP member, Senator Susan Collins of Maine, introduced a resolution in January 2007 reaffirming the Constitution's protection of sealed mail from warrantless search.[122] Should such a resolution be enacted, any future presidentialist who wanted to cite the 2006 Bush signing statement as some sort of legal legitimation for the President's authority to inspect the mail, would have to acknowledge Congress's formal disagreement. Whether responses like this would temper signing statement practice is uncertain, but they can certainly diminish the utility of the signing statement mechanism as an opportunity for the President to erect without challenge an edifice of unilateral utterances to stand as ersatz legal authority for unsubstantiated claims of executive authority. What happened from 2001 to 2006 was Bush Administration exploitation of congressional passivity to generate a series of documentary artifacts that can impersonate as legal authority for unilateral presidentialist legal interpretation.

It might well be asked how much all of this lawyerly complexity really matters. Even if we concede that the President is fabricating baseless constitutional objections to the statutory qualifications for Postal Rate Commissioners or the obligation of the Secretary of Agriculture to listen to an advisory board on specialty crops, this may not seem worthy of public agitation. But it does matter, in two important respects.

First, as the next chapter discusses, the signing statements are intended to help legitimate a specific form of presidentialist initiative that is less known to the public than such matters as wiretapping and war making, but, in terms of day to day governance, arguably more significant. This is the recent revolution in the President's relationship to the policy-making bureaucracy—the agencies that regulate virtually every aspect of Americans' social and economic activity, including critical matters of public health and safety. Our recent Presidents have asserted unprecedented authority to determine how all such policy is made,[123] and their signing statements could be used as something that looks like legal authority for executive usurpation. They are formal documents, officially anthologized and electronically searchable. They are connected to an assigned presidential role in the constitutional order. Legally speaking, their content is discretionary with the President. If they say something often enough, these presidential utterances, thus solemnized, may begin to look like law. They are duly executed and ceremonially delivered. They are citable. They are precedents of a sort. One is tempted, however, to say that they are faux law in just the way creation science is faux science. Left unchallenged, they may still have the power to cow Congress and shape the behavior of executive underlings.

But the second point is that the Bush 43 signing statements and the Administration's litigiousness over executive privilege are part of the more general presidentialist ethos of government described in earlier chapters.

Presidentialism is a form of institutional ambition that feeds on itself, and presidential signing statements are both a reflection of and encouragement to a psychology of constitutional entitlement. The future of specialty crops may be less newsworthy than Guantanamo or NSA wiretapping, but the sense of unilateral authority that fuels the President's stance on obscure matters helps to maintain the attitudes—the norms of governance—that lead to other, more consequential claims of unilateral executive authority. An important function of the Bush 43 signing statements is that they serve as reminders to Administration members, and especially to Administration lawyers, of how the President wants the Administration to behave: claim maximum power, concede minimum authority to the other branches.

This is how the thin, formalist rule of law reflected in the signing statements relates to the slipshod, sometimes unethical government lawyering described in chapter 4. The Bush 43 Administration's repeated utterance of its constitutional philosophy was calculated to shape executive branch behavior by solidifying allegiance to norms of hostility to external accountability. Like the torture memo or the rationalizations for warrantless wiretapping, the signing statements embody both a disregard for the institutional authorities of the other branches—especially Congress—and a disregard for the necessity to ground legal claims in plausible law. Such is the legal face of contemporary presidentialism.

6

The President's Personal Bureaucracy: Administrative Accountability and the Unitary Executive

War, national security, and executive privilege represent hotly disputed territory when it comes to the allocation of power between Congress and the President. Much less familiar, however, and much less well understood, are the increasingly heated contests over domestic policy making authority. There are at least two reasons for this. One is that the mechanics of administrative policy making are simply obscure. Institutions like the Environmental Protection Agency and the Federal Communication Commission may be familiar. Americans are presumably aware administrative agencies like these make binding rules about important subjects. It seems a safe guess, however, that few people have a detailed understanding of how these rules get made, the relationship of these rules to the laws Congress enacts, and the nature of the interactions between the administrative agencies and other institutions of government—Congress, President, and judiciary. The second is that debates over administrative policy making authority seem more subtle. The trade-offs between war and peace, or secrecy and openness, that often attend debates over foreign affairs and national security policy making presumably evoke at least some general, even if only visceral understanding. This is less likely when the issue becomes whether the President commands the administrative bureaucracy or merely supervises it.

To repeat a distinction to which I have earlier referred, the central question is whether, as chief executive, the President is "the overseer" or "the decider" when it comes to the federal bureaucracy. President Bush popularized the "decider" label in defending his 2006 decision to retain Donald Rumsfeld as Secretary of Defense: "I hear the voices, and I read the front page, and I know the speculation. But I'm the decider, and I decide what is best. And what's best is for Don Rumsfeld to remain as the secretary of defense."[1] The distinction refers most specifically to two conceptions of the President as "chief executive." The overseer model interprets the President as having general oversight of the executive branch and numerous powers to shape indirectly the behavior of all executive branch subordinates. Under this model, he sometimes has the power to command his subordinates directly, but only if they are either assisting the President in the discharge of one of his constitutional functions (such as negotiating a treaty) or discharging an administrative function conferred by some congressional statute under which Congress has also provided, implicitly or explicitly, that presidential command is permissible. The decider model imputes to the President the power to dictate how his subordinates discharge any and all of their discretionary functions, whether rooted in the Constitution or in statutes enacted by Congress and without regard to any limitations Congress might try to impose on the President's power of command. Presidentialists argue that the President is thus commander-in-chief of the civilian bureaucracy just as he is of the military. Presidentialists often defend the decider model in terms of electoral accountability, on the hypothesis that giving all policy control to the President gives the general public more influence on policy because the public can vote a President out of office, at least once. But treating the President as the decider is both profoundly antidemocratic and deeply dangerous. There is virtually no aspect of the economic, social, or political lives of Americans that is untouched by federal bureaucratic activity. Unduly subjugating the routine regulatory decisions of administrative agencies to the political agenda of a single figure—even a figure as important as the President—can result in hardships, injuries, and even deaths as surely as unsound military policy making. The difference is primarily that we cannot identify the victims as easily.

Up until at least 1981, if a federal administrative lawyer were asked to describe the relationship between the President and the administrative bureaucracy of the United States, the lawyer would probably say something like this: The President has powerful influence over the federal bureaucracy. He appoints the heads of all agencies (albeit with Senate advice and consent). Under the administrative laws enacted by Congress, the President can also fire most agency heads at will—and he can discharge any of them for good cause, such as lawbreaking. An agency's failure to attend respectfully to the President's concerns may elicit punishment in the preparation of the agency's future budget. And, of course, the President is the President. By virtue of his office and his personal influence, what he says always carries great weight.

But that lawyer would have added a crucial final point: The President cannot actually order administrative agencies to issue the precise rules and regulations he wants. Agencies can issue rules and regulations that bind the public only insofar as they have legislative authority from Congress to do so. That authority may leave the agency with substantial room for exercising its own judgment in how to develop the very best regulation. In exercising discretion, no sensible agency will be oblivious to the President's policy agenda. But the decision of how best to exercise agency judgment remains with the head of the agency, not the President. That means the President may fire an agency head if he is disappointed too often, but he cannot insist beforehand that the agency head follow the President's policy preferences. This is the overseer model.

If you asked a member of the Bush 43 legal team to describe the President's relationship to the administrative bureaucracy, you would get an answer diametrically opposed on precisely that point. As discussed in chapter 2, under the theory of the unitary presidency that the presidentialists embrace, the President is entitled to tell all administrators how to exercise their discretionary powers. Contemporary presidentialists believe that the authority explicitly granted by Congress to agency heads is, under this theory, power actually delegated to the President. This is not just a matter of what Congress wants. It is what the Constitution compels. Congress could not provide otherwise. This is the decider model.

Because the overseer model recognizes the President's authority to fire most administrators at will, you might not suspect much difference in operation between the pre-1981 view and the view of the presidentialists. Won't an administrator subject to at-will discharge always follow orders? But the answer is no. An agency head fearful of disappointing the President, even at risk of being fired, is constrained also by other constituencies. She will worry about the congressional committees that oversee her agency. She will worry about industry or public interest groups that monitor and publicize her performance. She will worry about maintaining personal credibility within her agency, with future clients or employers and with the larger public. She will know that the President can fire her, but only at political cost to the President. Thus, the difference between the President as overseer and the President as decider can shape many a key decision. Moreover, the choice between overseer and decider models will have other ramifications. Most obviously, the pool of people willing to be agency heads under the decider model may not include figures with the personal stature or political clout of those willing to take administrative jobs under the President as overseer. So, how did we get to our current situation, and what does it mean?

From Overseer to Decider: A Brief Institutional History

The federal executive branch has no inherent authority to issue general rules on the air we breathe, the water we drink, the food we eat, the drugs we take, the cars we drive, the conditions under which we work and play, our susceptibility to discrimination in schools, in public accommodations, and in the workplace, our entitlements to health care, disability insurance, and income security in our old age—or on any of the other aspects of our individual or collective welfare that are currently subject to administrative regulation. The reason the executive branch does regulate in these areas is that Congress, exercising the constitutional powers of the legislative branch, has decided to create administrative agencies and to empower those agencies to issue binding rules as Congress's instruments for accomplishing the legislature's constitutionally authorized objectives.

Both the scope of the modern regulatory state and the use of legally binding administrative rules to carry out Congress's purposes are relatively new. Prior to 1960, agencies typically implemented their statutory authority through systems of licensing and other administrative action that evolved legal standards case by case, or on what lawyers would call an "adjudicative" basis.[2] Things changed, however, with the advent of the civil rights revolution, the Great Society, and the environmental and consumer movements. Congress very substantially increased the number and jurisdiction of federal agencies and made clear their authority to issue broad, legally binding rules as a more efficient and effective means of achieving solutions to social problems.

There are really only two key differences between such administrative rules and the statutes that Congress enacts directly. One of those differences is simply that administrative rules are written outside the legislative branch and do not have to follow the constitutional requirements of legislative process This means, for example, that, in promulgating a rule, an agency does not need to assemble the kind of geographically broad political coalition in support of its policies that would be necessary to achieve a majority vote in Congress. The second key difference is that, while Congress's authority to make law is constrained only by the Constitution, an agency is constrained by both the Constitution and the congressional statute that empowers the agency. An agency empowered by Congress to regulate securities markets may not regulate air pollution. An agency authorized to regulate broadcast indecency may not issue rules for federal disability insurance.

Nonetheless, agencies empowered to make rules pursuant to their statutes typically have the authority to make very significant policy judgments in the process of making those rules. To simplify a real example, Congress has constitutional authority to empower some federal agency—most likely, it would choose the Environmental Protection Agency—to issue rules limiting the emission of sulfur dioxide by coal-burning power plants. In principle, such power plants could lower their emissions by moving to other fuels, switching from high-sulfur to low-sulfur coal, or building smokestacks and related technology to cleanse pollutants out of their fumes. Unless Congress has limited the agency's options—if all Congress has commanded is, "Reduce sulfur dioxide in the air!"—then the agency might choose to allow all of these approaches, some of them, or perhaps an entirely different alternative. It might choose to nudge power plants toward reform by taxing their pollution, or it might command them directly to take particular pollution-reducing steps. All of this is likely to matter a great deal in the short term, especially if you are a coal miner (or, even more, a coal miner in a state producing high-sulfur coal) or a manufacturer of "scrubbing" equipment. And the agency's choices could affect the cost of energy to both businesses and residences, inducing additional economic effects in both the short and longer terms. Agency rule making frequently entails policy choices of this kind, involving substantial, politically sensitive tradeoffs between competing values and interests.

This is the sort of discretion at stake in the choice between overseer President and decider President. An overseer President who dislikes specific command-and-control regulations would undoubtedly try to influence the EPA to adopt a regulatory strategy that leaves power plants with a lot of flexibility in achieving pollution reduction. The President would presumably appoint an EPA Administrator who shares the President's regulatory philosophy. White House staff would consult, perhaps both privately and publicly, with EPA staff in order to bring to bear their arguments in favor of a flexible regulatory approach. It might be made clear that the President would support the EPA Administrator's desire to have Congress expand the agency's regulatory authority if the President saw that the agency was exercising its authority in a flexible way. But, no matter how numerous these measures, the final regulatory decision would remain with the EPA Administrator. The President might ultimately fire an Administrator who disappoints the White House too often, but only if the President were willing to take the political heat that would undoubtedly follow from such a move. The decider model is more straightforward. In the presidentialist view, the President could simply tell the EPA what regulation to adopt. He could do so confidentially, shielded by executive privilege. He could perhaps even change the agency making the decision by ordering that

EPA follow the regulatory preference of the Department of Commerce. Politically, acknowledging presidential authority of this magnitude would mark a radical centralization of policy making power within the executive branch.

As the missions of the federal bureaucracy expanded, and especially as Congress began to mandate serious environmental regulation, with its exceptionally large potential economic impacts, Presidents became correspondingly more concerned about the policy output of the administrative agencies. Without abandoning the overseer President model, Presidents Nixon, Ford, and Carter all took the position that, as overseer, they could require most agencies to consider at least some prespecified set of factors in reaching their rule making decisions. For example, Carter issued an order providing that administrative officials with regulatory authority should issue a significant rule only after "the direct and indirect effects of the regulation have been adequately considered" and "public comments have been considered and an adequate response has been prepared."[3] Although the line might not always be clear, these factors were chiefly articulated in terms that were "administrative" rather than "political." That is, these presidents' approaches were defended in terms of general values that did not seem, on their face, to be strongly determinative of any particular rule making outcome. Instead, new analytic or deliberative processes were offered as efforts to insure that agencies took account of one another's missions in terms of issuing their own rules or that the economic impacts of regulation be fully considered. These are the kinds of general administrative accountability virtues that would be hard to attack on their face, irrespective of one's more specific regulatory philosophy.

President Richard Nixon responded to the newly emerging world of federal rule making by creating a process with the somewhat obfuscatory name of "Quality of Life Review." This move was the first to seek to introduce the Office of Management and Budget—previously involved mainly in executive branch fiscal management—into agency regulatory processes in a systematic way. OMB is one of the best known units with the Executive Office of the President, which is a kind of mini-bureaucracy atop the bureaucracy that Congress created in order to help the President to manage the executive branch. (It also includes the National Security Council Staff and the Council of Economic Advisors.) In essence, Quality of Life Review was an informal consultation process through which the Environmental Protection Agency was required to vet its proposed regulations with representative of other agencies, under the auspices of OMB. The presumed aim was to discourage interagency conflicts by deterring EPA from the promulgation of regulations that would interfere with the administrative objectives of other agencies.[4] Gerald Ford broadened this concern for external regulatory impacts, requiring all agencies to prepare Inflationary Impact Statements for all significant proposed regulations. This exercise was intended to deter agencies from imposing regulations that would lead to unintended and adverse economic effects.[5]

By the election of Jimmy Carter, "regulatory reform" had become a significant—and significantly bipartisan—political theme. In March 1978, Carter issued an executive order entitled "Improving Federal Regulations," which required every agency other than the "independent regulatory agencies" to develop a plan for conducting more systematic analyses of the costs and benefits of economically significant regulations.[6] Every time an agency proposed a significant rule, it would have to do such an analysis of all regulatory approaches under consideration and provide a public rationale for its ultimate choice. President Carter also gave the Executive Office of the President two major new roles with regard to regulatory oversight. First, he charged OMB—the largest domestic agency within the Executive Office of the President—with overseeing implementation of the new executive order. Additionally, he created a Regulatory Analysis Review Group, headed by the Chair of his Council of Economic Advisors, which would annually examine a limited number of especially significant agency rules and their supporting analyses.[7]

Structurally, the initiatives of these three Presidents—Nixon, Ford, and Carter—had two critical and interrelated points in common. First, their initiatives purported to leave the policy making discretion of the agencies as Congress provided. Even Carter's order—although directing that agencies consider "alternative approaches" and ensure that "the least burdensome of the acceptable alternatives has been chosen"—was hardly a constraint on agencies pursuing their individual statutory missions. Any proposal an agency head did not want to adopt could simply be discarded as not one of the "acceptable alternatives." Second, the formal commands to agency heads did not go further, in essence, than "consult," "analyze," and "consider." EPA had to listen to the views of other Nixon Administration agencies, but not necessarily to comply with them. Gerald Ford's agencies had to make an effort at determining inflationary impacts, but what to do about those impacts remained up to the agencies. Carter insisted on rules that were "adequately considered" and "written in plain English and . . . understandable to those who must comply" with them.[8] That sort of initiative did little to move final decision making authority from agencies to the White House.

Things changed dramatically with the Reagan Administration, although—in comparison with his successors—Reagan's moves now seem
modest. Reagan withdrew the Carter order on federal regulations and
replaced that order with a more stringent requirement that all executive
agencies perform cost-benefit analyses of all proposed regulations. He required each agency—to the extent permitted by congressional statute—to
adopt whatever regulatory approach toward accomplishing its objectives
maximized net social benefits and minimized net costs. For the first time,
Reagan required, as a matter of presidential command, that each agency
submit its analyses to OMB for review and not promulgate final rules until
OMB had "signed off" on the relevant agency regulatory analyses.[9] OMB
would perform this function through one of its subunits, the Office of Information and Regulatory Affairs, known through Washington by its ini-
tials, pronounced "Oh, Ira."

In issuing this order, Reagan revolutionized the rule making process by
routinizing White House oversight of proposed agency rules and specifying a general regulatory philosophy that agency heads would be required
to follow, to the extent permitted by law. The Justice Department signed off
on the proposed order, however, only on the understanding that the President was not disturbing the statutory authority of the individual agencies;
the regulatory philosophy he imposed would leave each agency's discretion
substantially intact. A Justice Department memorandum supporting the
legality of the proposal stated this view explicitly; President Reagan's order
would not "empower the [OMB] Director . . . to displace the relevant agencies in discharging their statutory functions or in assessing and weighing
the costs and benefits of proposed actions."[10] The OMB Director's "power of
consultation would not . . . include authority to reject an agency's ultimate
judgment, delegated to it by law, that potential benefits outweigh costs, that
priorities under the statute compel a particular course of action, or that
adequate information is available to justify regulation. . . ."[11] In short, while
President Nixon, Ford, and Carter took the position that Presidents may
require agencies to take certain factors into account, President Reagan took
the position that Presidents may actively manage agency rule making processes to make sure that the specified administrative factors are taken into
account rigorously. This was a significant move away from overseer to decider, if only because by mandating a cost-benefit framework, the President
effectively tilted the playing field in the direction of deregulation and placed
a central agency, OMB, in the position of policing agency implementation
of the President's regulatory philosophy.

It is tempting to be cynical about the analytical process and structure that Reagan decreed. Reagan ran on a platform promising business "regulatory relief." Lurking behind the highly rationalistic language of his executive order, which called for maximum "net benefits" and "least net cost," was a more generalized political hostility toward the regulatory state. In operation, however, the kind of data-driven, highly rationalized analytic process Reagan's order contemplates does function differently from direct political command. Indeed, it is evidence of this that the Reagan Administration's antiregulatory constituencies were critical of the Administration for using its political capital to improve the rule making process rather than trying to limit the bureaucracy's capacity to make rules at all.

For the function of *political* oversight, that is, making sure that agencies were maximally responsive to the President's political agenda, the Reagan Administration continued to rely chiefly on the agency heads. In his second Administration, Reagan issued an additional executive order that required agencies, subject to OMB supervision, to adopt a regulatory planning process. As part of that process, the head of each agency was required to submit to OMB an annual "overview of the agency's regulatory policies, goals, and objectives for the program year and . . . information concerning all significant regulatory actions of the agency, planned or underway, including actions taken to consider whether to initiate rulemaking; requests for public comment; and the development of documents that may influence, anticipate, or could lead to the commencement of rulemaking proceedings at a later date."[12] The Director of OMB, in turn, was authorized, "[i]n reviewing each agency's draft regulatory program" to "(i) consider the consistency of the draft regulatory program with the Administration's policies and priorities and the draft regulatory programs submitted by other agencies; and (ii) identify such further regulatory or deregulatory actions as may, in his view, be necessary in order to achieve such consistency."[13]

On its face, it may sound as if what the order intends is a significant movement of political authority from agencies to OMB, but its actual motivation was rather different. The primary function of requiring agencies to submit regulatory plans was to make sure that agency heads were notified early and comprehensively about regulatory proposals percolating up through the career civil service. The motivation for creating agency head accountability to the Director of OMB was really to give agency heads a powerful lever to demand accountability from lower levels of the bureaucracy.

The Administration of President George H. W. Bush changed the claims of executive authority in two ways. President Reagan's initial regulatory

executive order had created a "Presidential Task Force on Regulatory Relief" to oversee the OMB/OIRA review process.[14] In June 1990, President
Bush 41 assigned that body's tasks to the President's Council on Competitiveness, chaired by Vice President Quayle.[15] The Reagan process of analytical oversight, even bolstered by the regulatory planning process intended
to make the agencies more politically responsive, was still resulting in a
significant volume of regulation during the Bush 41 Administration. Hoping to bolster the Administration's credibility with the Republican right
wing and to establish a meaningful portfolio for Vice President Quayle, the
Council sought to impose its deregulatory philosophy much more directly
than the OIRA analytic model. The Council identified particular regulatory areas of interest—most notably, clean air and wetlands protection—on
which to focus its attention. Rather than operating through career desk
officers in OMB, the Council operated chiefly through the personal staff
of the Vice President. In contrast to the elaborately specified executive order directions for OMB review, the Council followed no published, regular
procedures. It gave Congress and the public no access to documentation
of its deliberative activities. It did not establish any controls on the degree
or nature of its substantive contacts with special interest representatives
outside the Administration. Its basic function was to pressure agencies to
follow the political preferences of the business constituencies supporting
the Administration.[16]

The first way in which this approach escalated the claims for executive
authority was by allowing the Council to involve itself not just in the name
of neutral-sounding administrative values, but also on the basis of straight-
out political preference. The Council's apparent mandate was to make regulatory policy friendlier to big business. Second, it was evidently the Council's view that it could do more than tell agency what factors to consider.
It could direct outcomes. As summarized by *Washington Post* reporters
Bob Woodward and David Broder, the Council diluted or killed "regulations . . . relating to commercial aircraft noise, bank liability on property
loans, housing accessibility for the disabled, clothing makers' right to work
at home, disclosure requirements on pensions, protection of underground
water from landfill runoff, reporting requirements for child-care facilities
located in religious institutions, and fees for real estate settlements."[17] The
same was true for EPA regulations aimed at limiting pollution from mu-
nicipal incinerators, protecting wetlands, and preventing air quality deg-
radation. Thus was the decider President model born, but with an obvious
hitch: the point of the Council's secret operations was to disguise White
House influence. As explained by Woodward and Broder, its intention was

to impose a business-oriented approach to regulation while "leaving . . . 'no fingerprints' on the results of its interventions."[18]

The performance of the Council on Competitiveness antagonized the Democratic leadership in Congress, not least because the Council sought to pervade the Administration's political preferences through what seemed to be a distortion of the highly analytic administrative oversight process inherited from the Reagan Administration. Critics argued that fidelity to the Administration's political agenda had come to take precedence over the agencies' legislative mandates and that the Council had become a potential vehicle for private special interests to hold sway over regulatory decision making without disclosing their involvement.

When President Clinton took office in 1993, he made it a priority to reform the OMB process and return it to a professional and analytic mode. He revised the Reagan executive order to take specific account of Congress's key objections.[19] To avoid allegations that the process was simply subterfuge for regulation bashing, he reworded the governing regulatory philosophy to be equally hospitable to arguments for and against new rules.[20] His order specifically states that nothing in it is to be "construed as displacing the agencies' authority or responsibilities, as authorized by law."[21] The order mandates a more transparent review process, including requirements for the disclosure of correspondence between OMB and the agencies and for the public logging of all external communications that pass through OMB regarding agency rule making. Responding to fears that OMB might use its consultation powers to delay rule making on political grounds, the Clinton order specifies deadlines within which OMB must respond to agency proposals and submissions.[22]

Yet, Clinton did not retreat from the Bush 41 position that the President could directly require agency heads to take regulatory action pursuant to their statutory mandates. He issued numerous mandates to agencies related to his administrative reform agenda. In the name of enhanced efficiency, for example, Clinton issued a September 1993 executive order requiring each agency to try eliminating, within three years, half of its internal regulations "not required by law" that pertain to that agency's organization, management, or personnel matters.[23] Many of Clinton's orders were more substantive, however, and included directives ordering the commencement of rule making proceedings. As recounted by Harvard Law School Dean Elena Kagan, who formerly served in both Clinton's Office of White House Counsel and on his Domestic Policy Staff, the orders covered a wide range of social initiatives, such as a directive to the Secretary of Labor to propose a rule authorizing states to permit paid leave to new parents through the unemployment insurance system; a directive to the Administrator of the EPA and the Secretaries of Agriculture and the Interior to propose enhanced rules on water pollution; and a directive to the Secretaries of Health and Human Services and the Treasury to adopt enhanced standards and enforcement policies regarding the safety of imported foods. Such directives were especially notable in the fields of health care and firearms control. They were accompanied by other strategies, including the staging of press conferences and other public events that effectively appropriated the regulatory actions of the agencies as the President's own, thus significantly constraining the agencies' options, at least politically.[24]

That Clinton embraced unitary executive behavior by exerting increased political control of the agencies—behavior that significantly accelerated from the last year of his first Administration forward—is clear. Clinton anticipated that the actions he sponsored would be politically popular and wanted to share in the public's good opinion of those initiatives. Moreover, such unilateral action gave him a vehicle for maintaining his political relevance after the 1994 midterm elections turned Congressional control over to the Republicans—leadership that Clinton sensed was embracing a series of domestic positions far less popular, in fact, than his own.

Although Clinton's independent initiatives were clearly a policy challenge to Congress, they did not pose what might be considered a constitutional challenge. That is because the Clinton legal team did not insist that his administrative vigor rested on inherent constitutional power. It argued that Clinton was going no further than Congress itself had implicitly permitted in terms of presidential direction of administration. Dean Kagan, whose detailed scholarly defense of Clinton's administrative vision presumably also represents the Clinton Administration's legal thinking, defended the Clinton record in terms of his statutory authority. Kagan wrote that she "accept[s] Congress's broad power to insulate administrative activity from the President, but argue[s] . . . that Congress has left more power in presidential hands than generally is recognized."[25] She urges that a "statutory delegation to an executive agency official . . . usually should be read as allowing the President to assert directive authority, as Clinton did, over the exercise of the delegated discretion."[26] That is, the Clinton Administration recognized and accepted that Congress had the power to delegate in both general and specific terms, but argued that, unless Congress conspicuously insulated an agency administrator from presidential direction, the President was acting within his own statutory powers in telling the agency administrator how to implement the agency's authority. Under such a rubric, the President became a decider, not an overseer, except as prohibited by Congress. The exception Kagan recognizes involves the so-called independent agencies, which are agencies within the executive branch whose administrators can be fired by the President only for good cause, and not at will. As to these agencies, the President would remain an overseer only.

From 1970 to 2001, the domain of domestic regulation thus experienced the same kind of conspicuous, but incremental, increase in the concentration of executive power that the United States has witnessed in foreign and military affairs since the end of World War II. We can trace a trend line from the start of compulsory interagency consultation and regulatory analysis under Nixon, Ford, and Carter, to the centralized management of regulatory analysis under Reagan, and then to the intensification of presidential political input into rule making under Bush 41 and Clinton. This trend line, like the foreign and military affairs trend line, marks a bipartisan phenomenon. But in this domain, once again, the Bush 43 Administration, which enabled the marriage of increasing executive power with the unrelenting policy ambitions of the Republican right wing, represented an acceleration of presidentialist practice that was breathtaking.

Unlike the Clinton Administration, the Bush 43 Administration embraced the constitutional theory of the unitary presidency that would grant the President inherent power to dictate to all executive branch officials how they should exercise their discretionary power. This theory acknowledges no authority in Congress to insulate any discretionary administrative policy making from direct presidential command. As noted in chapter 5, George W. Bush, during his first six years in office, inserted 363 objections into signing statements indicating that provisions he was signing into law were potentially in violation of this unitary executive power.[27]

Perhaps even more important, Bush demonstrated early his intent to exercise control over administrative decisions of key importance to his right-wing base. He issued a series of executive orders creating so-called Centers for Faith-Based and Community Service within executive departments, charged with coordinating "agency efforts to eliminate regulatory, contracting, and other programmatic obstacles to the participation of faith-based and other community organizations in the provision of social and community services."[28] Another order directed the Attorney General; the Secretaries of Agriculture, Education, Health and Human Services, Housing and Urban Development, and Labor; and the Administrator of the Agency for International Development to amend existing policies of their respective agencies to conform to the Administration's stance on nondiscrimination against faith-based organizations in the competition for federal financial assistance to social service programs.[29] Perhaps most famously, President

Bush decided in August 2001 that federal funding should be available for embryonic stem cell research, but only using embryonic stem cell lines that were already in existence at this time.[30] Of course, there is no statute vesting this decision in the President. Decisions regarding federal funding for research under the auspices of the National Institutes of Health are made by the Director of NIH, under supervision of the Secretary for Health and Human Services.[31] Yet, under the constitutional views of the Bush Administration, Congress could not deprive the President of ultimate control of this policy choice, so long as any discretion over the matter is left to executive branch resolution at all.

President Bush also implemented his view of the unitary presidency through aggressive deployment of the OMB/OIRA regulatory oversight process first launched by the Reagan Administration. From 2001 to 2006, OIRA was led by Dr. John Graham, a distinguished conservative regulatory economist. Critics who believed that the Reagan and Bush 41 Administrations had used OIRA to stifle health and safety regulations levied the same criticisms against Graham. Insofar as OIRA impeded regulation, however, it did so not through political directive, but through what critics charged were politically motivated additional layers of administrative scrutiny, often derided as "paralysis through analysis." Thus, although Bush retained the Clinton executive order intact, OIRA promulgated a series of guidelines and "circulars" regarding information quality, scientific peer review, and risk assessment that made agency analysis significantly more complex, even though it was hardly clear that the additional complexity improved the quality of regulatory output. A 2004 circular on how agencies should develop their regulatory analyses for proposed rules takes fifty single-spaced pages to lay out its requirements.[32]

The major surprise, for a conservative Republican Administration, is that OIRA, acting on behalf of the President, occasionally used his executive order process to prod agencies into either issuing new regulations or tightening existing rules. It developed a mechanism called a "prompt letter" to communicate its recommendations for proactive regulatory initiative. One such letter effectively urged the Food and Drug Administration to require food labeling to indicate trans fat content. Other letters involved OIRA in developing rules regarding automated external defibrillators, fuel efficiency standards for automobiles, and pollution from diesel engines in off-road vehicles.[33] Although these letters did not purport to command agencies how to exercise their discretion, the intensification of OIRA's proactive regulatory role represented another step forward in the exercise of White House authority over administrative agencies.

The White House also exercised its unitary executive theory surreptitiously. Reports that emerged between 2005 and 2007 showed dozens of scientists in a variety of federal agencies had been pressured to eliminate or soften references to "climate change" and "global warming" from a range of documents, including press releases and communications with Congress.[34] One White House official, a former oil industry lobbyist with no scientific background, acknowledged personally making 181 changes in three government reports on climate in order "to align these communications with the Administration's stated policy."[35]

With John Graham's 2006 departure from government, critics feared that, as under the Bush 41 Administration, Graham's successor would abandon Graham's public stance of analytic neutrality and begin using the executive order process to intensify White House political pressure on the agencies under the guise of regulatory analysis. Two developments intensified those fears in early 2007. One was the issuance of a Bush executive order amending the OIRA process that seemed to portend a further politicization of regulatory oversight.[36] The second was the use of a recess appointment to install Graham's successor, Susan E. Dudley, whom the Administration apparently thought too controversial to go through a promised Senate confirmation hearing.[37]

In "unitary executive" terms, the most seemingly significant of the Bush amendments to the Clinton executive order was a requirement that each agency "designate one of the Agency's Presidential appointees" to serve as the agency's "regulatory policy officer," namely, the point person within the agency who would promote agency compliance with the executive order regulatory review process.[38] Indeed, under the Bush amendments, no proposed rule making could be included in an agency's regulatory plan unless approved by the regulatory policy officer or "specifically authorized" by the head of the agency. By requiring the approval of a presidential appointee, whether the agency head or a lower-level administrator, it appeared to be the President's intention to assure that someone with close and direct political ties to the White House always have authority to cut off a regulatory initiative. Under the Clinton order, each covered agency had been directed to choose such a regulatory policy officer who would report to the head of the agency, and this individual was not assigned any gatekeeper role in the initiation of regulatory activity and did not have to be a presidential appointee. The point of the changes thus appeared to be the President's insistence that, in principle, decision makers regarding regulatory activity should have direct political accountability to the White House, not just to Cabinet secretaries or other agency administrators.

In principle, this steady accretion of Presidential authority over domestic regulatory activity threatened a radical transformation of our constitutional lawmaking process. Given the amount of policy making discretion that Congress vests in administrative agencies, the annual volume of legally binding rules that emanate from the federal bureaucracy currently exceeds the output of the legislative branch in terms of rules that legally bind the public. The President's insistence that he has unitary control over all such discretionary decision making by administrative agencies suggests a transformation of the President not only from overseer to decider, but from chief executive to chief lawmaker. Becoming the sole decider with regard to the vast output of legally binding administrative regulations would potentially give the President a single-handed role dwarfing the role of Congress in prescribing rules that Americans are compelled to obey. Such rules, whether focused on environmental protection or worker safety, involve policy judgments and economic trade-offs no less profound than those entailed in most congressional statutes. Centralizing presidential control over this lawmaking activity is arguably presidentialism in its most audacious but, for most Americans, its least visible manifestation.

How the Unitary Executive Impedes Administrative Accountability

The institutional history just summarized substantiates a critical warning I voiced in chapter 2: the theoretical argument that the Constitution does not compel the presidentialist vision is not enough to defeat the growth of presidentialism in practice. Through statutory enactments and case-by-case judgments, Congress and the judiciary, respectively, can show so much deference to the executive branch that the President will enjoy as much scope for the exercise of unilateral power as if the Constitution did enshrine the unitary executive. In this sense, it hardly matters whether anyone believes the Bush 43 statements that claim inherent Article II power to direct the policy making discretion of his subordinates. For most government agencies, the system of regulatory oversight that has evolved over the last quarter century gives the President very nearly the leeway that unitary executive theory would demand.

There are at least three reasons why so radical a transformation of our system for public policy making has proceeded virtually unimpeded under both Republican and Democratic Presidents, dealing with both Republican and Democratic Congresses. The first is that proponents of the unitary executive in this form have been successful in making the argument that the system somehow enhances accountability. It would be hard to contend that coordination in government is always a bad thing, so executive claims that increased presidential involvement in regulatory policy making makes the system more accountable has superficial plausibility. The second is that Americans are ideologically inclined to believe that government agencies are likely to impose more regulations than can be justified in cost-benefit terms, and the current system of White House regulatory oversight advertises itself as a way of reducing regulatory costs and increasing regulatory benefits. The third is that, for both Democrats and Republicans, winning the presidency becomes a yet more valuable prize if a President, once elected, can unilaterally determine an ever-larger set of public policy outcomes. At any given moment, a number of key Senators and would-be Senators from both parties clearly imagine themselves to be potential Presidents. Hence, a potentially vocal set of possible opponents to presidentialism are more muted in their criticisms than their position as congressional leaders would suggest that they should be.

The accountability argument is truly empty. The alternatives are not a unitary executive and anarchy. The alternatives are presidentialist government and pluralist government, and in either case there are identifiable actors who can be held politically accountable. Under one model, our elected President is "the decider," getting to dictate to all executive branch policy makers how their discretion shall be exercised. Under the pluralist model, the elected President still exerts powerful influence over each agency, but final decision making authority on matters that the Constitution allows Congress to regulate would rest in those agencies to which our elected Congress delegates decision making authority.[39] Congress is no less responsible or responsive to the electorate than presidents; agency administrators, although concededly not elected, are highly attuned to the political agendas of the elected President who appoints them and the elected legislators who vote their appropriations. Agencies are also subject to review by courts, which are well positioned to insure agency fidelity to the legal mandates enacted by our elected legislators.

When our administrative system is viewed as it really is, it is clear that Congress has designed the pluralist system well in order to promote accountability. Vanderbilt law dean Edward Rubin has sensibly said, "Accountability can be roughly defined as the ability of one actor to demand an explanation or justification of another actor for its actions and to reward or punish that second actor on the basis of its performance or its explanation."[40] Key elements of accountability in the pluralist system include the requirements that administrators appear annually before Congress in order to justify their budget requests and respond to periodic demands from congressional oversight committees to explain and justify their decision making in public testimony. Before agencies can promulgate regulations, they generally have to publish their proposals and solicit public input.[41] Final rules must be accompanied by a public statement of basis and purpose that lays out the agency's legal authority and the policy rationale upon which it acted. Agency rules may be challenged in court on a variety of bases, including whether or not the agency has followed the statute it was required to implement and reacted in a nonarbitrary way to significant issues that public comment brought to the agency's attention. Significant information about the agency's rule making rationale and underlying support is available to the public through the Freedom of Information Act, which facilitates scrutiny of agency decisions by the press, regulated parties, issue-oriented advocacy groups, and members of the general public.

Indeed, the openness of agency decision making to public scrutiny—the relative transparency in terms of process—is itself a guarantee of public accountability. This transparency is endangered by more intense presidential involvement in regulatory oversight because increased presidential involvement elevates the likelihood that Presidents will assert executive privilege regarding White House communications within the executive branch that actually determine policy outcomes. Under current law, executive branch lawyers may claim privilege in court for any so-called predecisional documents that reveal the preliminary deliberations of the executive branch on any official matter, but many such documents are also quite freely shared.[42] Even though FOIA might allow them to do so, agencies do not always withhold from either Congress or the general public the documents that reveal their preliminary thinking about regulatory policy. Should Presidents become more directly involved in regulatory decision making, documents related to those deliberations would more likely be covered by the constitutionally based "presidential communication" privilege, which extends not only to predecisional documents exempted from mandatory disclosure under FOIA, but to all confidential presidential communications and many documents prepared by senior staff in fulfilling their role of advising the President. To the extent the President and his senior staff become more directly involved in regulatory policy making, executive privilege of this sort is more likely to be invoked and such claims may prove hard to overcome.[43] To the extent secrecy actually impedes accountability, increased presidential involvement is potentially a step backward, not forward.

The presidentialist claim that presidential oversight increases accountability with respect to regulatory policy rests largely on the argument that White House–directed policy making is more likely than decentralized policy making to enhance executive branch fidelity to the current policy preferences of the electorate at large. The claim is that Presidents will be more forthcoming than agency heads with public explanations or justifications for their actions, and thus the public would be better empowered to punish presidents whose explanations fail to respond to the weight of public opinion. These claims rest on faulty assumptions. The unitary executive offers no promise that presidents will explain their actions more fully or publicly than do subordinate administrators, and there is no reason to believe that the President, at any given moment, will embody more effectively than do his agency appointees as a group a set of policy predilections, across a wide set of issues, that is held by a contemporaneous majority—or, more accurately, by contemporaneous majorities—of Americans. For example, the Reagan and both Bush Administrations used centralized regulatory oversight to weaken environmental regulation, even though consistent and overwhelming majorities of Americans subscribed to the view that the quantity of U.S. environmental regulation was appropriate or too low.

The most obvious reason why the President is unlikely to be more responsive to public sentiment than is the bureaucracy as a whole is that the President is a single person.[44] Fans of the unitary Presidency are fond of pointing to the Framers' explicit decision not to vest executive power in a multimember body, such as some sort of executive council. As much as anything, however, that decision reflects an implicit rejection of political representativeness as an intended feature of the chief executive. Had representativeness been the goal, surely a multiple-headed presidency would have been preferable, given the vast array of important policy questions about which different coalitions of Americans are likely to hold different views.[45] A collective body would have a far greater capacity, through its own internal shifting coalitions, to mirror the diversity of public opinion across a wide array of policy debates.

The incentives of our one-person chief executive to follow the polls in any close way are also not as strong as is often assumed. After all, despite common references to a presidential candidate's unique "national constituency," a presidential candidate is subject to election only twice—and only once after the country has actually witnessed the President's performance. With the possible exception of the 2004 election, which seemed to be dominated by issues of national security, two considerations seem to outweigh all others in recent choices of Presidents—public satisfaction (or the lack of it) with economic performance under the most recent incumbent and a general sense of an incumbent President's personal performance. During both an initial campaign and another for reelection, a presidential candidate knows that his detailed stances on matters of policy are not likely to make decisive differences in his political fortunes. And, of course, following a successful reelection campaign, there is no further prospect of confronting the electorate to discipline a President's policy judgments. If bureaucratic accountability to elected politicians is to be used as a structural mechanism aimed at achieving direct responsiveness to public opinion, it would probably make more sense to intensify the influence that Congress—especially the House—has over the agencies. Members of Congress are eligible for reelection indefinitely; a common observation of the House is that its members are in a constant election campaign. One would thus expect the policy output of Congress to track public opinion more conscientiously than would the President's day-to-day agenda, as it long did, for example, with regard to the war in Iraq during the Bush Administration.

Another version of the accountability argument emphasizes responsiveness not to the public at large, but rather to those persons most likely to be affected by particular regulations. Such eminent political scientists as Robert Dahl have described American democracy as a pluralist system in which different elites are influential with regard to different issues, depending on their focus.[46] Responsiveness to those most affected by bureaucratic decision making might even seem to be a preferable accountability goal, especially if we are confident that all those who stand to gain or lose substantially through a particular decision are represented with equal effectiveness in policy making processes.

Of course, we know that is not the case. Industry is far more effectively represented in administrative policy making than the general public. Although the full range of interests affected by truly significant regulatory decisions are likely to be numerous and diverse, the parties with adequate resources and organization to make themselves effectively heard within the administrative process are far more likely to be the antiregulatory voices of big business than even well-known public interest groups such as the Sierra Club or the Natural Resources Defense Council.[47] Given this reality, any tight concentration of power in the White House over bureaucratic decision making would seem to impede, rather than advance, the cause of accountability.[48] If not represented by industry lobbyists, the parties likely to be affected by regulation (or the lack of it) need realistic opportunities to secure the effective representation of their views and meaningful mechanisms for a policy dialogue that seriously takes account of all that is at stake in an administrative decision. Neither of these accountability preconditions is well served by rigid hierarchical decision making. It is precisely the large size and relative openness of Congress that makes it realistic to hope that all interests relevant to a policy decision will find some effective legislative representation and voice. The same is true of our sprawling bureaucracy. If ultimate policy making power were lodged in a single individual, such an arrangement would necessarily increase the chances that one interest or set of interests will have disproportionate access and influence.

Looking at the problem of agency accountability from the perspective of affected parties, it is perhaps most troubling that the presidentialist model would so easily permit a President to disturb the equilibrium that such interests have reached in striking a bargain over authorizing legislation. It is only when Congress, the President, and public interest groups enjoy rough parity in their capacity to shape agency behavior that the political environment is likely to replicate the conditions that produced whatever legislation the agency is implementing. Vesting policy authority in an administrator who enjoys independent discretion, but who also faces politically pluralist decision making conditions, is most likely to produce policy outcomes consistent with the array of political forces embodied in a statute.[49] By contrast, neither Congress nor those members of the public most affected by regulatory decisions can seriously hope to discipline the abandonment by a unilateralist President of an earlier compromise once a piece of authorizing legislation is enacted. To see this, imagine that Congress decides to authorize a series of federal grants to public school districts that are "culturally disadvantaged." Assume that the bill's sponsors were unable to muster a majority to make grants available solely to districts that were "economically disadvantaged." To pick up votes they needed from members of the House representing relatively affluent districts, the sponsors agreed to the broader standard of "culturally disadvantaged," which might include a district that is well off financially but geographically remote from any symphony orchestra. The President signs the law. But imagine, then, that the President orders the Secretary of Education to adopt a definition of "culturally disadvantaged" that limits the category of eligible districts to districts that are "culturally disadvantaged for reasons of poverty." Such a regulatory policy would upend the bargain made in the House of Representatives, but would presumably not animate a two-thirds legislative congressional majority to pass a new statute—over the President's certain veto—that would overturn his regulation. Moreover, his abandonment of particular interests in a specific episode is not likely to be so important to his reelection prospects—if he has any—to deter a President determined to go his own way.

There is, of course, yet another political tradition within which to construct an ideal of accountability. People sometimes speak of a dispassionately determined "public interest" that may or may not coincide with polling results of the current moment. To the extent any such public interest is ascertainable—a public interest that is also genuinely democratic in that it fairly mediates the interests of all affected citizens with equal regard—then perhaps we should most value accountability to just that ideal. Such, of course, was James Madison's goal. Recall that he argued for a constitutional design intended above all to constrain the influence of "faction," defined as "a number of citizens, whether amounting to a majority or minority of the whole, who are united or actuated by some common impulse of passion, or of interest, adverse to the rights of other citizens, or to the permanent and aggregate interests of the community."[50] Defenders of presidentialism, both liberal and conservative, often cite Madison's anxiety about factions as a basis for preferring unitary presidential control. But the chief constitutional instrument for elevating the public interest over faction is our checks and balances government design, with its emphasis on vigorous and open dialogue and reasoned deliberation. Administrative decision making in the public interest requires an extension to the executive branch of a policy dialogue that is robust, thorough, and reasoned. And, as Professor William Luneberg has argued, the President's capacity to tell subordinate administrators what to do is far more likely to inhibit, rather than advance, robust intrabranch policy debate.[51] To achieve public interest–centered dialogue within the executive, it is important not to tighten the reins on subordinates excessively, but to provide incentives for administrators to speak freely and for the President actually to listen to diverse voices despite the predictable dominance of his own.

Besides the virtues of dialogue, those who believe in the ascertainability of a "public interest" beyond opinion polls—and, at least on some issues, I surely count myself among them—are likely also to trumpet the virtues of expertise as a central feature of administrative decision making. Expertise provides a foundational rationale for the entire phenomenon of specialized agencies under different administrators. Each agency, because of its discrete jurisdiction and sustained immersion in particular categories of problems, is expected to develop a base of knowledge and methodological sophistication intended to protect against decision making based solely on passion or "interest." The ideal of expertise argues strongly for diffusing policy making authority to specialized agencies with the capacity and incentive to master their own policy domains. Relatively autonomous expert agencies are likely to pursue policy making that, while deeply political, also has a serious, well-trained, technically sophisticated, and disciplined eye on a reality apart from politics. If we want administrative decision making that is attentive to "the permanent and aggregate interests of the community," thoughtfully determined, then decision making structures should maximize opportunities for transcending partisanship and ideology. Tightly hierarchical structures do not.

The final point often urged to link presidentialism to accountability is that the unitary executive centers responsibility in a single, responsible official. The argument is that presidentialism solves the supposed problem that, in a politically pluralist system, those authorized to hold decision makers to account are nonetheless often unable to identify the relevant decision makers. The foundation of this claim is that the bureaucracy is diffuse, opaque, and impersonal, while the president is distinct, public, and identifiable—he is thus more likely to be held accountable. The Framers expressly noted this problem in deciding to vest executive power in a single, rather than in a plural, President. In the words of Alexander Hamilton: "[O]ne of the weightiest objections to a plurality in the executive . . . is that it tends to conceal faults and destroy responsibility. . . . [T]he multiplication of the executive adds to the difficulty of detection. . . ."[52] The unitary executive is supposed to make a special contribution to accountability by increasing transparency.

Despite the surface appeal of this argument, it is in one sense operationally unlikely and, in another, operationally insignificant. It is operationally unlikely because, to a great extent, even the vesting of ultimate decisional authority in the President will not eliminate the ubiquitous possibilities that a complex bureaucracy affords the President to disavow responsibility for unpopular choices and to claim the chief credit for successes. Recall, for example, that a major goal animating the Bush 41 Council on Competitiveness was to give the President the prerogative—at least in friendly audiences—to embrace the Council wholeheartedly for advancing his values, while keeping intact—presumably in other audiences—the plausibility of denying direct responsibility for any particular thing the Council had done.

The argument is also insignificant because, even without plenary power to second-guess all bureaucratic policy makers, the President may well be held generally and properly accountable for overall bureaucratic performance in any event. That is because voters know the President has appointed all key policy makers and the most important managers of executive affairs; their appointments of outstanding and awful FEMA Administrators, respectively, is why President Clinton's approval numbers went up after the bombing of the Oklahoma City federal building, but President Bush's went down after Hurricane Katrina. The President's value structure is likely to dominate the bureaucracy even if he is not formally able to command all important policy decisions. Because agencies know that the President's support may be critical on everything from annual budget requests to negotiations with Congress over enhanced administrative authorities, it is presumably the rare agency head who, having been appointed by the President, will then be oblivious to the President's governing philosophy.[53]

There is, in addition, another reason for thinking that any link between presidential policy control and decisional transparency is a red herring. As noted earlier, the alternative to presidentialism is political pluralism, not genuine agency independence. Presidents always have influence, but, in a pluralist world, they have to compete on a more level playing field with Congress in keeping the heat on agency administrators. Conversely, if the President were to enjoy more and more complete control over the content of domestic policy, then the weaker the identifiable link would become between legislator effectiveness and government performance. There seems to be a kind of "conservation of accountability" law at work here, under which decisional transparency on one end of Pennsylvania Avenue becomes plausible deniability on the other. The more public leverage over the President becomes an effective lever over bureaucratic output, the less effective congressional elections would seem to be in achieving policy accountability. Unitary executive theory threatens to weaken substantially the democratic efficacy of congressional elections.

We have identified at least three political measures against which to hold government decision making accountable: the majority views among voters, the dominant sentiments among affected parties, and an objectively determined public interest. Our governmental system contains a variety of instruments that could plausibly be used to secure some correspondence between bureaucratic decision making and any of these measures. These include presidential elections, congressional elections, presidential oversight, congressional hearings, appointments and removals, confirmation proceedings, administrative procedures, judicial review, and grassroots public pressure.

But what accountability requires, under all the theories mentioned, is a set of political conditions that is fairly complex. Perhaps the most important is widespread access to information about the nature of the decisions at issue. A second is policy dialogue, and a third, a multiplicity of opportunities for dialogue to be well informed and salient to actual decision making. A fourth is flexibility in the value structure of bureaucratic decision making. The more procrustean the decision making environment, the less accountable it is to anyone but to the ultimate decision maker.

This strongly suggests that the Clinton executive order process—without further presidential control of subordinate administrators' discretion—

represents the high-water mark of what ought to be tolerable in terms of centralization. The order envisions considerable openness in the regulatory process and relatively broad public access to relevant intrabranch and outside communications. It tolerates diffuse policy making influence, limiting OIRA's capacity to strong-arm agencies through both the formal description of its powers and through its susceptibility to deadlines. By contrast, both Bush Administrations have provided cautionary lessons in what the unitary executive could look like in domestic regulatory affairs.

Under Bush 41, we saw dysfunctional presidentialism in the form of the Council on Competitiveness. The Council was not effective in increasing the correspondence between agency outcomes and popular opinion. Its insistence on environmental deregulation consistently defied majority popular sentiment. Nor does the Council seem to have improved the government's responsiveness to the full range of interests affected by regulation. Pious denials notwithstanding, the alignment of the Council's agenda with that of organized business strongly suggests that some interests were treated as invariably weightier than others. This last fact also strongly undermines any suggestion that the Council made a positive contribution to aligning policy outcomes more consistently with a dispassionately determined public interest. The Council seemed not to suppress special interest factionalism, but to cater to it, submerging, rather than elevating, policy dialogue. Its policy directives sometimes tended to ignore contrary expert judgment in favor of an overwhelming ideological commitment to deregulation for its own sake. Such a result is unsurprising given that the Council's chair, Vice President Quayle, described himself as a "zealot" for deregulation. Zealotry and the public interest would seem unlikely companions.[54]

Under Bush 43, perhaps the most damning evidence for presidentialism involved White House control of regulatory activity related to global warming. The pressure on agency experts to downplay the threat of global warming and White House intervention in the editing of documents to portray the scientific consensus as weaker than it is can be understood only as accountability to the oil industry. This influence was largely surreptitious, undermining the argument for transparency. It did not result in policy making faithful to the public or to the public interest, dispassionately determined. And, following the 2004 election, the President no longer faced the discipline of electoral pressure to punish him for the Administration's performance. What we have seen of the unitary executive in practice fully supports the theoretical case in favor of policy making pluralism. Tightening White House control over regulatory policy making does not enhance accountability in any meaningful sense; it reduces it.

The Hidden Costs of the Unitary Executive

The nuts-and-bolts presidentialist argument urged most often for central-ized oversight of bureaucratic administration is that regulatory agencies, left to their own devices, will supposedly overregulate as a matter of rou-tine; should this be so, the public ought to benefit when some central au-thority holds agencies accountable, permitting them to intervene in private behavior only when necessary to accomplish a public purpose and only at the lowest net cost consistent with Congress's statutory commands. Given that this is the rationale for the aggrandizement of presidential control over administration, it ought to give all Americans pause that, after twenty-five years in operation, no one can actually demonstrate that the system has paid off. That is, no one can show that we have achieved greater net social benefits than the United States likely would have enjoyed under a more pluralistic, less centralized regulatory system. On the contrary, given what we know about the OMB review process in operation and OMB's own esti-mates of the costs and benefits of regulation, involving the White House in regulatory review would have to reduce the annual net costs of regulations that agencies propose by somewhere between 7 and 37 percent on average in order to justify White House involvement in economic terms. That is, unless White House involvement in regulatory oversight is reducing net costs somewhere in that range, the combination of direct costs imposed by the review process—the salaries for increased staff, for example—and the indirect costs of delaying implementation of socially beneficial regula-tions would exceed the amount saved by piling White House cost-benefit review on top of the cost-benefit review that agencies already conduct. This is demanding a fairly impressive rate of return for the process, even assum-ing that the costs of delay are low and the overall price tag of the rules is high.[55]

Upon reflection, the difficulty of demonstrating that OIRA reduces regu-latory costs enough to justify the costs associated with a centralized system of regulatory review should not be surprising. The argument that agencies will regulate excessively or inefficiently left to their own devices—that is, in a more pluralistic policy making environment—rests on a series of dubious and unproven assumptions. It has variously been theorized that agencies left on their own will overregulate in order to expand their resources and aggrandize their authority. They will respond too precipitously to perceived health and safety risks. They will fall sway to ideologically driven bureau-crats. Or they may be "captured" by proregulatory forces. But there is no proof that any of these things is systematically the case.[56]

The theory that agencies will overregulate in order to build their own empires is typically associated with the work of William Niskanen.[57] By disguising the real costs of regulation, administrators can supposedly deceive Congress into providing their agencies with inefficiently extravagant budgets. Other political scientists have called this argument into serious question, however.[58] As an empirical matter, rather than engaging in deception of their elected overseers, agency administrators appear to be highly responsive to political pressures applied to them by the President and Congress. Moreover, even if we deem agency administrators to be rational maximizers of their individual self-interest, it is not clear what personal benefits they would derive from expanding their agency budgets—and thus why they would be motivated by this factor alone. Expanding agency resources will not typically line administrator pockets. There is no reason to think the tenuous personal rewards linked with agency budget expansion are more motivating than the satisfactions (and professional esteem) that might be associated with actually accomplishing the agency's assigned mission in an effective manner.

Finally, even if agencies did overregulate in order to elicit stronger budgetary support, it would be reasonable to expect such agencies to promulgate a large number of relatively lenient rules rather than rules that impose excessive costs or unrealistic goals. Agencies will most likely succeed in enhancing their resources if they can show both an active agenda and success in implementing and enforcing their regulatory programs. Unduly stringent rules will undermine compliance and make enforcement—and enforcement success—much harder to demonstrate. The now-classic illustration of this phenomenon is the shift in the National Highway Traffic Safety Administration from promulgating significant safety regulations to managing vehicle recalls. Congress funded NHTSA generously for this latter purpose, which imposed few costs on industry and had no shown connection to actual safety improvement. It was nonetheless a highly visible mission that provoked little resistance and created the appearance of genuine concern for the public interest.[59]

A more plausible case for agency overregulation is that administrators may turn out to be more cautious in the face of uncertain risks to health and safety than later science may prove to have been warranted. It is not at all clear, however, that caution in the face of uncertainty is irrational. For example, the benefit-cost ratio for the regulation of particulate matter in the air turns out to be hugely favorable. Yet, it is not clear that a positive cost-benefit analysis would have been possible when EPA's rules were put into effect because the full range of harms due to particulate matter was not appreciated until years later.[60] Likewise, EPA's regulation of leaded gasoline has turned out to be enormously beneficial in terms of curbing a variety of adverse health effects, perhaps most notably the reduced learning capacity associated with elevated lead levels in the blood of children. Early in the Reagan Administration, cost-benefit analysis proved critical in persuading EPA not to loosen the regulation of leaded gasoline by delaying the phase-down requirements for small refineries. However, that cost-benefit analysis depended on data yielded from the regulatory experience of the 1970s. When the phase-down rules were first issued, it is unlikely that cost-benefit analysis, based on then-available data, would have supported the regulatory effort.[61] In short, it may well be that an agency's precautionary stance—although responding less to contemporary expert opinion than to public fear—may turn out to be well founded. Although mistakes will be made, it is not clear that an overemphasis on known costs over speculative benefits will produce a socially more optimal level of regulation.

For this very reason, there is another explanation why agencies regulate stringently in the face of uncertainty. Congress repeatedly commands it. Congress tells EPA to regulate with a "margin of safety." It tells OSHA to control work exposure to toxic substances "to the maximum extent feasible." It generally applies a zero tolerance approach to food and drug additives shown to be carcinogenic in humans or animals. These may or may not be socially optimal policies, but they are the law. White House pressure to reduce agencies' precautionary commitments runs counter to the mandate enacted by our democratically elected legislative branch.

The precautionary stance of health and safety agencies may be justified for yet a further reason. Many health and safety risks are likely to be latent and widely diffused, while the costs of regulating may be readily apparent and concentrated (at least in the first instance) on well-organized business interests. This gives antiregulatory forces a huge advantage in organizing politically to oppose regulation. Agency precaution in the domain of health and safety can serve as a valuable counterweight to this distortion of the policy making process.

The idea that agencies regulate out of ideological zeal is a common accusation, but dubious. Career administrators may well be committed personally to the causes on behalf of which their agencies work, but their personal rewards are likely to turn very substantially on the quality of their work and their conformity to the ethical norms that prevail in the professional bureaucracy. Urging zealous regulation based on flawed analysis would likely incur political opposition and make life significantly more unpleasant for one's political superiors. The fact that agency bureaucrats identify with their agencies' missions does not by itself suggest a serious threat of overregulation.[62]

It is sometimes cited as proof of the overregulation argument that the political appointees who head government agencies often appear, over time, to become more sympathetic to the policy views of the career bureaucracy. In other words, under the sway of the career bureaucrats who are ideologically committed to their respective agencies' missions, political appointees are supposedly diverted from the President's agenda to that of the bureaucrats. The likeliest reason, however, why a political overseer is apt to change his or her views over time is that increased exposure to the workings of a particular agency—the nature of the challenges it faces both in terms of the problems it is supposed to address and the difficulties of addressing those challenges consistent with limited agency resources—leads to a fine-tuning of the political official's initial policy proclivities. There is very little evidence that administrators become less sympathetic over time to the President's policy values or less interested in bringing those values to bear on his or her agency's performance. Their view simply becomes better informed about the agency's mission and resources.[63]

The final argument why agencies allegedly would overregulate, if not subject to some form of central discipline, is that they are susceptible to "capture" by organized groups who exert undue influence over an agency by virtue of their superior information sources and effective organizing. The problem with this theory, however, is that the groups best positioned to capture agencies by virtue of their resources, focus, and effective organization are not proregulatory public interest groups, but the much better-funded and more narrowly focused business groups that oppose regulation.[64] Not surprisingly, industry groups are commonly the most visible and vigorous players in terms of commenting on proposed rules and challenging in court any final rules they oppose.[65] Given the actual distribution of advocacy resources among groups organized for the purpose of helping to shape public policy, a distribution that heavily favors industry, centralized review aimed at reducing economic costs—the proffered objective of the Reagan-Bush system—seems only to aggravate an existing imbalance. It would probably promote more balanced decision making if centralized review were committed to amplifying the voice of public interest groups and avoiding the likelihood of unjustified industry objections to health and safety rules.

Indeed, the "capture" justification for White House regulatory review is ironic for another reason. If the capture scenario is plausible, then industry capture of OIRA seems at least as likely as industry capture of an individual agency. Collective action is easier for concentrated groups—like industry trade associations—that have deep pockets and relatively few members with lots at stake and whose shared points of view do not have to be reconciled and accommodated and harder for more diffuse groups, like those concerned with the environment, which have smaller lobbying budgets and large numbers of members with a wider variety of opinions and individually smaller stakes. If industry groups invest their resources in capturing individual agencies, then they would surely be willing to bid for OIRA's favor, as well. And, because OIRA is arguably an even bigger prize—its domain extends over a wide range of government regulatory activity—its price would presumably be higher, meaning that the less-well-financed public interest groups representing fairly diverse membership will be at an even greater disadvantage in trying to dominate OIRA's policy output. Moreover, because agencies operate more transparently than OIRA—under federal law, they can typically take no major regulatory action without ample opportunities for public comment and review—OIRA is likely to be more vulnerable than the agencies to the distorting effects of behind-the-scenes pressures.

Of course, no matter what the regulatory environment, presidentialist or pluralist, agencies will sometimes make regulatory decisions that cannot be well justified under a retrospective analysis of costs and benefits. Although very little effort is devoted to revisiting agency cost-benefit analyses to determine their accuracy, the evidence we have suggests that mistakes routinely occur. What is not so clear is that mistakes invariably go in the same direction. Agencies not only underestimate costs, they overestimate them. They not only overestimate benefits, they underestimate them. The cost to society of delaying the issuance of socially beneficial rules will quite plausibly exceed any reduction in implementation costs achieved by subjecting those rules to lengthy review by OMB. From a societal point of view, the delays currently imposed by White House regulatory review on the issuance of regulations can be justified only if agencies left on their own would generally propose regulations that, despite the incentives not to do so, cost substantially more than is actually necessary to achieve their benefits. There is no evidence that more autonomous agencies would make mistakes of the necessary magnitude to justify OIRA review.

An even more immediate point for our purposes—even if some centralized review of regulatory activity turns out to be a good idea—is that the policy case for some form of OMB review is all but unrelated to the presidentialist case for a unitary presidency. Because he does sit atop the entire regulatory bureaucracy, the President might well be positioned to play a role that the original Reagan order on federal rule making promised, but which OIRA has never truly played—namely, a coordinating role. It might be beneficial for a centralized body to look at the entire range of federal regulations relevant to some particular set of social goals in order to determine how they fit together as a whole, whether their distributional impacts are fair, and whether portions need updating (or, indeed, repeal).[66] This is a role no one single-mission agency can play, and it is what President Carter apparently intended by creating the Regulatory Analysis Review Group under his Council of Economic Advisors.

The potential for such a salutary centralized function, however, does not establish the case for a unitary presidency. The hallmarks of the unitary presidency in operation—the preference for executive discretion over legislative direction, the elevation of presidential policy preference over individual agency decision making, and the correspondingly increased concern for confidentiality surrounding policy communications that may involve the President or his close aides—are all unnecessary for the functioning of an effective system of coordination and in tension with the goal of genuine administrative accountability. Meanwhile, the substantial regulatory delays entailed in White House review impose billions of dollars of "social cost"—a euphemism for the illness, injuries, and even deaths that could have been forestalled had agencies been permitted to proceed with greater independence. The elevation of the President from "overseer" to "decider" simply cannot be shown to serve the public interest overall. Presidentialism promises to offer not only bad theory, but bad government.

A perfect example appears in a March 2008 EPA decision to change the regulatory standard for ozone in the ambient air to 0.075 parts per million (ppm) from the current level of 0.084 ppm. In July, EPA had suggested a range of 0.070–0.075 ppm in its original proposal to tighten up the ozone rule. EPA bowed to White House pressure in adopting the least stringent requirement in this range. According to EPA analysis, changing the primary standard to 0.075 ppm would prevent at least 260 premature deaths, 890 heart attacks, and 200,000 missed school days every year starting in 2020. However, had EPA adopted a standard of 0.070 ppm, the analysis shows the more stringent standard could have prevented an additional 300 premature deaths, 610 heart attacks, and 440,000 missed school days each year.[67] These all may be seen as the costs of White House review.

March 2008 also marked the release of a report of the Government Accountability Office revealing how White House–coordinated intervention involving OMB reviewers, EPA political appointees, and even other agencies eroded the independence of EPA scientists charged charged with determining the health dangers associated with toxic chemicals widely found in polluted areas, including soil, lakes, streams, and groundwater.[68] Cancer risk assessments for nearly a dozen major chemicals were found to be years overdue because of additional forms of bureaucratic clearance imposed on the agency by the White House. Not surprisingly, more than half of nearly 1,600 EPA staff scientists who responded online to a detailed questionnaire by the Union of Concerned Scientists said they had experienced incidents of political interference in their work.[69] Meanwhile, some of the chemicals on which the government has delayed action for years, such as trichloroethylene, a widely used industrial degreasing effort, have already—in reports by the National Academy of Sciences, the National Academy of Engineering, the Institute of Medicine, and the National Research Council—been linked to cancer and other health hazards.

The injuries we suffer in domestic policy making because of presidential regulatory involvement that is excessively unilateral are no doubt less dramatic than the harms inflicted in foreign and military policy. When an overreaching President abuses his freedom of action to launch unjustified military attacks with insufficient planning for their aftermath, we see the carnage. Lists of the American dead are available. By way of contrast, we never know who precisely is sicker than they otherwise would have been or who had an accident that could have been avoided had federal regulation not been unduly impeded by the überbureaucracy of presidential oversight. That does not mean, however, that the costs are less real or the risks to American democracy less serious. If an OMB-centered system of regulatory review is warranted, it should focus on genuine coordination, not just cost reduction, and it should operate not as a conduit for White House political control, but with as much transparency and access for public input as possible.

7

Recovering the Madisonian Dream: Visions of Democracy, Steps to Reform

Healthy checks and balances in a separation of powers system like ours depend on informal practices of cooperation and mutual respect among the branches of our federal government. At least since 1981, many of these key informal practices, which have long helped to sustain effective governance in the United States, have withered. They have fallen prey to partisanship, most conspicuously—though not exclusively—the drive for complete policy control by the hard-right wing of the Republican Party, whenever its members have had effective authority over any of the three branches of government.

The most dangerous of the threats to checks and balances have appeared when the aggressive, norm-breaching tendencies of the Republican Right have joined with a trend toward increased executive power that has been notable since the New Deal, irrespective of the President's party. Under George W. Bush, the merger of partisanship and executive ambition finally crystallized into a theory and practice of a unilateral presidency that truly threatened—and, if it persists under his successors, will continue to threaten—American democracy. His was a presidency in which the chief executive was assertedly entitled to direct personally all of the government's policy making discretion exercised outside Congress and the courts and in which the President claimed expansive independent powers over foreign and military affairs that are largely immune from judicial review or legislative oversight. The results were hugely dysfunctional government—predictably bad decision making in the domains of military planning, foreign policy, and national security; contempt for the rule of law among government lawyers; presidential efforts to generate a phony appearance of legitimacy for executive resistance to accountability; and presidential usurpation of administrative agency decision making that is costly both economically and in terms of the health and safety of the American people. In short, since 1981, American democracy has been hit by something of a "perfect storm." The question is what to do about it.

The answer, not surprisingly, has multiple parts. To understand the answer most fully requires us to create a modern version of the Madisonian frame of mind. Madison dreamed of a constitutional system in which mechanisms of checks and balances would prevent any faction—whether a majority or a minority of "We, the People"—from running roughshod over the interests of their fellow citizens. But the viability of checks and balances would depend on more than the design of government on parchment. It would depend also on the ways in which government officials, once in place, would be motivated to act. Virtue alone could not be the source of their motivation. The social and political background conditions against which the President and members of Congress were chosen would also be critical.

For Madison, the most decisive social and political condition relevant to the constitutional system was geography. He blamed the "turbulence and contention" afflicting direct democracies, in part, on the relatively small number of citizens who could effectively be governed within such a system. In Madison's view, "the greater number of citizens and extent of territory which may be brought within the compass of republican than of democratic government . . . is [the] circumstance principally which renders factious combinations less to be dreaded in" large republics than in small democracies.[1] According to Madison:

The smaller the society, the fewer probably will be the distinct parties and interests composing it; the fewer the distinct parties and interests, the more frequently will a majority be found of the same party; and the smaller the number of individuals composing a majority, and the smaller the compass within which they are placed, the more easily will they concert and execute their plans of oppression. Extend the sphere, and you take in a greater variety of parties and interests; you make it less probable that a majority of the whole will have a common motive to invade the rights of other citizens; or if such a common motive exists, it will be more difficult for all who feel it to discover their own strength, and to act in unison with each other.[2]

The remedy in designing the legislative branch was straightforward: drawing congressional districts large enough so that each member of Congress would be answerable to a diversity of local interests would mean that no representative could ever be captured by a single group. As a political imperative, the necessity of building coalitions would thus make every representative a kind of honest broker for the public interest. (In a similar vein, the design of the electoral college and the requirement that electors in each state vote for at least one out-of-state candidate would propel to the forefront only presidential candidates of sufficient eminence and good character as to win the approbation of a broad national coalition.[3]) Madison's focus on coalition building and the need for accountability to diverse points of view held out hope that norms of mutual accommodation and a balancing of competing interests would ensue in both the selection of our national leaders and the actual workings of day-to-day government.

In the twenty-first century, geography is insufficient to sustain the Madisonian promise. The hardening of our national two-party system, changes in electoral rules that favor incumbents and reduce electoral competition, and the force of mass media in helping to manufacture public opinion have all been powerful forces in favor of factionalism. No one deliberates over good character in the electoral college. Incumbent representatives in gerrymandered districts enjoy reelection rates that Soviet parliamentarians would have envied. Corporate-dominated media narrow the range of significant opinion presented on some critical issues and all but ignore others altogether. I argued in chapter 1 that the post-1980 Republican embrace of "presidentialism" seems at least as much a matter of opportunism as conviction. What created that opportunity was not just the failure of those formal institutions that the Constitution specifies, but also changes in the larger social and political context that altered the incentives and motivations operating for the men and women Americans elected to federal office.

The changes we now need must thus be of two sorts. First, there is a roster of changes that could be made within government right now to help reinvigorate political pluralism and mitigate the trend toward presidentialism. Tools of this sort are available to each of the three branches of government. The aims uniting these tools are the strengthening of interbranch accountability—most especially, the accountability of the President to Congress and to the courts—and the revitalization of pluralism in government policy making.

But, if these aims are to endure, we must also change the larger social and political context that creates incentives and motivations for our leaders. We need a government in which partisan competition is tempered by a sense of shared national fate. Building on Madison's insight that checks and balances need to be sustained by a politics of coalition building that resists factionalism, we need to rebuild a governmental system in which political leaders can thrive only by assembling coalitions among Americans with differing interests and perspectives. Toward that end, political checks and balances need to be the dominant fact of every public official's political life. It is not as if such a diversity of interests and perspectives is absent within our states and congressional districts. But, through a variety of rules and institutional practices, many voices within our national democratic conversation have been artificially suppressed. What we need is more democracy to level the playing fields of electoral competition and democratic deliberation.

It may at first seem paradoxical that the cure for excessive partisanship is more democracy. But such a proposal appears paradoxical only if we mistakenly treat partisan elections as the essence of democracy, rather than as an instrument for democracy's foundational aim—legitimating government decision making through processes that respect the value of both political freedom and political equality. Once we sort out more clearly what we mean by democratic legitimacy in this sense and the role of the presidency in achieving that legitimacy, the nature of the reforms we need—some internal to government, others directed to our larger political culture—becomes clear.

Democratic Legitimacy and the Role of the President

Most Americans regard democracy as the foundational principle of government legitimacy. By "legitimacy," I mean the moral entitlement of any government to rule. It is the quality of government that makes it acceptable for a relatively few members of a society to make decisions that bind the rest of us.[4] For most people, democracy presumably makes government legitimate because, as compared to other systems, it promises to do better at accomplishing two tasks. One is assuring that, when public policy decisions are made, the interests of everyone potentially affected by government action are given serious consideration. All citizens are treated equally in the sense that the interests of all are equally worthy of being taken into account and government deliberations aimed at determining the public interest do not simply disregard the interests of anyone. The second is providing individual citizens the most meaningful individual experience of political self-determination. Our system is successfully democratic to the degree it supports the experience of individual citizens as autonomous actors who are free to participate meaningfully in public acts contributing to our collective political life.[5] Voting, of course, is a key way in which we exercise our political autonomy. But it is not at all the only way. We also petition, deliberate, write letters to the editor, picket, organize, and in countless other ways engage with the processes by which the political direction of society is determined.

Under the theory of presidentialism, it is the election of Presidents that most critically establishes both sides of democratic legitimacy. Americans exercise their political freedom by choosing the President, and the President assures equal respect for competing interests by bringing to bear on government decision making his unique embodiment of a national perspective that excludes no one. According to presidentialists, only the President can be trusted to temper the impulses of faction because, unlike other government actors, he is electorally accountable to a diverse national constituency, no part of which he can safely ignore. The President's singular authority and visibility make him uniquely accountable, both in principle and in fact, to the national majority that elected him. Armed with the ambitious scope of executive power that presidentialists impute to him, the President is able to resist vigorously the ambitions of Congress to usurp executive power and to overstep the faction-ridden legislative role.[6]

There are, however, at least two problems with this account of democracy and the President's role in it. First, in defending aggressive executive power, presidentialists seem to use the President's electoral accountability to a national constituency both to establish his unique concern for the interests and perspectives of all Americans and, paradoxically, his democratic entitlement to ignore the political views of nonsupporters. The latter stance was expressed in its purest possible form in a much-celebrated interview on March 20, 2007, between television satirist Jon Stewart and John Bolton, the former United Nations ambassador who had secured his position in 2005 through a recess appointment calculated to avoid a Senate confirmation vote. Stewart asked Bolton why President George W. Bush did not include in his Cabinet a wider array of political philosophies and perspectives on governance. Bolton said:

The President ought to have people philosophically attuned to his way of thinking, and if you've got a problem with that, I would suggest you have a problem with democratic theory. . . . The whole point of electing a President to preside over the Executive branch is to give the people a choice over the direction the entire executive branch is running in. . . . That's what a President is for under the Constitution. . . . The President has a responsibility to be true to the people who voted for him . . . Otherwise, what's the point of having elections?[7]

Far from the President being equally accountable to all Americans, Ambassador Bolton suggested a special presidential accountability limited to his supporters. Yet, it is difficult to see how a President whose core political responsibility is "to be true to the people who voted for him" is going to be a trustworthy fiduciary for the interests of the American people as a whole.

But a deeper problem with presidential theory is the implausibility of its account of the President's unique national accountability. Chapter 6 already took note of the obvious problem that a two-term President is subject to re-election only once. This plainly attenuates any pressure on the President to respond to a broad-based national coalition during the second term. More-over, as George W. Bush proved in 2000 and John Kerry almost showed in 2004, the electoral college enables candidates to become President in any event who do not actually represent a numerical majority of the country. They may represent a factional minority perspective that is nonetheless geographically so distributed as to produce an electoral college victory. In addition, there is simply no reason to believe that Presidents will be equally concerned with the interests even of all those subcommunities within his winning coalition. Major financial contributors, whose interests are quite unlikely to mirror those of the country as a whole, will surely enjoy dis-proportionate access to the President, whose policies may well be skewed accordingly.

The pluralist account of democratic legitimacy—which is incidentally truer to the founders' vision—is more nuanced and more credible. Its fundamental insight is that governmental legitimacy—the commitment of government to promote individual autonomy and the equal consider-ation of all citizens' interests—demands a complex network of competing, but interdependent sources of authority. For the Framers, it was only their new amalgam of different political institutions, constructed as competing branches of government, that could hope to fulfill their republican or, in our word, "democratic," aspirations. These institutions were intentionally designed to be different in a variety of ways—in their precise constituen-cies, in their decision making processes, in the scope of their authorities, in their capacities for action, and in their modes of organization and selection. But the three branches of the national government were also designed to have three things in common, which are essential to the accomplishment of democratic legitimacy. First, each branch is constituted by a process gov-erned either by "the people" themselves or by those chosen by the voters to assemble the institution in question. Second, each is bound to the people as a trustee for the public interest. Third, each participates in a process of mutual support and constraint that is essential to what Hamilton called "government from reflection and choice."[8] Legitimacy in a government so designed would thus depend equally on the proper operation of each of these branches; the executive branch was not simply to be treated as a first among equals.

The Philadelphia delegates recognized that they wanted a government characterized by an extraordinary and dynamic pursuit of balance. The famous historian Gordon Wood has called it a "kinetic theory of politics."[9] On one hand, a new national legislature was to embody, through the House of Representatives, "an immediate dependence on, and an intimate sympathy, with the people."[10] At the same time, the legislature was to temper the passions and the inexperience to which popular assemblies might fall prey with a more stable perspective based on experience and expertise. Such was the job of the Senate. In order that national needs might be addressed effectively, Congress was to enjoy broad discretion in the making of law, and the executive was to have the energy necessary for sound administration—the "true test of a good government," according to Alexander Hamilton.[11] Both of our elected branches, Congress and the President, would be accountable in turn to an unelected judiciary, protected as to both tenure and salary and authorized "to guard the Constitution and the right of individuals."[12] The Framers, recognizing the bewildering diversity of interests among the people, eschewed any reliance on the fiction that public sentiment embodied in a single plebiscite could capture the public interest. They instead configured the government's principal institutions to reflect different constituencies, whose representatives would be engaged in a complex ongoing dialogue to determine where the public interest lay. All of our national institutions were calculated to insure that local, state, and national perspectives would be distinctly articulated and given due weight in the calculation of the public interest.

Under the founders' vision—the pluralist vision—democratic legitimacy depends not only on the popular choice of our elected leaders, but on the continuing dedication of our public officials in all branches to give due consideration to all relevant interests in calculating what the public interest ultimately requires. This dedication is to be realized through complex processes of bargaining and deliberation. The minority of voters who lose in an election contest thus do not lose their expectation that their interests—their lives and well-being—will continue to be respected even by those officials they did not support in the election. Toward this end, no feature of government is more essential to democratic legitimacy than the ongoing pervasiveness within government of free and open dialogue. Checks and balances were intended to protect the republic by restraining the capacity of any one branch to rule tyrannically by "checking" unwise initiatives. But they were also supposed to advance the public interest by assuring government through dialogue and reason, "balancing" interests against one another in an ongoing pursuit of consensus.

In government's ongoing deliberative process, it is a fair enough statement that the President, because of his unique visibility and national political base, will contribute a perspective that is different from and more nationally oriented than that of any individual legislator. It is because of his unique perspective that the Framers gave the President veto power. But the idea that the President's perspective, from a Madisonian point of view, will always be less faction-driven and thus superior to the legislative perspective, suffers from a critical error. That is, the congressional perspective with which the President competes is not the parochial perspective of any individual legislator, but the collective judgment of the legislative branch as a whole. Not only is Congress's collective view going to reflect its own national coalition, but the legislators who form that coalition are more democratically accountable than is the President. Members of the House face reelection every two years, not every four, and, because every member of Congress is entitled to seek reelection indefinitely, legislators do not routinely have the insulation from accountability that the President enjoys in his or her second term.

Presidentialists make their strongest case against Congress with regard to the appropriations process. It is well known that members of Congress chase dollars shamelessly for their districts, and not so rarely on behalf of dubious projects. Legislators have been accused of becoming "ever more creative in funneling federal resources back to their constituencies while imposing the cost in federal taxes, borrowing, or regulation on someone else's constituency or on the nation as a whole."[13] If presidentialists had a strong empirical case that Presidents uniquely embody the national interest, we should be able to observe their salutary influence on this fractious, bargaining-intensive process. When Senator X supports Senator Y's National Toothpick Museum because Senator Y is helping Senator X get funding for her state's Salt Water Taffy Research Institute, Presidents could easily stand up to such nonsense. They could veto appropriations bills that contained wasteful spending. Even after an overall appropriations bill is enacted, the President has statutory authority to ask Congress formally to go back and "rescind" those items of spending that cannot be justified on sound policy grounds.

Presidents almost never do this. And the reasons are straightforward. Every appropriations law contains at least some spending authority that the President wants. A thoroughgoing presidential attack on pork spending for particular districts will put his own projects at risk, antagonizing the representatives of particular districts or states and, by extension, their constituents. These are legislators whose support the President needs to enact his own agenda. On the other hand, the amounts saved are not likely to be large enough to win the President a lot of political points for fiscal discipline. As a result, we simply do not see in the appropriations process Presidents resolutely imposing the uniquely national, faction-resistant perspective that presidentialists advertise. And, with regard to other forms of congressional policy making—laws that do not entail direct expenditures and for which "logrolling" is thus harder to achieve—there is simply no reason to believe that the political values and philosophy guiding individual legislators are less oriented toward the public interest than are the President's values and philosophy.

Madison's great insight about faction is the realization that, at any given moment, our dispassionately determined "public interest" may or may not coincide with the desires of voters as those desires get expressed on a single election day. The people's representatives determine the public interest through an extended democratic conversation during which multiple interests and perspectives are brought to bear and momentary passions are perhaps cooled with time for reflection. Animating the pluralist view of checks and balances—a more genuinely Madisonian vision of democracy—is thus the realization that our best instrument for elevating public interest over faction is open, vigorous government dialogue that effectively airs contending positions and multiple points of view and tests competing perspectives against the best available knowledge. From a pluralist, Madisonian point of view, this dialogue should be a pervasive feature both within the executive and in interbranch relations.

Unfortunately, the more centralized a President's control over subordinate officers, the more inhibited intrabranch policy debate is likely to be. Likewise, the greater the President's capacity for unilateral action, the more impoverished will be his policy dialogue with Congress. Even our unelected judges have a critical democracy-reinforcing role to play in insuring conscientious executive branch attentiveness to the public interest as embodied in both the Constitution and the democratic enactments of the legislature. Seen from this perspective, robust checks and balances are key to implementing a genuinely Madisonian view of democracy. By fostering dialogue among government institutions, checks and balances create the maximum space for meaningful democratic expression by individual citizens and the greatest likelihood that all relevant interests will be genuinely considered in making policy trade-offs. None of this will work perfectly—it will just work better than the ethos of presidentialism.

It is easy enough to anticipate one presidentialist response to this vision: Won't all this government dialogue induce paralysis? If the presidency is everywhere checked and balanced, how will urgent business get done? Part of what makes government legitimate in the eyes of the public is effectiveness. The cost of dialogue and consensus building may just be too high in terms of the transaction costs of governing. The trains have got to run.

There are two answers to this. The first is that the urgency argument is easily overstated. It is often uttered most compellingly in foreign and military affairs. Yet, on large questions of policy—such as whether to invade Iraq—there is most often ample time for dialogue and well-considered judgment to emerge. The supposed "urgency" of many presidential decisions is frequently of the President's own making and largely concocted to limit debate. On other questions, such as global warming or the high cost of health care—where the government has seemed to act with agonizing slowness in the face of public need—it is not actual policy dialogue that has slowed things down, but the largely behind-the-scenes influence of special interests. But even this cloud has its silver lining. By the time government does move meaningfully on issues such as global warming and health care reform, the public impetus for change will have become so great that the government can move ahead with far greater confidence of widespread support.

The second answer, however, is perhaps even more important. The pluralist vision of democracy may deny the President the constitutional scope for unilateral action that modern presidentialists advocate. But it leaves open the possibility that both court and Congress, in the exercise of their own authorities, may become persuaded to give the President significant leeway for action. The facts that Congress is allowed to delegate authority narrowly and the courts may review the President with some intensity do not constrain them to do so on every issue. In many contexts, the American public might well benefit from the organizational unitariness of the presidency, the hierarchical structure of the executive branch, and the President's usual capacity to engage more successfully than could a plural body in delicate international relations. There will be occasions when courts should defer to the President in areas of legal uncertainty and on which Congress should authorize presidential initiatives on terms that give the President significant policy latitude. Thus, even if the pluralist vision of the Constitution is the right one, the President is likely to find himself frequently vested with sufficient power to act independently in many key areas. The difference is that, when he acts independently, he will also have to act with the awareness that he may be appropriately called to account to the other branches of government for how he decides to exercise whatever discretion they confer. And the other branches' deference to the President should not be automatic, but should follow from vigorous debate on the wisdom, in specific contexts, of allowing the President to act energetically.

Legal awareness that executive authority is significantly at the sufferance of Congress and the courts should lead a President to act with greater prudence and integrity. Presidents should be reluctant to take actions that they are unwilling to justify explicitly and publicly if they know that Congress is legally regarded as within its rights in calling upon the executive to defend those actions. Unilateralism legitimates secrecy, and secrecy promotes effective decision making in the public interest only in exceptional circumstances. An Administration's conspicuous availability to have its performance subjected to public scrutiny will improve both the quality of that performance and public confidence in the executive branch.

Combining a pluralist understanding of the president's limited inherent powers with a readiness to accept fairly regular congressional acquiescence in presidential discretion is actually the arrangement that promises our greatest hope for policy making in the interest of the public at large and above the factional appeals of "special interests." An ethos of government that embraces both Congress's legal entitlement to regulate the President in significant ways and the President's capacity, if given broad discretion, to advance the public interest effectively in some critical domains, creates a political context within which the branches have the greatest likelihood of achieving a balance between constraint and discretion that actually makes sense.

In contrast to the presidentialists, constitutional pluralists concededly offer a messier vision of democracy. It is a vision of democracy in which government rule is legitimated by the vigor of policy discussion, within both the government and the citizenry at large, and by the accountability of President, Congress, and the courts to one another. The President does not stand in this account as a unique seer of the national interest, but as a critical motivator of the dialogue that should characterize a healthy democracy. He has unique resources to insure that policy makers attend to the interests of all Americans and that proposals on the national agenda take the fullest account of best available knowledge. Contrary to John Bolton, he promotes democracy not just by being "true to the people who voted for him," but by faithfully executing the law and promoting a synthesis of policy judgment that represents the best direction for all the American people.

Madisonian Democracy for the Twenty-First Century

To restore Madisonian checks and balances, we have to be prepared to think like James Madison. We have to design formal rules and processes that, if implemented, can strengthen pluralist dialogue and interbranch accountability within government. To animate and sustain those reforms, we need to restructure the larger political and institutional setting in which government acts; if pluralism and dialogue are to be the hallmarks of policy making by those in power, then our systems of political communication and electoral competition must be organized in a way that makes it necessary for those in power to respond to plural voices.

Fortunately, there is no shortage of measures available to each branch of government to halt, if not reverse the trend, toward unchecked presidentialism. Perhaps fittingly, the process could start with a new President determined to use the unilateral powers of the office to reverse course on unilateralism.

One starting point is the nominations process for both administrative policy makers, including Cabinet secretaries, and for judges. Presidents need to have people working in the executive branch who share the President's general political outlook, but within broad parameters, partisanship should be scaled back and independent stature valued more. People should be appointed to high office because their records of public achievement have already earned them high marks for integrity, initiative, and accomplishment in the areas of administration they are currently being asked to serve. A new Labor Secretary should have done work that advances the welfare of workers. A new Secretary of the Interior should have a record of conservation leadership. And so on. To get such people to accept public office, the President may well have to promise nominees a significant range of decision making autonomy once appointed. That is precisely the point. The President should be surrounded by administrators of sufficient stature to be more than mere acolytes in the development of public policy.

With regard to the judiciary, different approaches are called for at both the lower court and Supreme Court levels. To downplay partisanship and emphasize performance, the President should revive the Carter Administration's system of regional commissions to screen nominees for the U.S. Court of Appeals. Such commissions could work in concert with the Senators of affected states, thus maintaining a significant senatorial role in the selection process. On the other hand, giving distinguished panels the authority to evaluate the character, legal ability, and professional achievement of judicial candidates should broaden the range of acceptable choices and assure the public that judges are not being chosen predominantly on the basis of ideological litmus tests.

The Supreme Court, however, is different. Although procrustean tests of judicial philosophy may be inappropriate, the fact is that Supreme Court Justices do make law, and their philosophical predispositions matter to the resolution of legal questions. Judicial candidates sometimes protest that politics will not shape their decisions; they will merely remain faithful to neutrally chosen methods of constitutional interpretation that will produce the results in individual cases. But this is naive. The very choice of interpretive methods may well be shaped by the political outcomes judges expect their methods to yield.[14]

Given the impact of the Supreme Court on American law, it is critical that our highest bench itself be a site of democratic pluralism. The coexistence on the Court of the liberal Warren and the conservative Harlan or the liberals Brennan and Marshall and the conservatives Burger and Rehnquist produced a creative and healthy jurisprudential dialogue. It is hardly a secret, however, that, as of 2009, Justices Warren, Brennan, and Marshall have no true contemporary heirs. With Chief Justice Roberts and Justices Scalia, Thomas, and Alito all embodying a hard-right conservative view of American constitutionalism, there is no one on the Court urging a progressive view of equivalent scope, depth, and coherence. In choosing a lawyer of superb character and marked achievement to sit on the Court, a new President should also give priority to restoring that progressive voice. Every Administration should make sure that the Court has available to it Justices from a variety of outlooks, philosophical commitments, and background experiences.

A new President can also, on independent initiative, engage in more concerted interbranch coalition building in order to move a legislative agenda forward. The Clinton Administration's Health Care Task Force, which assembled in secret and without congressional participation, to forge a legislative proposal on universal health care was truly a crystalline example of how not to proceed. Although the President is not a Prime Minister, and the line between lawmaking and legal implementation is a hallmark of the separation of powers, there is no reason why Presidents could not act more consultatively with congressional leadership in order to hammer out legislative proposals that attract broad-based support and for which all can take credit.

A third set of reforms would reexamine the process of regulatory oversight in the Office of Management and Budget. Instead of superimposing yet additional layers of cost-benefit analysis on agencies already engaged

188 · Chapter Seven

in that analytic exercise, it would be useful to shift the OMB role from cost reduction to interagency coordination. As argued in chapter 6, it could be helpful for OMB (or some other agency within the Executive Office of the President) to identify high-priority regulatory subjects and reexamine the entire range of regulations within each domain to determine how they fit together as a whole, whether their distributional impacts are fair, and whether portions need updating or replacement.[15] President Carter's model of a Regulatory Analysis Review Group may be more appropriate than the current model of review by the Office of Information and Regulatory Affairs.

Yet a fourth and truly critical set of reforms would seek to promote pluralist dialogue and executive branch accountability by returning to an ethos of open government. Almost every step in this domain will entail the rather straightforward reversal of an information policy adopted unilaterally by the George W. Bush Administration. For example, Congress enacted an Open Government Act of 2007,[16] intended to enhance enforcement of the Freedom of Information Act, or FOIA. To increase public access to government records, the Act created an office of FOIA Ombudsman in the National Archives and Records Administration, an agency widely respected for its professionalism and political neutrality. President Bush relocated the office to the Justice Department, the agency charged with defending government decisions to withhold records from disclosure. The office should be moved back to NARA.

In a similar vein, the Bush Justice Department promised federal agencies that the Department would defend decisions not to disclose records upon public request whenever such decisions to keep records secret could be sustained by formal reliance on a statutory exemption from the rule of mandatory disclosure under FOIA. This reversed a policy of the Clinton Justice Department to defend agency failures to disclose only if they were defensible both on a legal basis and on a policy basis, that is, only if the agency had not only technical legal authority for withholding a document, but also a plausible explanation why making the document public would harm the public interest. A new Administration should go back to the Clinton policy.

A new Administration should revoke Bush's Executive Order No. 12,233, which complicated the release of records from prior presidential Administrations. The order should be rewritten to simplify the release of historical records under the Presidential Records Act. A new order should eliminate the prerogative for anyone other than a president or former president to claim executive privilege and should renounce the notion of vice presidential privilege.

A comprehensive analysis should be undertaken of all government information withdrawn from the World Wide Web in the wake of September 11, and any information whose public disclosure does not pose a genuine risk to national security should be restored to easy public access. In a similar vein, the executive order on the classification of national security documents should be redrafted to restore the Clinton Administration's insistence that equal priority be attached to the declassification of documents whose confidentiality is unnecessary to American security. Vice presidential records should again be subject to mandatory declassification review by the National Archives and Records Administration.

The new Administration should catalogue and reexamine all agency practices of withholding unclassified information based upon categories of "sensitivity" not authorized by law. Such systems should be eliminated, unless they are fully in compliance with the Freedom of Information Act.

A new President can likewise make and keep a series of critical pledges to put a halt to creeping presidentialism. The constitutional theory of the "unitary executive" should be categorically renounced. The President should repudiate the use of "signing statements" to reinterpret congressionally enacted statutes, except in those rare cases where statutory provisions may violate clearly established principles of constitutional law. The President should pledge good faith negotiation with Congress regarding requests for executive branch information, to insure that Congress is able to conduct its legislative and oversight responsibilities effectively. The President should order the Justice Department to limit the invocation of the state secrets privilege to defeat judicial review only when actually necessary to protect the foreign policy or national security interests of the United States in specific cases. The President should support the independence and authority of agency inspectors general and order agencies to cooperate fully with the investigative authority of the Government Accountability Office. Finally, the President should broaden consultation with Congress in the making of national policy within areas of shared constitutional responsibility and candidly seek congressional authorization for any increased discretionary authority the executive branch may need to respond to national needs more effectively.

Congress, of course, will also be a critical actor in the restoration of checks and balances—whether in deploying its own independent powers, drafting legislation, or reestablishing informal norms of communication with the executive branch. For example, Congress, like the President, needs to rethink its role in the appointments process. The Senate should take seriously its role not merely to consent, but to advise—and should give weight not only to the character and records of achievement of presidential nominees, but also to their commitment to implementing the law within their jurisdiction and their determination to operate in an open and accountable manner. With regard to judicial nominations, the members of the Senate Judiciary Committee should commit themselves to a merit-centered focus on lower court appointees and should support presidential nominations that emanate from a process of independent review.

With regard to Supreme Court nominees, the Senate Judiciary Committee needs to rethink its hearing process from the bottom up. Members should appropriately concern themselves with both the merit of individual appointees and the representativeness of the Court as a whole. Unfortunately, the quality of committee questioning in recent hearings has been lackluster at best, with members either trying fruitlessly to "nail" a nominee on a controversial question of constitutional interpretation or to exact pledges of fidelity to law that are either so general as to be meaningless or simply oblivious to how the Justices' judicial philosophies actually animate their work. In this context, the Committee could usefully provide an extended period for questioning of the candidates led by staff attorneys, some of whom might even be litigators hired for the specific hearing. People who practice or teach constitutional law for a living would simply be better equipped to ask questions that would be more revealing and harder to evade and to follow up meaningfully when answers appear incomplete or ambiguous. The Committee should also remain committed to seeking external input through the American Bar Association Standing Committee on the Federal Judiciary, which has long provided a useful independent assessment of judicial nominees' qualifications.

In the wake of controversial dismissals of U.S. attorneys in politically questionable circumstances, Congress should rethink whether U.S. attorneys should be dischargeable by presidents at will. The public interest in nonpartisan law enforcement might be served better by U.S. attorneys appointed for four-year terms and removable only for good cause, such as malfeasance or an inability to discharge the responsibilities of office. Keeping terms relatively short would assure Presidents of a law enforcement apparatus philosophically compatible with the Justice Department's political leadership, but limiting the removal power to instances of "good cause" would protect the independence of prosecutorial decision making in sensitive cases.

Congress should also think systematically about its oversight powers. Although hearings to ferret out specific wrongdoing may occasionally be called for, priority should ordinarily be determined according to the potential of various inquiries to shed light on the need for new legislation. At this point, the need is urgent for a set of retrospective hearings on the separation of powers practices of the Bush Administration. The point should not be to assign blame for particular mistakes, but to clarify the nature of the controversies that persist between the branches and to determine specific areas where legislative reforms need to occur. Congress should consider, for example, whether a statute expressly limiting the legal effect of presidential signing statements is appropriate. A statutory process for the orderly resolution of interbranch executive privilege disputes might be in order. The State Secrets Protection Act proposed in 2008[17] to provide an orderly process for assessing in civil litigation whether invocations of the state secrets privilege are justified should be enacted. Congress should reconsider whether the trend toward deepening the levels of political agency management should be reconsidered and the role of and protections for the career civil service instead be intensified.

In the area of military policy making, the War Powers Resolution, in its current form, has simply proven inadequate to discipline executive branch unilateralism. A "Use of Force Act," proposed in 1995 by then–Senator Joseph Biden of Delaware, remains the most promising reform proposal so far advanced.[18] The Biden proposal would replace the War Powers Resolution with a more detailed and potentially more restrictive regulation of presidential power and, perhaps most significantly, institutionalize ongoing consultation between the President and key Cabinet members with a statutorily designated bipartisan congressional leadership group to focus on foreign and national security policy.

In terms of new interbranch norms, Congress and the President should follow through on an innovative 2008 suggestion by then-presidential candidate Senator John McCain: implement an American version of what is known in Great Britain as "question time" for the head of government. In parliamentary systems, "question time" is the occasion during legislative proceedings when members of Parliament who are not themselves government ministers are allowed to pose questions—whether friendly or challenging—to the Prime Minister. C-SPAN regularly broadcasts such sessions in the British Parliament to the United States, perhaps causing some bemusement on this side of the ocean whether the American Revolution actually deprived us of some significant measure of democratic accountability. Questioning our head of government on the floor of Congress would be potentially far more illuminating of executive branch thinking on key policy issues than White House press conferences that too easily become manipulable rituals of obfuscation and evasion.

To its credit, the Bush Administration did make one conspicuous attempt at promoting government openness—its so-called electronic rule-making initiative, the public face of which is a Web site called Regulation. Gov. A federal statute entitled the Administrative Procedure Act requires federal agencies to create opportunities for public comment before implementing most significant administrative rules.[19] The process, though, can be notably arcane for Americans who are unaware of how rules are made or what rules are being considered at what time and by which agencies. The vision behind Regulations.Gov is a one-stop portal that would enable members of the public to identify quickly the rules on any subject that are being proposed and deliberated by any agency within government and to take advantage of a simple online process for providing public input.

Unfortunately, the initiative never reached its potential because Congress never provided it with sufficient appropriations or a sound governance structure. Instead, design of this potentially powerful tool for pluralistic dialogue became enmeshed in a seemingly endless process of push-and-pull among various agencies, typically resisting OMB efforts to force uniformity of practice on agencies with very different regulatory missions and cultures. If Congress wants to empower Americans through the Internet to participate more meaningfully in a pluralistic policy dialogue within the executive branch, it will have to provide the project a clear legislative mandate and adequate financial and personnel resources.[20]

Congress should go even further to make the executive branch transparent to the public. Presidents have long claimed that "predecisional documents," memoranda that reveal the substance of policy-oriented discussions within government that precede public administrative initiatives such as the promulgation of a regulation, are presumptively immune from mandatory disclosure whether in court, Congress, or any other forum. As written, the federal Freedom of Information Act currently permits the executive branch to implement that position with regard to everyday public requests for information, although the need for such secrecy is questionable.[21] For example, the Reagan Administration relied on FOIA to shield information regarding its program of presidential regulatory oversight, even though that information is now routinely available, with no apparent adverse effect on government decision making, on an OMB Web site.[22] With that in mind, Congress should now reconsider the range of decision making documents that the executive branch is entitled to withhold from the public under the Freedom of Information Act. A strong presumption against secrecy should prevail whenever release of a document has no implications for military affairs, foreign policy, or law enforcement.

Of course, empowering citizen input into representative government through enhanced transparency is not a strategy that ought be limited to the executive branch. Congressional practices that disguise the responsibility of individual legislators, such as the process in the Senate of secret "holds" on nominations, should be categorically abolished. Congress also needs to attend to the imperative of opening up its own deliberations. A Library of Congress Web site currently provides free and comprehensive access to information about pending legislation, committee proceedings (including full text reports), and the *Congressional Record*.[23] But users need to know a lot about Congress in advance in order to take real advantage of the Web site. And, of equal importance, the site fails to offer "one-stop shopping" for citizens interested in the legislative process. It offers nothing, for example, about members' position statements and voting records.

As of late 2008, several excellent Web sites exist—most notably, OpenCongress.org and GovTrack.us—that support the tracking by non-specialists of individual pieces of legislation and the votes of individual legislators. These Web sites, however, are dependent on a combination of advertising and philanthropic largesse. Given the importance to democratic accountability of the kinds of information such sites make available, they ought to receive public funding and assurance of institutional permanence. Citizens should be able to access easily not only political information about members of Congress, but also institutional research, committee reports, drafts of bills, and floor debates. Americans would be far better positioned to participate meaningfully in politics if they had access to all the decisions that were being made in their name.

Of the three branches, the judiciary has the least capacity to participate in an aggressive and systematic way in a recalibration of checks and balances and a taming of presidentialism. That is because courts cannot determine for themselves which questions and controversies will be brought before them for resolution, and uniformity of judicial response can be achieved only through decisions of the U.S. Supreme Court, which in recent years has decided fewer than one hundred cases per term.

Nonetheless, it is relatively easy to spot three areas of public law doctrine where the evolution of a new approach (or resuscitation of an old one) would help advance the cause of pluralism and keep checks and balances healthy. First, the Supreme Court should affirm, on the earliest relevant occasion, that presidential signing statements have no jurisprudential weight in determining the meaning of statutes enacted by Congress. Congress, not the President, is the legislative branch, and the Court should simply reject at its earliest opportunity the proposition that the scope of a law's impact may be authoritatively altered through presidential interpretation.

In the same vein, the Court should rethink the scope of what administrative lawyers know as the *Chevron* doctrine.[24] This rule provides that, when Congress authorizes a government agency to make and implement policy, but does so through a statute that is ambiguous in its terms, the executive branch can give the statute any interpretation it wants, so long as that interpretation is not out-and-out irrational. In other words, even if a federal court is persuaded, all things considered, that the executive branch has not given a statute its most plausible reading, the court is supposed to defer to the preferences of the executive branch agency unless the court has determined that Congress has essentially outlawed the agency's interpretation.

The *Chevron* doctrine actually makes sense when an ambiguous statute is interpreted by the agency that is charged with its implementation and has expertise in the subject matter of that statute. Congress has affirmatively decided that it wants that agency to make policy, and the agency is likely to be more knowledgeable than a federal court about how that statute fits best within the full range of legislation the agency is charged with enforcing, as well as the implications of different interpretations for the effective discharge of the agency's mission. If, however, an agency has resolved an ambiguous statute in a particular way, not because of its independent and expert judgment, but because it was essentially compelled to do so by the White House, that rationale disappears. When it is the White House, not an agency, which offers a court a doubtful statutory interpretation, the court should scrutinize that interpretation with care to make sure that fidelity to Congress and not to the President's unilateral policy agenda is the governing consideration.

But perhaps the most important step the Court could take toward enhancing political pluralism in the United States is reversing its presumption against judicial involvement in challenges to the partisan gerrymandering of legislative districts.[25] The apportionment of legislative districts with the primary purpose of protecting incumbents is perhaps the single political practice that most effectively entrenches factionalism in a Madisonian sense. The adoption of an apportionment plan animated chiefly by the desire to preserve safe seats and dampen electoral competition should be regarded as unconstitutional.

Nearly all the reforms I have thus far recommended would operate fairly directly either to intensify interbranch accountability or to animate checks and balances by elevating the importance of pluralistic democratic deliberation within government. To endure, however, and to be maximally effective, these changes need to reinforced by more structural reforms in our systems of politics and political communication that will promote shifting coalitions and vigorous debate and discussion, while precluding a hardening of factions around any single dimension of common interest. Outmoded government structures and conditions of modern communication have limited what should be the effects on government of the diversity of views and interests among American voters. America thus needs to address the political and institutional contexts that have enabled and promoted the spirit of faction-ridden government that Madison decried. Rather than placing our hopes entirely in enlightened leaders to bring us the needed reforms, Americans should embrace the following as a platform for a broad-based, inclusive social movement for democratic revitalization.

Repairing Elections

A logical starting point would be reforms aimed at effectively enfranchising as many of the American people as possible. Our current system unjustifiably disqualifies millions of adults from voting and places many millions more in situations where their votes are politically all but meaningless. To the extent large swaths of the voting age public are excluded from exerting meaningful pressure on political officials through their votes, it cannot help but decrease accountability among our officials and increase the likelihood of government by faction. Four reforms would be critical steps toward repairing this situation:

1. Secure Universal Suffrage. Millions of competent adult Americans are ignored in federal policy making in that they are simply not allowed to vote. This includes, for example, over 430,000 adults who live in the District of Columbia and have no voting representation in Congress. There is no contemporary principled justification for their disenfranchisement. Wyoming, with a smaller population, enjoys two votes in the Senate and one in the House, while the District of Columbia has no votes at all. This unfairness works an obvious distortion in the balance of interests brought to bear on federal policy making.

A far larger number of disqualified potential voters consists of disenfranchised felons—persons convicted of nonmisdemeanor crimes and who, in all but two states, are subject to some denial of voting rights, whether temporary or permanent. The most careful recent attempt to estimate the magnitude of this phenomenon is the work of sociologists Jeff Manza and Christopher Uggen, who calculate the number of persons legally disenfranchised on Election Day 2004, at roughly 5.3 million, or roughly 2.7 percent of the nation's "voting eligible" population.[26] Compared to the U.S. population as a whole, this group is disproportionately poor and minority. As a result of felon disenfranchisement laws, an estimated 13 percent of black men are ineligible to vote—a figure that cannot help but have a devastating impact on the capacity of this community as a whole to achieve an effective voice in national policy making.[27] The work of Uggen and Manza reveals that felony disenfranchisement has played a critical role in determining a number of recent Senate elections and is probably responsible for at least one Republican presidential victory.[28]

The prevalence of felon disenfranchisement not only diminishes the quality of American democracy, but quite likely undermines society's interest in the effective reintegration of offenders into the mainstream of civic life. This belief is hardly confined to liberals. In the spring of 2007, Florida's Republican Governor, Charlie Crist, led that state's efforts to restore voting rights to nonviolent offenders and would have reportedly gone further, except for the vehement opposition of the state's Attorney General.[29] If American democracy is to approximate the legitimating ideal of taking seriously the interests of all Americans, this is a practice that must be eliminated. Florida's progress demonstrates its political feasibility.

2. *Eliminate the Influence of the Electoral College.* Beyond the problem of Americans unjustifiably excluded from voting is the more prevalent problem of voters positioned so that their votes have no political impact. We elect Presidents through an electoral college system in which every state is accorded a number of votes equal to the size of its delegation in the House of Representatives plus two; forty-eight of the fifty states—all but Nebraska and Maine—award their votes entirely to the winner of the state's popular election for President. Because many states are overwhelmingly Republican or Democrat, dissenting voters in those states can have virtually no impact

on the selection of the President, and political activity in those states surrounding the presidential election is artificially suppressed as a result. The upshot, as demonstrated in 2000 and nearly again is 2004, is that a candidate can be chosen as President who does not represent the plurality of voters actually going to the polls on Election Day.

Although the public typically favors getting rid of the electoral college,[30] it has long been conventional wisdom that the veto power of small states over the constitutional amendment process has made abolition impossible. National Popular Vote, a nonprofit corporation with a distinguished bipartisan advisory board of political heavyweights, believes, however, that it has figured out how, without a formal constitutional amendment, we can guarantee that the national popular vote winner will always win the electoral college. The plan is elegantly simple. It requires a number of states whose collective electoral votes would amount to a majority in the electoral college to form an "interstate compact." Through identical legislation enacted by all of its members, each state would promise—once the requisite number of states signed up—that it would appoint electors in each presidential election committed to voting for the national popular vote winner.[31] Maryland has already enacted the plan and, as of mid-2007, the idea has legislative sponsors in forty-seven states.

Securing sufficient support to bring the NPV plan into being will entail significant effort, but nothing like the effort required to amend the Constitution. An amendment would require a vote by two-thirds of each House of Congress, including the support of a significant number of Senators and Representatives from states that currently benefit from disproportionate clout under the electoral college system. Their handiwork would then have to be ratified by three-quarters of the states, including yet more of the small ones. By contrast, NPV could go into effect if adopted by as few as a dozen states. If ratified by a congressional majority, it would even become an "interstate compact" that one state could seek to enforce in the Supreme Court against any other state that neglected to follow the agreement.

The NPV plan for dealing with the electoral college would have a huge benefit beyond the impediment to future minority-vote presidents. It would mean that presidential candidates would benefit from competing seriously for the votes in every state.

3. Increase the Competitiveness of Congressional Elections. The problem of meaningless voting exists throughout the country for congressional districts. The Supreme Court insisted forty years ago that the Constitution demands congressional districts of nearly equal size so that, mathematically, a vote in one district should count the same as a vote cast in every other district, at least within the same state.[32] But this has not produced competitive elections. That is because, now aided by computers, state legislatures have figured out how to sort each state's Democrats and Republicans into districts that have "safe" majorities for either the Democratic or Republican candidate. Given the huge financial advantage to incumbents in reelection races, it is not surprising that, aided by the gerrymandered districting system, congressional incumbents who seek reelection are typically victorious in over 90 percent of their races—often in nearly 98 percent of their races.[33] Against this background, it is also hardly surprising that many voters throughout the country find that their representatives are more or less indifferent to their points of view. When a district is designed to guarantee one party's victory, the incumbent does not need to worry about the interests or perspective of the median voter; what counts is courting the base of whichever party is all but inevitably going to win each election.

The most popular idea for reforming the pattern of excessively partisan districting has been to remove the job of legislative apportionment from state legislatures and place it with independent redistricting commissions. It is important to recognize, however, that the districting process is inherently political and entails sensitive trade-offs, no matter who is in charge. A national coalition of reform groups has judged that there are at least ten states where redistricting reform seems politically plausible in the near future.[34] By engaging in coalition building across party lines, constructive ideas can evolve in each state for making elections more competitive without unduly disregarding other values, such as the integrity of municipalities or preserving effective participation for racial minorities. Evidence suggests that the idea of redistricting reform is attractive to voters if not cast in a way that raises suspicions that sponsors are seeking to advantage one political party over another.[35]

4. Create National Standards for Registration and Voting. Amazingly enough in twenty-first-century America, there is still doubt whether the Constitution actually assures the right to vote. Elections for federal officials are not only conducted by state and local authorities, but they are administered under a bewildering patchwork of rules and regulations that result in the hugely unequal treatment of votes and voters from different states and counties.

The Constitution ought to be amended to make explicit the guarantee of a federally protected right to vote in all popular elections. Such an amendment should likewise empower Congress to impose uniform national standards for registration and voting to insure that all Americans have an equal opportunity for effective political voice through the electoral process.[36] These standards should mandate voting technology that is simple, trustworthy, and susceptible to verification.

Equally important are national standards for the rules governing voter registration. A 2001 MIT/CalTech study estimated that registration problems disenfranchised 3 million voters during the previous year. Congress should be in a position to mandate same-day registration opportunities on Election Day itself.[37] The only legitimate governmental purpose for registration is to forestall election fraud, and computing technology now makes it practicable to run clean elections with same-day registration. States that permit Election Day registration see voter turnouts higher than the national average—12 points higher in the 2004 presidential elections—but only six states now permit the practice.[38] Opportunities for adult Americans to cast effective ballots and have them accurately counted in the states and precincts in which they actually live should not depend on the vagaries of local law.

Fair Play in the Market for Ideas

Reforms in the formal rules and practices related to elections can increase the pressure on elected officials to consider the full range of perspectives and interests relevant to the solution of problems. But reforming the machinery of voting is not enough. Unchecked, unbalanced government is also encouraged by background social conditions. Two such conditions are primary. The first consists of distortions in the marketplace of ideas—the fact that the communication resources available to proponents of contending ideas may be so unevenly distributed as to prevent a fair hearing for those ideas, regardless of their merit or capacity to persuade. The second are media practices that exaggerate polarization within the voting public and discourage mutual engagement and consensus building by failing to present contending ideas fully and fairly. Three further avenues of reform address these conditions:

5. *Curb Corporate Power over Politics.* In the landmark reapportionment case of *Reynolds v. Sims,* the late Chief Justice Earl Warren articulated a bedrock assumption of electoral democracy: "Legislators represent people, not trees or acres. Legislators are elected by voters, not farms or cities or economic interests."[39] In contemporary America, however, there can be little doubt that corporations, using advantages conferred upon them by

the laws under which they are organized and regulated, exert a measure of influence over our political system that subverts the connection between policy makers and individual voters. Millions of dollars devoted to lobbying, campaign contributions, and independent advocacy expenditures make it difficult to elicit government support for policies that are antagonistic, to any real degree, to the ideology and self-interest of corporate CEOs. The most compelling evidence of this fact is the near absence of the very issue of corporate influence from discussion in our mass media, which are themselves largely controlled by corporate conglomerates.

The most straightforward path to change would seem to be the imposition of direct restrictions on the capacity of corporations to spend money on the political process. Corporate speech and political spending may be protected by the First Amendment, but should be susceptible to regulation to a significant degree beyond what would be constitutionally permissible for the regulation of individuals.[40] In the context of political campaigns, there should be strict limits not only on corporate political contributions, but also on the amount of corporate funds that can be spent "independently" on behalf of candidates. Supreme Court doctrine that limits the regulation of corporate speaking on behalf of "issue elections," such as initiatives and referenda should be overturned. Unfortunately, in our current legal and political environment, such changes in the regulation of corporations are unlikely.

There is somewhat more movement in the direction of lobbying reform, limiting the scope of what public officials can accept from corporations by way of various favors. Strict limits on the receipt of corporate largesse should extend across all branches of government, barring—for example—corporate-sponsored travel and corporate involvement in the political action committees through which individual legislators dole out support to one another. Once again, however, it is probably safe to estimate conservatively the willingness of incumbent political officials to cut off their own access to such resources.

Two other avenues may prove more practicable politically. The first is continuing to expand legal disclosure requirements. All corporate political spending, including issue advocacy and independent election campaigning, should be explicitly tagged as such. The avenues that now exist for corporations to mask their activity in the guise of grassroots politics should be closed. When, for example, legislators and the voters they represent hear from groups like Consumers for Cable Choice, the New Millennium Research Council, Hands Off the Internet, and TV4US, on issues of telecommunications reform, they ought to be informed that each of these groups is substantially supported by AT&T.[41] No nonprofit advocacy organization should be able to retain tax-free status unless it discloses fully the extent of its backing by private corporations.

The second route is to shore up the capacity of other speakers to devote significant resources to noncorporate points of view. Most notably, federal law should be changed to ease collective bargaining and to facilitate the easier organization of unions. With only 13.8 of its wage and salary employees in unions (and only 8.6 percent in the private sector), the United States lacks the kind of organized counterweight that exists in other Western democracies to the most extreme public policy influence of the superrich. Yet, one recent poll shows 60 million Americans would join unions if they could. Legal changes, such as requiring employers to recognize unions once a majority of workers sign authorization cards, and strengthening penalties for violations of the rights of workers seeking to form unions, would likely promote significant increases in the number of unions and strengthen a public policy voice more representative of the working and middle classes in the United States.[42]

6. *Reduce Media Costs for Candidates.* It is not just disproportionate corporate power that distorts the market for ideas or threatens the connection between elected officials and individual voters. Running for office has become so expensive that office holders must devote extraordinary time, energy, and attention to fund-raising, and the range of potentially viable candidates—especially for federal office—is limited to the wealthy or those with access to significant wealth.

Probably the fastest growing expenditure item for federal candidates has been the cost of mass media. Although a few leading candidates get some free coverage of their views through news programs, the opportunities to convey a message to voters lasting more than a few seconds are few and far between—especially on the broadcast networks. Political advertising, for those who can afford it, has become a vast source of revenue both for the networks and for local television stations throughout America.

A major step to reducing the cost of elections, thus opening up the range of potential dialogue and public engagement, would be expanding the availability of free and reduced-cost media time for political candidates. A constructive proposal in this regard is the proposed "Our Democracy, Our Airwaves Act," introduced in 2003 by Senators John McCain and Russ Feingold.[43] The Act would require radio and television broadcasters to carry at least two hours per week of candidate- or issue-centered programming for a total of six weeks preceding a primary or general federal election. At least half these segments would have to air between 5 p.m. and 11:35 p.m., and no credit would be given for programming between midnight and 6 a.m. In addition, the Act would create a voucher program to be financed by a spectrum use fee levied on broadcasters. Political parties would receive up to $750 million in vouchers to be given to federal candidates, thus effectively providing them free media time. Qualifying federal candidates will also be eligible to receive $3 in vouchers for every dollar raised in private contributions. Steps in this direction would bring the public more information and a wider range of candidates, while enabling office holders to pay more attention to ideas and less to money.

7. Promote Opportunities for Media Ownership and Issue Coverage. A final, profound distortion in the marketplace of ideas is the consequence of concentration in the ownership of America's media firms. Studies have shown that the deregulation of media ownership has reduced the extent of local radio news coverage and reduced the range of formats available to radio listeners.[44] "Localism" hearings sponsored by the FCC in 2003 and 2004 brought in testimony that media consolidation results in less independently produced programming, increased censorship of divergent views, less political discussion, and fewer opportunities for women and minorities to become broadcast owners. There seems little doubt that reducing the number of owners reduces the number of voices actually heard via the mass media. Among television networks, industry consolidation has greatly reduced the prospects for independent producers to get shows aired. Every major network is now integrated with one or more production studios under common ownership.

Critics of the view that media concentration is a problem typically provide economic arguments for the competitiveness of the media market as a whole. They argue that, without both vertical and horizontal integration, media firms cannot generate the resources they need to provide strong, independent voices for the public interest. The fact remains, however, that where media ownership is narrowly restricted, those of us who do not own newspapers, broadcast stations, or cable channels are significantly dependent on the biases of a few powerful actors to have our point of view meaningfully presented in public deliberation.[45]

Another way to think of this is that economic efficiency in communications is not the sole or even primary aim of a communications system in a democratic community. Democracy requires widespread citizen access to a public sphere in which all competing ideas can be effectively presented to a sizeable audience. Access, in other words, is a kind of "public good" that even a genuinely free market cannot guarantee.

Contrary to advocates of deregulation, the Internet does not make up for the increasing concentration among owners of radio and television broadcast networks, television production companies, and major newspapers. Although it reduces the cost of distributing content to nearly zero, it gives a tremendous advantage to those with disproportionate resources to produce more appealing content. Likewise, networked "consumers" of information goods are more likely to turn to distributors with well-known off-line brands and seek out sites that they expect others—such as friends and coworkers —will also see. Hence, the number of noncommercial Web sites that get nontrivial attention is infinitesimal in comparison to the number of sites available, and even the most frequented commentary sites are seen by a fraction of the audience that reads major newspapers or follows radio and television news.[46]

The reduction in voices resulting from increased media consolidation has been exacerbated by the repeal of the FCC's Fairness Doctrine. Until the mid-1980s, a condition of holding a radio or television broadcast license in the United States was the obligation to provide significant coverage of important public issues, with reasonable opportunities for the audience to hear contrasting viewpoints.[47] Abolition of this so-called Fairness Doctrine led to a proliferation of radio outlets carrying a menu of one-sided demagogic programs of political commentary, entirely unrebutted by any contending point of view.

A campaign on behalf of what Professor C. Edwin Baker has called the "maximum practical dispersal" of media ownership[48] would likely be more effective in democratizing the communications market than resuscitating the Fairness Doctrine. In operation, though probably salutary overall, the doctrine was highly manipulable and difficult to enforce except in the most extreme cases. By contrast, dispersing ownership to the maximum practical extent compatible with maintaining economically viable media entities would expand the number of outlets controlled by persons of different outlooks or at least interested in catering to the concerns and information needs and desires of different groups. Diffuse ownership would provide checks and balances within the information sphere that are critical to supporting a political culture in which ideas contend on their merits, not the economic resources available to their sponsors.

Empowering Citizens

Beyond reforming electoral rules to accomplish effective universal suffrage and redressing distortions in our media-saturated marketplace for ideas, we can also build democratic legitimacy by making it easier for individual citizens to become active participants in the world of politics. We can organize our collective life in real space to proliferate opportunities for citizens of different backgrounds, beliefs, and aspirations to encounter one another in constructive discourse. We can also use the Internet to lower the barriers to civic engagement, given its unparalleled capacity to foster human networking and the creation and sharing of knowledge. In short, we can increase the likelihood that competing institutions of government will reflect the full spectrum of public views and interests by maximizing the opportunities for individuals to express those views and interests in meaningful ways.

8. Resuscitate the Culture of Political Dialogue. An obvious reason why more voices are not heard in the halls of power is that many citizens prefer to avoid active engagement in political discussion. Survey work suggests that people avoid political discussion because they fear its unpleasantness and suspect its inefficacy.[49] Many people doubt that citizens with fundamentally different viewpoints can reason their way productively to persuasive solutions to public problems. They further doubt that, to the extent such discussions were successful, politicians would implement the insights that citizens generate. Deliberation research offers strong reasons to regret this state of affairs. Such research shows that, when deliberative experiences are well organized, participants enjoy themselves and frequently produce a good job at developing proposed budgets and policy recommendations across a wide range of issues.[50] Moreover, examples from around the world demonstrate that it is possible to effectively institutionalize broad-based citizen deliberation as part of a program of government-initiated outreach that offers to take serious account of public views in making formal policy decisions.[51]

Professors Bruce Ackerman and James Fishkin have offered one especially creative proposal to rekindle the public appetite for community deliberation. Their proposal is a new national holiday—more specifically, a two-day quadrennial holiday linked to each presidential election—called Deliberation Day.[52] A lot of the good that Deliberation Day could accomplish might be achieved through more modest efforts organized in local communities, perhaps through public libraries. Libraries have long been our most trusted public institutions, and their efforts to organize civic discourse—in possible partnership with public television stations, universities, and nonpartisan community groups—might have special credibility, even among members of the public who learned only after the fact what their fellow citizens had said and thought. If such events became a staple of community calendars across the country, it could well lay the framework for something as ambitious and productive as what Ackerman and Fishkin have proposed.

Informal social networking can also help to increase our willingness to take time for civic dialogue with others. An intriguing example, albeit on one side of the political spectrum, is an initiative called Drinking Liberally, which advertises itself as an effort to give "like-minded, left-leaning individuals a place to talk politics."[53] According to its Web site, "You don't need to be a policy expert and this isn't a book club—just come and learn from peers, trade jokes, vent frustration and hang out in an environment where it's not taboo to talk politics."[54] As of September 2003, it claimed 293 chapters in all fifty states and the District of Columbia. One wonders, given the availability of the Internet to sustain social networking initiatives, whether something called "Drinking Together"—an organization devoted to social interaction among people who are *not* like-minded—might also thrive.

The point is to start a kind of virtuous, democracy-building spiral. As people accustom themselves to sharing political ideas with fellow citizens, they should come to demand more attentiveness from their representatives. As representatives hear from a wider and wider range of their constituents, they should find it necessary to cater less to their base and more to a larger public interest. The social impetus to push for a public-regarding consensus should lead Congress and the President to play their roles vigorously, but through mutual engagement, not separation of powers brinksmanship. Over time, government "of the people, by the people, and for the people" should begin to feel increasingly like reality.

9. Make Broadband Universal and Affordable. People in every sector of the computing business typically yearn for the must-have software application or "killer app" that will drive consumer demand for computing capacity to untold new heights. The "app" for which people yearn, however, is probably written into our biology; it is human connection. It is no accident that the most pervasive use of new digital information and communication technologies is e-mail. E-mail has exploded the range of opportunities for human contact, whether within organizations or across the globe. But e-mail's capacity to make human beings "present" to one another is obviously limited.

People want audio and, especially, video. In terms of democratic revival, this is very good news.

Think for a moment of the collective capabilities that would enable rich and inclusive democratic discourse via the Internet. People would presumably want "space" to meet one another—that is, to be present to one another through sight, sound, and text—in both "real time" and asynchronously. They would want ready access to information that they could share and dissect with one another. They would probably benefit from skilled moderation. To a university faculty member such as myself, what this sounds like is obvious. This democratic forum is more or less identical to what we would call a "virtual classroom." We are talking about an "app" that enables people to meet in real time forums or online communities, leave messages for one another to be reviewed at leisure, create and access libraries, and collaborate in the generation of both individual and collective insight.

As awareness of the Internet grew, so did concern for what has come to be called the "digital divide." In its original conception, the "divide" referred to differential access to hardware. Some people had computers; others did not. And, quite predictably, the distribution of computing capacity was disproportionately associated with race and class. Even as the access divide has partially eased, however, there remain other "divides" that are seemingly less tractable in terms of motivating universal Internet use. The more enduring inequalities seem to be inequalities of skill and confidence, especially confidence that time spent with computers can bring things of value to the user.[55] Survey research has found that differences in use of the Internet to participate in political discourse relate more substantially to these variables than the mere fact of access to a computer or even whether people otherwise characterize their lives as "busy."[56]

The technology divide and the divide in motivation are related. That is because the computers over which it is easiest for people to derive value from the Internet are computers that have a so-called broadband connection to the worldwide network of networks. Broadband refers to high-speed Internet connections that can accommodate the instantaneous exchange of text, voice, and video. It is broadband that makes communications-rich democratic forums on the Internet plausible, and it is the proliferation of broadband (and the accompanying access to video) that is most likely to motivate universal Internet use for purposes of social interconnection.[57] The better the connection, the easier it becomes to navigate the Internet and the lower the barriers to finding genuine value for each user through their online activity.

The United States is currently lagging in the world of broadband. Although we have the largest absolute number of broadband subscribers in the world,[58] among the thirty members of the Organization for Economic Co-operation and Development, which represents most postindustrial democracies, we rank twelfth in terms of the number of broadband subscribers per 100 inhabitants, behind Canada and Scandinavia, as well as South Korea.[59] The International Telecommunications Union, which includes a larger number of nations, ranks us fifteenth, and we fall to twenty-first in the ITU "digital opportunity index," which takes price and other factors into account.[60] But even this does not tell the full story. The broadband capabilities marketed to the American public allow users to download information at a maximum rate of 1–5 megabytes per second, but to transmit information at 500 kilobytes per second or less. In a recent survey, the median U.S. broadband subscriber could download at 1.9 megabytes per second and upload at 371 kilobytes per second.[61] By way of contrast, most South Korean residents can receive or transmit information at 50–100 megabytes per second, a rate available also in places as diverse as Denmark, Romania, and Japan.[62] Iceland makes 100 megabytes per second service available for $26 a month,[63] and Singapore is planning to create 1 gigabyte per second capacity for its citizens by 2015.[64] As matters stand now, 31 million American households lack any Internet connection,[65] and broadband access is highly correlated with income.[66] Rural broadband penetration lags behind urban areas and, while growing, still lags about 8 percentage points behind the national average.[67]

The advent of universal and affordable broadband access—comparable to the universal provision of telephone service that Americans have enjoyed for most of a century—would bring countless benefits not only to individual users, but to society as a whole. The expansion of any information network makes the network more valuable for all its users. A broadband network would afford opportunities for creative self-expression, economic entrepreneurship, and civic interaction of a quality we can barely imagine today. Connecting every American household to genuine broadband would thus probably be the single most transformative step we could take toward enabling inclusive, pluralistic democratic conversation among citizens and between citizens and their government.

What unites these ideas is pluralism, the conviction that checks and balances work best when those who hold office must also hold themselves accountable to a wide variety of constituents with varying interests and different outlooks. Each officeholder would have to become a sort of broker or mediator for ongoing political dialogue and will be more likely to insist that the branch he or she represents will have its say in the actual formulation of public policy.

These proposals hardly exhaust the roster of reforms that could have a transformative impact on political dialogue and coalition building in America. After all, Americans could participate more meaningfully in deliberative politics if our schools were better. We would probably regard one another's interests with more sympathy if wealth and income inequalities were reduced and if people thus felt their material interests were less opposed. People would likely become both more rational and more expansive in their outlook if they were less insecure about their own future; it could thus be argued that universal health care and government guaranteed job retraining would help create a more promising political context for public-interested compromise on economic issues. In short, anything that would make Americans more knowledgeable, more tolerant, and more confident in the future—our own and our children's—would likely enhance our democracy, too.

And make no mistake—the practice of constitutionalism within the halls of American government will be shaped, most profoundly, by changes in the quality of our collective democratic life in society at large. If healthy governance relies on informal understandings and norms of interbranch accommodation within government, then we should wish for norms of trust, cooperation, forbearance, and self-restraint to prevail in the larger society. Madison wrote: "If men were angels, no government would be necessary."[68] But he might have added: "If men are never angels, no good government is possible." Those who govern us are more likely to exhibit the values on which the system depends if those values live robustly throughout the public sphere.

As citizens, we must also recognize that choosing an interpretation of our constitutional heritage is something more than selecting a legal theory that lives only in courtrooms and law reviews. The values and assumptions implicit in our constitutional law shape the self-understanding of our Presidents, legislators, judges, and administrators. Told that the Constitution sanctions vigorous unilateralism, they will pursue it. Taught that our system demands dialogue and accountability, they will, to a greater extent, engage in that alternative. To get past the spirit of faction that has produced a Bush 43 Presidency and the dysfunctional decision making that attends it, we need to insist on a reawakening to the Madisonian vision as an ethos of governance and of civic life more generally.

None of this is beyond us. The leaders who gathered in Philadelphia, as James Madison recorded, were statesmen of extraordinary vision and worth. But the far greater resources on which we can currently draw in our own century—economic resources, communications resources, and resources of national experience and deliberation—give us enormous advantages with which to confront the future. Efforts to turn back the excesses of executive power can easily start now. They should take root in a national conviction that the theory and practice of constitutional pluralism, not presidentialism, hold the greatest promise for transforming Madison's founding dream of virtuous republicanism into an effective operating philosophy for American democracy in the twenty-first century.

Notes

Chapter One

1. GARRY WILLS, JAMES MADISON 29–30 (2002).

2. Letter from James Madison to George Washington (Nov. 18, 1787), in JACK N. RAKOVE, ED., MADISON: WRITINGS 158–159 (1999) (hereafter MADISON: WRITINGS).

3. THE FEDERALIST No. 10, at 77 (James Madison) (Clinton Rossiter ed., 1961).

4. Id. at 78.

5. James Madison, *Vices of the Political System of the United States,* in MADISON: WRITINGS, *supra* note 2, at 69–80.

6. Id. at 79.

7. THE FEDERALIST No. 51, at 322 (James Madison) (Clinton Rossiter ed., 1961). .

8. James Madison, *A Sketch Never Finished Nor Applied,* in MADISON: WRITINGS, *supra* note 2, at 842.

9. The Clinton Justice Department provided a systematic overview of its separation of powers stance in an Office of Legal Counsel memorandum, The Constitutional Separation of Powers Between the President and Congress, 20 O.L.C. 124 (1996), *reprinted in* H. JEFFERSON POWELL, THE CONSTITUTION AND THE ATTORNEYS GENERAL 617 (1999). The memorandum expressly purported to supersede a Bush 41 memorandum, Common Legislative Encroachments on Executive Branch Constitutional Authority, 13 O.L.C. 299 (1989), in light of subsequent Supreme Court opinions and "certain differences in approach."

10. THE FEDERALIST No. 48, at 308–09 (James Madison) (Clinton Rossiter ed., 1961).

11. THE FEDERALIST No. 51, at 320 (James Madison) (Clinton Rossiter ed., 1961).

12. THE FEDERALIST No. 73, at 443 (Alexander Hamilton) (Clinton Rossiter ed., 1961).

13. THE FEDERALIST No. 10, at 78 (James Madison) (Clinton Rossiter ed., 1961).

14. Id.

15. See generally Allen Buchanan, *Political Legitimacy and Democracy,* 112 ETHICS 689 (2002). I explore ideas of democratic legitimacy in more detail in Peter M. Shane,

The Electronic Federalist, in PETER M. SHANE, ED., DEMOCRACY ONLINE: THE PROS-PECTS FOR POLITICAL RENEWAL THROUGH THE INTERNET 65–82 (2004).

16. Letter of Lord John Russell to Poulett Thomson (Oct. 14, 1839), available at http://www.constitution.org/sech/sech_133.txt.

17. Lu Hong & Scott E. Page, *Groups of Diverse Problem Solvers Can Outperform Groups of High Ability Problem Solvers,* 101 PROC. NAT'L ACAD. ARTS & SCI. 16385–89 (2004).

18. 42 U.S.C. § 1973–1973aa-6 (2006).

19. 42 U.S.C. 4321–47 (2006).

20. 418 U.S. 683 (1974).

21. The events of 1995 are recounted in detail in ELIZABETH DREW, SHOWDOWN: THE STRUGGLE BETWEEN THE GINGRICH CONGRESS AND THE CLINTON WHITE HOUSE (1996), on which the following summary is substantially based.

22. George Hager, *Day by Day: Talks Wax and Wane . . . as Anger, Miscues Punctuate Week,* 53 CONG. Q. WKLY. REP. 3876 (Dec. 23, 1995); George Hager, *A Battered GOP Calls Workers Back to Job,* 54 CONG. Q. WKLY. REP. 53 (Jan. 6, 1996).

23. George Hager, *Congress, Clinton Yield Enough to Close the Book on Fiscal '96,* 54 CONG. Q. WKLY. REP. 1155 (Apr. 27, 1996).

24. For example, a Los Angeles Times Poll National Survey, conducted January 19–22, 1995, asked 1,353 adults nationwide if they would favor cuts in spending for a variety of purposes. By the percentage margins indicated, respondents opposed cuts in the following: Medicare (88–9), Social Security (86–12), Medicaid (73–20), and the environment (67–27). Public Opinion on The Contract, available at http://oregonstate.edu/instruct/ps102/tutorial/congress/opinion.htmlP0111. A November 1995 CNN/USA Today/Gallup Poll found that Americans, by a 48 to 38 percent margin, thought it more important to protect Medicare funding than to balance the budget. CNN, Americans Blame GOP for Budget Mess (Nov. 15, 1995), at http://www.cnn.com/US/9511/debt_limit/11-15/poll/poll_txt.html [hereinafter CNN]. To be fair, the 1995 showdown was not the first occasion in recent decades when one house of Congress threatened to cut off appropriations across the board in order to force presidential agreement on a contested matter of policy. But the comparison between this and the prior occasion only demonstrates how dramatically the 1995 budget shutdown departed from conventional interbranch practice. In June 1973, the Democratic Senate Majority Leader Mike Mansfield told President Nixon he would block passage of any major appropriations bill for the next fiscal year—which, at the time, would begin the following July 1—unless Nixon agreed to a ban on any further funding for military operations in Southeast Asia. WILLIAM BUNDY, A TANGLED WEB: THE MAKING OF FOREIGN POLICY IN THE NIXON PRESIDENCY 389–90 (1998). Nixon relented. Mansfield had substantial bipartisan backing for his stance. Public support for rapid troop withdrawals from Vietnam had been growing since the late 1960s. BENJAMIN I. PAGE & ROBERT Y. SHAPIRO, THE RATIONAL PUBLIC: FIFTY YEARS OF TRENDS IN AMERICANS' POLICY PREFERENCES 234–237 (1992). Nixon's approval rating during the second quarter of 1973 stood at 44 percent and was heading downward as a result of the unfolding Watergate investigation. USA Today, Approval Ratings from

Ike Through Clinton (Jan. 14, 1996), available at http://www.usatoday.com/elect/eq/eqleg.062.htm (on file with author). Thus, although Mansfield's threat was a portentous exercise of checks and balances brinksmanship, he could plausibly assert the necessity of that strategy to force executive branch accountability to prevailing public sentiment.

25. Three of the more important accounts of the Clinton impeachment, told from different perspectives, are Joe Conason & Gene Lyons, The Hunting of the President: The 10-Year Campaign to Destroy Bill and Hillary Clinton (2000); Richard A. Posner, An Affair of State: The Investigation, Impeachment, and Trial of President Clinton (1999); and Jeffrey Toobin, A Vast Conspiracy (1999). My own summary relies largely on Toobin and his immensely helpful chronology compiled at xvii–xxii.

26. Toobin, *supra* note 25, at 61–81.

27. Robert W. Ray, Final Report of the Independent Counsel In Re: Madison Guaranty Savings & Loan Association Regarding Monica Lewinsky and Others, filed with the U.S. Court of Appeals for the District of Columbia Circuit, Division for the Purpose of Appointing Independent Counsels, Division No. 94–1 (2001), available at http://icreport.access.gpo.gov/lewinsky.html.

28. Clinton v. Jones, 520 U.S. 681 (1997).

29. See Linda Feldmann, *Democrats Hope for a Boost from Impeachment Fallout,* Christian Sci. Monitor (Dec. 29, 1998), at 1, available at 1998 WL 2372928 ("[T]he GOP has handed the Democrats a campaign issue they believe could tip some seats their way in 2000: the impeachment of President Clinton, a move the majority of the public opposed.").

30. President Clinton's approval ratings hovered in the "in the high 50s and low 60s" throughout 1997, but jumped to 69 percent after news first broke of the Monica Lewinsky investigation. It remained in the 60–70 percent range throughout the year and spiked to 73 percent after the House voted for impeachment. USA Today/CNN/Gallup Poll Results: A Year-By-Breakdown of President Clinton's Job Approval Ratings in the CNN/USA Today/Gallup Poll (Jan. 21, 2000), available at http://www.usatoday.com/news/p011020.htm.

31. Nixon v. United States, 506 U.S. 224 (1993).

32. Id. at 228.

33. Id. at 230.

34. Report of the Congressional Committees Investigating the Iran-Contra Affair, H. Rep. No. 100–433, at 395–99, 404–05 (1st Sess. 1987) [hereinafter, "Iran-Contra Report"]. On the lack of public support for Contra funding, see Public Opinion in U.S. Foreign Policy: The Controversy over Contra Aid 64–65 (Richard Sobel ed., 1993); Richard Sobel, *Public Opinion About United States Intervention in El Salvador and Nicaragua,* 53 Pub. Op. Q. 114, 124 (1989).

35. The Tower Commission Report: The Full Text of the President's Special Review Board 502–03 (N.Y. Times ed., 1987).

36. See Iran-Contra Report, *supra* note 34, at 414–16, 418–19.

37. Id. at 413.

38. See id. at 411–14.

39. See Peter M. Shane, *Presidents, Pardons, and Prosecutors: Legal Accountability and the Separation of Powers,* 11 Yale L. & Pol'y Rev. 361, 398–99 nn. 156–66 (1993).

40. United States v. Poindexter, 951 F.2d 369 (D.C. Cir. 1991); United States v. North, 910 F.2d 843 (D.C. Cir. 1990); United States v. North, 920 F.2d 940 (D.C. Cir. 1990).

41. John W. Dean, Conservatives Without Conscience (2006).

42. Jeffrey M. Stonecash et al., Diverging Parties: Social Change, Realignment, and Party Polarization 20–21 (2003).

43. See generally Jacob S. Hacker & Paul Pierson, The Republican Revolution and the Erosion of American Democracy (2005).

44. Gebe Martinez, *Democrats Cry Foul as GOP Eases Several House Rules,* 61 Cong. Q. Wkly. Rep. 90, 90 (Jan. 11, 2003). See also Jonathan Allen, *Effective House Leadership Makes the Most of Majority,* 61 Cong. Q. Wkly. Rep. 746 (Mar. 29, 2003).

45. Data on the 2000 presidential election results are taken from http://www.archives.gov/federal_register/electoral_college/electoral_ college.html. State population figures appear at http://www.census.gov/population/www/cen2000/phc-t2.html.

46. The Federalist No. 10, at 84 (James Madison) (Clinton Rossiter ed., 1961).

Chapter Two

1. The Limits of Executive Power: Restoring the Rule of Law, Speech of Al Gore to the American Constitution Society, Washington, D.C., Jan. 16, 2006, available at http://www.draftgore.com/exec_power.htm.

2. An excellent example of this view is Thomas O. Sargentich, *The Emphasis on the Presidency in U.S. Public Law: An Essay Critiquing Presidential Administration,* 59 Admin. L. Rev. 1 (2007).

3. For a view that the story is apocryphal, see Keith E. Whittington, Political Foundations of Judicial Supremacy: The Presidency, the Supreme Court, and Constitutional Leadership in U.S. History 33 (2007).

4. Massachusetts v. EPA, 549 U.S. 497 (2007).

5. Letter from EPA Administrator Stephen L. Johnson to Hon. Henry A. Waxman and Hon. Tom Davis (Mar. 27, 2008), available at http://oversight.house.gov/documents/20080327170233.pdf.

6. U.S. Const., Art. I, § 8.

7. Steven G. Calabresi & Christopher S. Yoo, *The Unitary Executive in Historical Perspective,* Admin. & Reg. Law News, Fall 2005, at 5.

8. U.S. Const., Art. II, § 3.

9. Kendall v. United States ex rel. Stokes, 37 U.S. 524 (1838).

10. Myers v. United States, 272 U.S. 52 (1927); Morrison v. Olson, 487 U.S. 654 (1988).

11. In 1988, the Office of Legal Counsel deemed unconstitutional a statute that required the Center for Disease Control to disseminate an informational pamphlet on

AIDS without vetting by the White House. In an opinion signed by then Assistant Attorney General Charles Cooper, the Justice Department insisted: "The Director of the CDC, as a subordinate executive branch officer within the Department of Health and Human Services, is subject to the complete supervision of the President with respect to the carrying out of executive functions." Statute Limiting the President's Authority to Supervise the Director of the Centers for Disease Control in the Distribution of an AIDS Pamphlet, 12 O.L.C. 47, 56 (1988). In asserting the President's role to edit CDC pamphlets, OLC said, "it matters not at all that the information in the AIDS fliers may be highly scientific in nature." Id. at 57.

12. Dan Eggen, *Accounts of Prosecutors' Dismissals Keep Shifting,* WASH. POST, March 17, 2007, at A1.

13. Letter from Fred F. Fielding, Counsel to the President, to the Hon. Patrick J. Leahy and the Hon. John Conyers, at 2 (June 28, 2007), available at http://judiciary.house.gov/Media/PDFS/Clemento70628.pdf.

14. 28 U.S.C. § 541 (2006).

15. The argument from the Vesting Clause was spelled out during the Reagan Administration in Statute Limiting the President's Authority to Supervise the Director of the Centers for Disease Control in the Distribution of an AIDS Pamphlet, 12 O.L.C. 47, 48–52 (1988).

16. Bill of Rights § 2, 1 W. & M. 2d Sess., ch. 2 (1689), *reprinted in* 4 PHILLIP B. KURLAND & RALPH LERNER, EDS., THE FOUNDERS CONSTITUTION 123 (1987).

17. J. ROHR, TO RUN A CONSTITUTION: THE LEGITIMACY OF THE ADMINISTRATIVE STATE 1–3 (1986).

18. See Peter M. Shane, *Independent Policymaking and Presidential Power: A Constitutional Analysis,* 57 GEO. WASH. L. REV. 596, 615–17 (1989), and the statutes there cited.

19. The new Post Office establishment was not even called a department. Its head, the Postmaster General, had a reporting relationship to the Secretary of the Treasury.

20. Gerhard Casper, *An Essay in Separation of Powers: Some Early Versions and Practices,* 30 WM. & MARY L. REV. 211, 240 (1989), *quoting* 1 Stat. at 65–66 (1789).

21. ROHR, *supra* note 17, at 22–23.

22. The President and Accounting Officers, 1 Op. Att'y. Gen. 624, 625 (1823).

23. F. McDONALD, NOVUS ORDO SECLORUM: THE INTELLECTUAL ORIGINS OF THE CONSTITUTION 258 (1985).

24. Casper, *supra* note 20, at 212, 224.

25. See, e.g., Steven G. Calabresi & Saikrishna B. Prakash, *The President's Power to Execute the Laws,* 104 YALE L.J. 541 (1994).

26. 487 U.S. 654 (1988).

27. Pub. L. 95-521, Title VI, 95th Cong., 2d Sess., 92 Stat. 1824 (1978), as amended and codified, 28 U.S.C. § 591–99.

28. 28 U.S.C. § 596(a)(1).

29. Morrison v. Olson, 487 U.S. at 677.

30. Id. at 691.

31. Id. at 691–92. It should be noted that, although an independent counsel could be discharged for cause only by the Attorney General, the President could fire an Attorney General who refused, contrary to the President's judgment, to exercise this discharge power properly.

32. James Risen & Eric Lichtblau, *Bush Lets U.S. Spy on Callers Without Courts*, N.Y. Times, Dec. 16, 2005, at A1.

33. Pub. L. 95-511, 95th Cong., 2d Sess., 92 Stat. 1783 (1978), as amended and codified at 50 U.S.C. § 1801–11, 1821–29, 1841–46, 1861–62.

34. Stanley I. Kutler, *Review of* Talking with David Frost: The Nixon Interviews, 81 J. Am. Hist. 1418–19 (1994).

35. In attributing a legal position to right-wing presidentialists, I am relying on legal positions actually expressed in executive branch documents, often amplified by the published academic writings of leading presidentialist legal scholars. The presidentialist position on war powers I am describing here is articulated both in the post–September 11 Office of Legal Counsel opinions I review in chapter 4 and in the scholarly work of one of those opinions' lead authors, Berkeley law professor John Yoo. See John Yoo, The Powers of War and Peace: The Constitution and Foreign Affairs After 9/11 (2005). This is not to say that presidentialist academics who have served in the executive branch would necessarily adopt, in their professorial role, the precise positions they articulated in their lawyerly work—although Professor Yoo does—or that conservative presidentialists agree on every issue. A number of leading presidentialist thinkers who have written supportively of the unitary presidency in domestic affairs—for example, Saikrishna Prakash—undoubtedly disagree with Professor Yoo's formulation of the President's war powers. I think it fair, however, to characterize the presidentialist school of thought according to those positions actually taken by the President's lawyers. To the best of my knowledge, the Bush 43 Administration invariably embraced the most ambitious claims of whatever presidentialist writing is likely to maximize its prerogatives.

36. See generally, Yoo, *supra* note 35, especially chap. 2 on war powers.

37. Id. at 190–95.

38. Id. at 211.

39. "Our analysis starts with the constitutional principle that responsibility for the conduct of foreign affairs and for protecting the national security are '"central" Presidential domains.' The President's constitutional responsibilities in both these areas flow from the specific grants of authority in Article II making him Chief Executive, U.S. Const. art. II, § 1, cl. 1, and Commander in Chief, id., art. II, § 2, c1. 1, as well as from the 'unique position' that the President occupies in the constitutional structure." Memorandum of Deputy Assistant Attorney General John C. Yoo, U.S. Department of Justice Office of Legal Counsel, for the Deputy Counsel to the President, Constitutional Issues Raised by Commerce, Justice and State Appropriations Bill (Nov. 28, 2001), available at 2001 WL 34907462 (O.L.C.).

40. Yoo, *supra* note 35, at 30–54.

41. John Hart Ely, War and Responsibility: Constitutional Lessons of Vietnam and Its Aftermath 3, 7 (1993); Louis Fisher, Presidential War

POWER 11 (1995); Jules Lobel, *"Little Wars" and the Constitution,* 50 U. MIAMI L. REV. 61, 75 (1995).

42. YOO, *supra* note 35, at 109.

43. 10 Annals of Cong. 613–14 (1800).

44. George Washington's Neutrality Proclamation, *reprinted in* STEVEN J. VALONE, ED., TWO CENTURIES OF U.S. FOREIGN POLICY: THE DOCUMENTARY RECORD 3 (1995).

45. Alexander Hamilton, *Letters of Pacificus,* No. 1, excerpted in PETER M. SHANE & HAROLD H. BRUFF, SEPARATION OF POWERS LAW: CASES AND MATERIALS 614, 615 (2d ed. 2005).

46. Id. at 616.

47. Id.

48. James Madison, *Letters of Helvidius,* Nos. 1–4 (Aug. 24–Sept. 13, 1793), *reprinted in* 4 THE FOUNDERS CONSTITUTION, *supra* note 16, at 67.

49. Id. at 71.

50. Id.

51. Id.

52. Id. at 76–77.

53. Id. at 69.

54. 343 U.S. 579 (1952).

55. Id. at 645 (Jackson, J., concurring).

56. Id. at 642.

57. Id. at 637.

58. Id. at 610–11 (Frankfurter, J., concurring).

59. Dames and Moore v. Regan, 453 U.S. 654 (1981).

60. Id. at 686.

61. David J. Barron & Martin S. Lederman, *The Commander in Chief at the Lowest Ebb—Framing the Problem, Doctrine, and Original Understanding,* 121 HARV. L. REV. 689 (2008); David J. Barron & Martin S. Lederman, *The Commander in Chief at the Lowest Ebb—A Constitutional History,* 121 HARV. L. REV. 941 (2008).

62. "In 1787 the world was a far larger place, and the framers probably had in mind attacks upon the United States. In the 20th century, the world has grown much smaller. An attack on a country far from our shores can impinge directly on the nation's security." Leonard Meeker, *The Legality of United States Participation in the Defense of Viet-Nam,* 54 DEPT. STATE BULL. 474 (1976), excerpted in SHANE & BRUFF, *supra* note 45, at 821.

Chapter Three

1. 50 U.S.C. § 1541–48.

2. Perhaps the strongest statement by a Framer in support of this functional view appears in THE FEDERALIST No. 70: "That unity is conducive to energy will not be disputed. Decision, activity, secrecy, and dispatch will generally characterise the proceedings of one man, in a much more eminent degree, than the proceedings of any

greater number; and in proportion as the number is increased, these qualities will be diminished." THE FEDERALIST NO. 70, at 424 (Alexander Hamilton) (Clinton Rossiter ed., 1961).

3. Jeffrey Rachlinski & Cynthia Farina, *Cognitive Psychology and Optimal Government Design,* 87 CORNELL L. REV. 549 (2002).

4. IRVING L. JANIS, VICTIMS OF GROUPTHINK: A PSYCHOLOGICAL STUDY OF FOREIGN-POLICY DECISIONS AND FIASCOES (1972); IRVING L. JANIS, GROUP-THINK: PSYCHOLOGICAL STUDIES OF POLICY DECISIONS AND FIASCOES (1982).

5. John M. Levine & Richard L. Moreland, *Small Groups,* in 2 DANIEL T. GILBERT, SUSAN T. FISKE, & GARDNER LINDZEY, THE HANDBOOK OF SOCIAL PSYCHOLOGY 415, 438 (4th ed. 1998) (hereafter SOCIAL PSYCHOLOGY HANDBOOK).

6. Philip E. Tetlock, *Social Psychology and World Politics,* in SOCIAL PSYCHOLOGY HANDBOOK, *supra* note 5, at 868, 887.

7. Id.

8. Marceline B. R. Kroon, Paul't Hart, & Dik van Kreveld, *Managing Group Decision Making Processes: Individual Versus Collective Accountability and Groupthink,* 2 INT'L J. CONFLICT MGMT. 91, 111 (1991). Law professor Gia Lee has argued, in part based on such research, that courts should be less deferential to presidential claims of confidentiality in litigation: "[T]here is reason to doubt that confidentiality-induced candor will improve presidential decisions." Gia Lee, *The President's Secrets,* 76 GEO. WASH. L. REV. 197, 261 (2008).

9. ROBERT S. MCNAMARA, IN RETROSPECT: THE TRAGEDY AND LESSONS OF VIETNAM (1995).

10. Id. at 39.

11. Id. at 39–40.

12. Id. at 43.

13. Id.

14. Id.

15. Id. at 47.

16. Id. at 48.

17. Id. at 50.

18. Id. at 52.

19. Id. at 53.

20. Id.

21. Id. at 107.

22. Id. at 120.

23. Id. at 171.

24. See id. at 174–77.

25. Id. at 162.

26. Id.

27. Id. at 196.

28. Id. at 197–98.

29. Id. at 306.

30. Id. at 203.

31. Id. at 323.

32. See id. at 306–07.

33. Id. at 322.

34. See id. at 266, 269.

35. Id. at 191–92.

36. See id. at 321–22.

37. WILLIAM BUNDY, A TANGLED WEB: THE MAKING OF FOREIGN POLICY IN THE NIXON PRESIDENCY (1998).

38. Id. at 55.

39. Id.

40. Id. at 57.

41. Id. at 58.

42. Id. at 152.

43. Id. at 498.

44. Department of Defense Report on Selected Air and Ground Operations in Cambodia and Laos 15 (Sept. 10, 1973), *reprinted in* Bombing in Cambodia, Hearings Before the Armed Services Committee of the U.S. Senate, 93d Cong., 1st Sess. (1973), available at http://www.dod.mil/pubs/foi/reading_room/27.pdf.

45. BUNDY, *supra* note 37, at 385.

46. Id. at 391.

47. Id. at 72.

48. Id. at 397–98.

49. Id. at 390.

50. Id. at 364.

51. Id. at 389.

52. Id. at 385.

53. THOMAS E. RICKS, FIASCO: THE AMERICAN MILITARY ADVENTURE IN IRAQ 242 (2006).

54. The factual accounts of the war in Iraq on which this section relies are chiefly RICKS, *supra* note 53, and MICHAEL R. GORDON & GENERAL BERNARD E. TRAINOR, COBRA II: THE INSIDE STORY OF THE INVASION AND OCCUPATION OF IRAQ (2006).

55. JOSEPH E. STIGLITZ & LINDA J. BILMES, THE THREE TRILLION DOLLAR WAR: THE TRUE COST OF THE IRAQ CONFLICT 9 (2008).

56. GORDON & TRAINOR, *supra* note 54, at 134.

57. JAMES RISEN, STATE OF WAR: THE SECRET HISTORY OF THE CIA AND THE BUSH ADMINISTRATION 76 (2006).

58. GORDON & TRAINOR, *supra* note 54, at 127–129; RICKS, *supra* note 53, at 52–53.

59. GORDON & TRAINOR, *supra* note 54, at 133.

60. Id. at 134.

61. Id.

62. RISEN, *supra* note 57, at 85–207.

63. RICKS, *supra* note 53, at 101.

64. GORDON & TRAINOR, *supra* note 54, at 64–65.

65. Id. at 6–10, 53.

66. Id. at 53.

67. Id. at 4.

68. Id. at 32, 45.

69. Id. at 32.

70. Id. at 28–29.

71. Id. at 33.

72. Id. at 8–9.

73. RICKS, *supra* note 53, at 96–100.

74. GORDON & TRAINOR, *supra* note 54, at 46.

75. Id. at 88.

76. On this stage of the prewar planning, see id. at 88–100.

77. Id. at 101–03.

78. Id. at 82–83.

79. Id. at 74, 105.

80. Id. at 140–41.

81. Id. at 141.

82. Id. at 142.

83. See generally id. at 143–58.

84. Id. at 162.

85. Id. at 484.

86. Peter J. Spiro, *War Powers and the Sirens of Formalism*, 68 N.Y.U. L. REV. 1338, 1348, 1352–53 (1993).

87. For an important argument as to how the presidency's "singularity" and "visibility" increase the vulnerability of the office, see Michael A. Fitts, *The Paradox of Power in the Modern State: Why a Unitary, Centralized Presidency May Not Exhibit Effective or Legitimate Leadership*, 144 U. PA. L. REV. 827 (1996).

88. MCNAMARA, *supra* note 9, at 101.

89. Id. at 165.

90. Id. at 192–94.

91. Id. at 52–55.

92. Id. at 156, 192–93.

93. Id. at 148.

94. Id. at 106.

95. Id. at 190–91.

96. My account is based on Alexander L. George, *The Case for Multiple Advocacy in Making Foreign Policy*, 66 AM. POL. SCI. REV. 751, 771 (1972).

97. Id.

Chapter Four

1. JAMES RISEN, STATE OF WAR: THE SECRET HISTORY OF THE CIA AND THE BUSH ADMINISTRATION 44 (2006).

2. Id.

3. The following account of the mid-1970s intelligence scandals is taken from PE-
TER M. SHANE & HAROLD H. BRUFF, SEPARATION OF POWERS LAW: CASES AND
MATERIALS 755–58 (2d ed. 2005).

4. Intelligence Activities and the Rights of Americans, Final Report of the Select Committee to Study Governmental Operations with Respect to Intelligence Activities, S. Rpt.
755, 94th Cong., 2d Sess., II: 277, 280–81 (1976).

5. Katz v. United States, 389 U.S. 347 (1967).

6. Pub. L. 90-351, 82 Stat. 197 (1968).

7. The text as originally enacted appears at Pub. L. 90-351, Title III, § 802, June 19, 1968,
82 Stat. 213. The current provision appears at 18 U.S.C. § 2511.

8. 82 Stat. 214 (formerly 18 U.S.C. § 2511 (3)).

9. 407 U.S. 297 (1972).

10. Id. at 308.

11. Id. at 322–23.

12. Pub. L. 95-511, 92 Stat 1783 (1978). FISA has been subject to a variety of amendments
since its original enactment, including a controversial series of changes adopted in the
FISA Amendments Act of 2008, Pub. L. No. 110-61, 122 Stat. 2436. The 2008 Amendments, however, did not reword the provisions of law discussed in the text, except to
occasionally relocate them. Where citations appear to FISA without a date specification,
the provision is located identically now and during the period discussed in the text.
Where the location has changed, I have cited the provision as it appears in the 2006 edi-
tion of the U.S. Code, as well as its current location.

13. 50 U.S.C. § 1802(a)(1)(B).

14. 50 U.S.C. § 1802(a)(1).

15. 50 U.S.C. § 1804(a). Under the FISA Amendments Act of 2008, United States persons may be subject to electronic surveillance even if they are not agents of a foreign
power as long as they are reasonably believed to be outside the United States at the time
of surveillance. Such surveillance must still be designed, however, to acquire foreign
intelligence information, and is still subject, except in emergencies, to the requirement
for prior authorization by the FISA Court. FISA Amendments Act of 2008, Pub. L. No.
110-61, § 101(a)(2), 122 Stat. 2438, codified at 50 U.S.C. § 1881a.

16. 50 U.S.C. § 1801(a) and (b).

17. 50 U.S.C. § 1804(a)(7) (2006), now codified at 50 U.S.C. § 1804 (a)(6).

18. 50 U.S.C. § 1801(e).

19. 50 U.S.C. § 1804(a)(5) (2006), now codified at 50 U.S.C. § 1804 (a)(4).

20. 50 U.S.C. § 1801(h).

21. 50 U.S.C. § 1801(h)(2).

22. 50 U.S.C. § 1811.

23. 18 U.S.C. § 2511(f). Prior to enactment of the FISA Amendments Act of 2008, Pub.
L. No. 110-61, 122 Stat. 2436, the exclusivity of FISA and Title III as legally authorized
methods of conducting electronic surveillance was stated explicitly only in the federal
criminal code, Title 18 of the U.S. Code, not Title 50, where the main body of FISA is
codified. The 2008 Act amended Title 50 to make the exclusivity point explicit in that

location, too. Id., § 102(a), 122 Stat. 2459, codified at 50 U.S.C. § 1812. As numerous critics pointed out, however, this did not change the law, but chiefly restated in a second location what FISA originally provided.

24. James Risen & Eric Lichtblau, *Bush Lets U.S. Spy on Callers Without Courts,* N.Y. TIMES, Dec. 16, 2005, at 1.

25. USA PATRIOT Act, Pub. L. No. 107-56 , § 206, 115 Stat. 282 (2001).

26. My account of the TSP relies generally on RISEN, *supra* note 1, at 39–60.

27. Id. at 51.

28. White House Press Briefing by Hon. Alberto Gonzales, Dec. 19, 2005, quoted in White House Press Release, Setting the Record Straight: Critics Launch Attacks Against Program to Detect and Prevent Terrorist Attacks (Jan. 4, 2006), available at http://www. whitehouse.gov/news/releases/2006/01/20060104-7.html.

29. Id.

30. Lowell Bergman, Eric Lichtblau, Scott Shane, & Don Van Natta, *Spy Agency Data After Sept. 11 Led F.B.I. to Dead Ends,* N.Y. TIMES, Jan. 16, 2006, at 1.

31. White House Press Release, President Bush: Information Sharing, Patriot Act Vital to Homeland Security (Remarks by the President in a Conversation on the USA Patriot Act, Kleinshans Music Hall, Buffalo, N.Y.), April 20, 2004, available at http://www.white-house.gov/news/releases/2004/04/20040420-2.html.

32. RISEN, *supra* note 1, at 57.

33. Daniel Klaidman, Stuart Taylor, Jr., & Evan Thomas, *They were loyal conservatives, and Bush appointees. They fought a quiet battle to rein in the president's power in the war on terror. And they paid a price for it,* NEWSWEEK, Feb. 6, 2006, at 34.

34. JACK GOLDSMITH, THE TERROR PRESIDENCY: LAW AND JUDGMENT INSIDE THE BUSH ADMINISTRATION 181 (2007).

35. Id.

36. U.S. Department of Justice, Legal Authorities Supporting the Activities of the National Security Agency Described by the President (Jan. 19, 2006), *reprinted in* David Cole & Martin S. Lederman, *The National Security Agency's Domestic Spying Program: Framing the Debate,* 81 IND. L. REV. 1355, 1374 (2006) (hereafter NSA Legal Authorities).

37. Letter from William E. Moschella, Assistant Attorney General, Office of Legal Affairs, U.S. Department of Justice to the Leadership of the Senate Select Committee on Intelligence and the House Permanent Select Committee on Intelligence (Dec. 22, 2005), *reprinted in* Cole & Lederman, *supra* note 36, at 1360.

38. Pub. L. No. 107-40, 15 Stat. 224 (2001) (hereafter AUMF).

39. NSA Legal Authorities, *supra* note 36, at 1379–90.

40. Id. at 1407.

41. AUMF, *supra* note 38, § 2(a).

42. Hamdi v. Rumsfeld, 542 U.S. 507, 518 (2004).

43. 18 U.S.C. § 2511(2)(f).

44. The Administration proffered an alternative version of this argument, under which FISA need not be implicitly repealed because FISA supposedly acknowledges that some

statute other than either FISA or Title III might authorize electronic surveillance. Specifically, 50 U.S.C. § 1809 makes it unlawful to conduct electronic surveillance except as "authorized by statute." Read in the context of FISA as a whole, however, it is patent that Congress meant to include in the phrase "by statute" only FISA itself and Title III. Unless that were so, the statement in 18 U.S.C. § 2511(2)(f) that FISA and Title III are the "exclusive means" by which electronic surveillance may be conducted would make no sense.

45. 50 U.S.C. § 1811.

46. NSA Legal Authorities, *supra* note 36, at 1407.

47. The first Supreme Court decision to construe electronic surveillance as a form of search under the Fourth Amendment was Katz v. United States, 389 U.S. 347 (1967).

48. February 2, 2006 Letter from Scholars and Former Government Officials to Congressional Leadership in Response to Justice Department Whitepaper of January 19, 2006, *reprinted in* Cole & Lederman, *supra* note 36, at 1420.

49. My account of Administration lawyering with regard to the warrantless surveillance issue is based on Klaidman et al., *supra* note 33, at 34.

50. GOLDSMITH, *supra* note 34, at 170.

51. Klaidman et al., *supra* note 33, revealed the fact of a hospital pilgrimage, but its full details later emerged through testimony by former Deputy Attorney General Comey to the Senate Judiciary Committee. Testimony of James B. Comey, Former Deputy Attorney General, U.S. Department of Justice to the Committee on the Judiciary, *Hearing on Preserving Prosecutorial Independence: Is the Department of Justice Politicizing the Hiring and Firing of U.S. Attorneys?—Part IV,* U.S. Senate, 110th Cong., 1st Sess. (2006), available at http://www.washingtonpost.com/wp-dyn/content/article/2007/05/15/AR2007051501043.html.

52. The key memos are reprinted in KAREN J. GREENBERG & JOSHUA L. DRATEL, THE TORTURE PAPERS: THE ROAD TO ABU GHRAIB 3–24, 38–222 (2005) (hereafter TORTURE PAPERS).

53. Rasul v. Bush, 542 U.S. 466 (2004).

54. Hamdan v. Rumsfeld, 126 S. Ct. 2749, 2794–96 (2006).

55. Id. at 2797–98.

56. Memorandum from Jay S. Bybee, Assistant Attorney General, U.S. Department of Justice to Alberto R. Gonzales, Counsel to the President, and William J. Haynes, General Counsel, Department of Defense, Re: Application of Treaties and Laws to al Qaeda and Taliban Detainees (Jan. 22, 2002), *reprinted in* TORTURE PAPERS, *supra* note 52, at 81, 110–11; Memorandum from Jay B. Bybee, Assistant Attorney General, U.S. Department of Justice to Alberto R. Gonzales, Counsel to the President, Re: Status of Taliban Forces Under Article 4 of the Third Geneva Convention of 1949 (Feb. 7, 2002), *reprinted in* TORTURE PAPERS, *supra* note 52, at 136.

57. Quoted in the January 22, 2002 Bybee memorandum, *supra* note 56, at 110, and in the February 7, 2002 Bybee memorandum, *supra* note 56, at 142.

58. January 22, 2002 Bybee memorandum, *supra* note 56, at 110–11; February 7, 2002 Bybee memorandum, *supra* note 56, at 142.

59. GOLDSMITH, *supra* note 34, at 148.

60. Memorandum of Jay S. Bybee, Assistant Attorney General, U.S. Department of Justice for Alberto Gonzales, Counsel to the President, Re: Standards of Conduct for Interrogation Under 18 U.S.C. §§ 2340–40A (Aug. 26, 2002), *reprinted in* TORTURE PAPERS, *supra* note 52, at 172, 207 (hereafter DOJ Torture Memo).

61. GOLDSMITH, *supra* note 34, at 150.

62. 18 U.S.C. § 2340

63. Id. at 176.

64. Id.

65. OLC relied on this analysis also in a subsequent March 14, 2003 opinion issued regarding the legal limits (or lack of them) on interrogations conducted by members of the Armed Services. See Memorandum from John C. Yoo, Deputy Assistant Attorney General, for William J. Haynes II, General Counsel of the Department of Defense, Re: Military Interrogation of Alien Unlawful Combatants Held Outside the United States 38–39 (Mar. 14, 2003), available at http://f11.findlaw.com/news.findlaw.com/hdocs/docs/doj/johnyooolc2003interrogationmemo.pdf.

66. 18 U.S.C. § 2340(2) (emphasis added).

67. See generally Walter E. Dellinger et al., *Principles to Guide the Office of Legal Counsel,* 81 IND. L.J. 1348 (2006), discussed in chapter 5.

68. GOLDSMITH, *supra* note 34, at 151.

69. Tim Golden, *After Terror, a Secret Rewriting of Military Law,* N.Y. TIMES, Oct. 24, 2004, at 1.

70. Klaidman et al., *supra* note 33, at 34.

71. Memorandum from John Yoo, Deputy Assistant Attorney General, U.S. Department of Justice, Office of Legal Counsel, to Timothy Flanigan, Deputy Counsel to the President, Re: Memorandum Opinion for the Deputy Counsel to the President (Sept. 25, 2001), *reprinted in* TORTURE PAPERS, *supra* note 52, at 3, 24.

72. Golden, *supra* note 69, at 12.

73. 66 Fed. Reg. 57831 (2001).

74. Golden, *supra* note 69, at 13.

75. Tim Golden, *Administration Officials Split over Stalled Military Tribunals,* N.Y. TIMES, Oct. 25, 2004, at 1, 8.

76. Golden, *supra* note 69, at 13.

77. This account is derived from Jane Mayer, *The Memo,* NEW YORKER, Feb. 27, 2006, at 32.

78. Id.

79. Working Group Report on Detainee Interrogations in the Global War on Terrorism: Assessment of Legal, Historical, Policy, and Operational Considerations (Apr. 4, 2003), *reprinted in* TORTURE PAPERS, *supra* note 52, at 286, 341–46.

80. Klaidman et al., *supra* note 33, at 34.

81. GOLDSMITH, *supra* note 34, at 22–23.

82. Memorandum of Daniel Levin, Acting Assistant Attorney General, Office of Legal Counsel, U.S. Department of Justice, to James B. Comey, Deputy Attorney General, Re:

Legal Standards Applicable Under 18 U.S.C. §§ 2340–40A (Dec. 30, 2004), available at http://www.usdoj.gov/olc/18usc23402340a2.htm.

83. Mayer, *supra* note 77, at 41.

84. RISEN, *supra* note 1, at 34–35; Jane Mayer, *Outsourcing Torture,* NEW YORKER, Feb. 14, 2005, at 106.

85. Remarks of Secretary Condoleeza Rice upon Her Departure for Europe (Dec. 5, 2005), available at http://www.state.gov/secretary/rm/2005/57602.htm.

86. Jules Lobel, *The Preventive Paradigm and the Perils of Ad Hoc Balancing,* 91 MINN. L. REV. 1407, 1409 (2007).

87. See, e.g., Stephen Grey & Renwick Mclean, *Spain Looks into C.I.A.'s Handling of Detainees,* N.Y. TIMES, Nov. 14, 2005, at A8; Ian Fisher, *Reports of Secret U.S. Prisons in Europe Draw Ire and Otherwise Red Face,* N.Y. TIMES, Dec. 1, 2005, at A14.

88. Ian Fisher & Elisabetta Povoledo, *Italy Braces for Legal Fight over Secret C.I.A. Program,* N.Y. TIMES, June 8, 2007, at A1.

89. Doug Struck, *Tortured Man Gets Apology from Canada,* WASH. POST, Jan 27, 2007, at A14 (indicated amounts are in Canadian dollars).

90. Draft Memorandum for Alberto Gonzales, Counsel to the President, from Jack Goldsmith, Assistant Attorney General, Office of Legal Counsel, Re: Permissibility of Relocating Certain "Protected Persons" from Occupied Iraq (March 19, 2004), *reprinted in* TORTURE PAPERS, *supra* note 52, at 367.

91. Convention Against Torture and Other Cruel, Inhuman or Degrading Treatment or Punishment, Art. 3, § 1, G.A. res. 39/46, [annex, 39 U.N. GAOR Supp. (No. 51) at 197, U.N. Doc. A/39/51 (1984)], *entered into force* June 26, 1987.

92. Will Sullivan, *Five Years and Counting in Cuba,* U.S. NEWS & WORLD REPORT, Dec. 31, 2006, available at http://www.usnews.com/usnews/news/articles/061231/8guantanamo.htm.

93. Joseph Margulies & Lawrence Wilkerson, *Guantanamo Prison Observes Sad Anniversary,* MIAMI HERALD, Jan. 28, 2007, available at http://www.constitutionproject.org/libertyandsecurity/article.cfm?messageID=285&categoryId=3.

94. Id.

95. Id.

Chapter Five

1. "In the weeks following the terrorist attacks on our nation, I authorized the National Security Agency, consistent with U.S. law and the Constitution, to intercept the international communications of people with known links to al Qaeda and related terrorist organizations." Radio Address by President George W. Bush, Dec. 17, 2005, transcript available at http://www.whitehouse.gov/news/releases/2005/12/20051217.html.

2. President Discusses Creation of Military Commissions to Try Suspected Terrorists, Press Release, Sept. 6, 2006, available at http://www.whitehouse.gov/news/releases/2006/09/20060906-3.html.

3. United States v. Nixon, 418 U.S. 684 (1974).

4. I gratefully borrow the dichotomy of "overseer" and "decider" from the work of Professor Peter Strauss. Peter L. Strauss, *The President as the "Decider" in Administrative Law,* 75 GEO. WASH. L. REV. 696 (2007).

5. The issues are well explored in Jeremy Waldron, *Is the Rule of Law and Essentially Contested Concept (in Florida)?* 21 LAW & PHIL. 137 (2002).

6. I have earlier explored some of the ideas of this section in Peter M. Shane, *Legal Disagreement and Negotiation in a Government of Laws: The Case of Executive Privilege Claims Against Congress,* 71 MINN. L. REV. 461 (1987).

7. 47 U.S.C. § 303.

8. 5 U.S.C. § 552(a)(6)(A)(i).

9. James G. March & Johan P. Olson, *Elaborating the "New Institutionalism,"* in R. A. W. RHODES, SARAH A. BINDER, & BERT A. ROCKMAN, THE OXFORD HANDBOOK OF POLITICAL INSTITUTIONS, at 3, 3 (2006) (hereafter OXFORD HANDBOOK).

10. Kenneth A. Shepsle, "Rational Choice Institutionalism," in OXFORD HANDBOOK, *supra* note 9, at 23, 27.

11. Id.

12. Id. at 30.

13. "Ordinarily, I would be content to say that it is not within the province of the Attorney General to declare an act of Congress unconstitutional—at least, where it does not involve any conflict between the prerogatives of the legislative department and those of the executive department—and that when an act like this, of general application, is passed it is the duty of the executive department to administer it until it is declared unconstitutional by the courts." Rendition of Opinions on Constitutionality of Statutes—Federal Home Loan Bank Act, 39 Op. Att'y. Gen. 11, (1937), *quoting* Income Tax-Salaries of President and Federal Judges, 31 Op. Att'y. Gen. 475, 476 (1919).

14. U.S. Const., Art. II, § 1.

15. U.S. Const., Art. II, § 3.

16. JACK GOLDSMITH, THE TERROR PRESIDENCY: LAW AND JUDGMENT INSIDE THE BUSH ADMINISTRATION 33 (2007).

17. Memorandum from Jay S. Bybee, Assistant Attorney General, U.S. Department of Justice, for Alberto R. Gonzales, Counsel to the President, Re: Standards of Conduct for Interrogation Under 18 U.S.C. §§ 2340–40A, *reprinted in* KAREN J. GREENBERG & JOSHUA L. DRATEL, THE TORTURE PAPERS: THE ROAD TO ABU GHRAIB 172 (2005).

18. Walter E. Dellinger et al., *Principles to Guide the Office of Legal Counsel,* 81 IND. L.J. 1348 (2006).

19. Id. at 1350.

20. Id. at 1353.

21. Id. at 1349.

22. U.S. Const., Art. I, § 8.

23. Lawrence Lessig & Cass R. Sunstein, *The President and the Administration,* COLUM. L. REV. 1, 106 (1994).

24. See generally Steven G. Calabresi, *Some Normative Arguments for the Unitary Executive,* 48 ARK. L. REV. 24 (1995).

25. Information Security Oversight Office of the National Archives and Records Administration, 2005 Report to the President 13 (2006), available at http://www.archives.gov/isoo/reports/2005-annual-report.pdf. In 2005, the number of classification decisions dropped again to about 14.2 million. Id.

26. Id. at 15.

27. John Podesta, *Need to Know—Governing in Secret,* in PETER M. SHANE, JOHN PODESTA, & RICHARD C. LEONE, EDS., A LITTLE KNOWLEDGE: PRIVACY, SECURITY, AND PUBLIC INFORMATION AFTER SEPTEMBER 11, at 11, 13 (2004).

28. Coalition of Journalists for Open Government, Federal Government Continues to Fall Behind in Responding to FOIA Requests, CJOG Finds (June 2006), available at http://www.cjog.net/documents/.pdf.

29. Id.

30. Cheney v. U.S. District Court for the District of Columbia, 542 U.S. 367 (2004).

31. Exec. Order No. 13,233, 66 Fed. Reg. 56025 (2001).

32. See, e.g., United States v. Reynolds, 345 U.S. 1 (1953).

33. See United States v. Nixon, 418 U.S. 683 (1974).

34. Letter from Attorney General William French Smith to President Reagan (Oct. 13, 1981), *reprinted in* PETER M. SHANE & HAROLD H. BRUFF, SEPARATION OF POWERS LAW: CASES AND MATERIALS 359, 360 (2d ed. 2005). Deliberative privilege is implicitly recognized in the Freedom of Information Act exemption from mandatory disclosure of government documents that would not be "available by law" to private parties in litigation with the government, 5 U.S.C. § 552(b)(5).

35. 418 U.S. at 705–06.

36. U.S. Const., Art. 1, § 5.

37. 418 U.S. at 705–06.

38. Id. at 706.

39. Id. at 708–13.

40. Letter from Attorney General William French Smith to President Reagan (Oct. 13, 1981), *reprinted in* SHANE & BRUFF, *supra* note 34, at 359, 361 (2d ed. 2005).

41. Letter from Attorney General William French Smith to Hon. John D. Dingell, Chairman, Subcommittee on Oversight and Investigations, Committee on Energy and Commerce (Nov. 30, 1982), *reprinted in* SHANE & BRUFF, *supra* note 34, at 349, 351.

42. Letter from Fred W. Fielding, Counsel to the President, to Messrs. Leahy and Conyers (June 28, 2007), available at http://leahy.senate.gov/press/200706/6-28-07%20ltr%20from%20WH.pdf.

43. Cheney v. U.S. District Court for the District of Columbia, 542 U.S. 367, 373 (2004).

44. Judicial Watch, Inc. v. National Energy Policy Development Group, 219 F. Supp. 2d 20, 42 (D.D.C. 2002).

45. 5 U.S.C. App. 2 §§ 1–16 and at § 3 (2).

46. Judicial Watch, Inc. v. National Energy Policy Development Group, 219 F. Supp. 2d 20, 54 (D.D.C. 2002).

47. In re Cheney, 334 F.3d 1096, 1104–05 (D.C. Cir. 2003).

48. Cheney v. U.S. District Court for the District of Columbia, 542 U.S. 367, 381–82 (2004).

49. In re Cheney, 406 F.3d 723 (D.C. Cir. 2005) (en banc).

50. Id. at 728.

51. Walker v. Cheney, 230 F. Supp. 2d 51, 55 (D.D.C. 2002).

52. Id. at 56.

53. Id. at 57.

54. Id. at 58.

55. Id.

56. U.S. Const., Art. II, § 2.

57. U.S. Const., Art. II, § 3.

58. Walker v. Cheney, 230 F. Supp. 2d 51, 59 (D.D.C. 2002).

59. Id. at 65–70.

60. The position of Vice President Cheney on executive privilege turned out to be more than a little ironic given a subsequent dispute between his office and the Information Security Oversight Office (ISOO) of the National Archive and Records Administration. The ISOO is charged under Executive Order No. 12958, as amended by Executive Order No. 13292, 68 Fed. Reg. 16315 (2003), with monitoring the activities of all executive branch agencies in dealing with classified information. In June 2007, it became well publicized that Cheney's office had refused to comply with the order for at least four years, even though the order expressly covers "any . . . entity within the executive branch that comes into the possession of classified information." Cheney argued that it was inappropriate to treat him as an executive agency because, as the constitutionally designated President of the Senate, he also performed significant functions for the legislative branch.

This was a stunning constitutional suggestion. Article I of the Constitution explicitly prohibits anyone from serving simultaneously in both the legislative and executive branches. Although Cheney avoided explicitly claiming that he is an officer of both branches, his argument is in transparent tension with the founders' express understanding of the government structure they were creating. It is also worth noting that the reason for positioning the Vice President as President of the Senate was not to render him an important legislative functionary, but to prevent the conflict of interest that would have been posed had a member of the Senate, selected to represent a particular state, been charged with taking on the more limited tie-breaking role as President, thus compromising his ability to represent his state in every Senate vote. Treating this role as somehow assimilating the Vice President's office to the legislative branch is quite a reach, to put it mildly. Understandably, the Vice President incurred substantial criticism from Congress and the press for seeming to fancy himself, alone among all officers of the United States, to be so clothed in executive power as to be invulnerable to Congress's claims of legislative oversight and simultaneously, so wrapped in legislative authority as to render him immune from accountability even to the President.

61. Exec. Order No. 13,233, 66 Fed. Reg. 56025 (2001).

62. Pub. L. 95-591, 92 Stat. 2523 (1978), codified at 44 U.S.C. §§ 2201–7.

63. 44 U.S.C. § 2203(f)(1).

64. 44 U.S.C. § 2204(a).

65. 44 U.S.C. § 2204(a)(5).

66. 44 U.S.C. § 2204(a)(6).

67. 5 U.S.C. § 552(b)(5).

68. 44 U.S.C. § 2204(c)(1).

69. 44 U.S.C. § 2204(c)(2).

70. 44 U.S.C. § 2204(b)(3).

71. 44 U.S.C. § 2206(2).

72. 44 U.S.C. § 2204(e).

73. 36 C.F.R. § 1270.46(d).

74. 36 C.F.R. § 1270.46(e).

75. Exec. Order No. 12,667, 54 Fed. Reg. 3403 (1989).

76. Id. § 2(a).

77. Id. § 2(b).

78. Id. § 4(b).

79. Exec. Order No. 13,233, § 10.

80. Id.

81. Id. § 3(d)(1)(ii).

82. Id. § 11.

83. Id.

84. Available at http://www.theonion.com/content/node/51140.

85. U.S. Const., Art. 1, § 7.

86. The following is typical of the genre: "While I am signing S. 1192, it contains a legislative veto provision which the Attorney General advises is unconstitutional. Section 114(e) of the bill would purport to authorize either of two committees of Congress to pass a resolution disapproving the expenditure of any sums in excess of $29 million from certain rail programs for the rehabilitation of Union Station. However, committees of Congress cannot bind the executive branch in the execution of the law by passing a resolution that is not adopted by both Houses of Congress and presented to the President for approval or veto. Accordingly, this language of section 114(e) must be objected to on constitutional grounds. The Secretary of Transportation will not, consistent with this objection, regard himself as legally bound by any such resolution." Statement on Signing the Union Station Redevelopment Act of 1981, 1981 Public Papers Pres. 1207.

87. Immigration and Naturalization Service v. Chadha, 462 U.S. 919, 968–69 (1983) (White, J., dissenting).

88. See generally RICHARD J. PIERCE, JR., SIDNEY A. SHAPIRO, & PAUL R. VERKUIL, ADMINISTRATIVE LAW AND PROCESS 62–68 (4th ed. 2004).

89. Immigration and Naturalization Service v. Chadha, 462 U.S. 919 (1983).

90. See generally Harold H. Bruff & Ernest Gellhorn, *Congressional Control of Administrative Regulation: A Study of Legislative Vetoes,* 90 HARV. L. REV. 1369 (1977).

91. CHRISTOPHER N. MAY, PRESIDENTIAL DEFIANCE OF "UNCONSTITUTIONAL" LAWS: REVIVING THE ROYAL PREROGATIVE 76 (1998).

92. Report of the American Bar Association Task Force on Presidential Signing Statements and the Separation of Powers Doctrine, at 10 (Aug. 2006), available at http://www. abanet.org/op/signingstatements/aba_final_signing_statements_recommendation-report_7-24-06.pdf.

93. T. J. Halstead, Presidential Signing Statements: Constitutional and Institutional Implications 3 (CRS Report for Congress Apr. 13, 2007).

94. Id. at 5.

95. Id. at 6.

96. The Bush Administration's signing statement practices were first brought effectively to light in a series of Pulitzer Prize–winning articles by *Boston Globe* reporter Charlie Savage. See, e.g., Charlie Savage, *Bush Challenges Hundreds of Laws, President Cites Powers of His Office,* BOSTON GLOBE, Apr. 30, 2006, available at http://www. boston.com/news/nation/washington/articles/2006/04/30/bush_challenges_ hundreds_of_laws/. (Credit for early spotting also goes to Dahlia Lithwick of *Slate.* Dahlia Lithwick, *Sign Here: Presidential Signing Statements Are More than Just Executive Branch Lunacy,* SLATE, Jan. 30, 2006, available at http://www.slate.com/id/2134919/.) Savage integrated his research on signing statements into a far more comprehensive account of the ways in which the Bush 43 Administration sought to consolidate executive branch power. His account treats Vice President Cheney as the key leader in the campaign to resuscitate the Nixonian view of the Presidency, largely as a reaction to his personal discontents with congressional reactions to Watergate and the Iran-Contra affair. CHARLIE SAVAGE, TAKEOVER: THE RETURN OF THE IMPERIAL PRESIDENCY AND THE SUBVERSION OF AMERICAN DEMOCRACY (2007). It was Savage's articles that gave impetus to the research Neil Kinkopf and I conducted, on which this section is based.

97. Neil Kinkopf & Peter M. Shane, Signed Under Protest: A Database of Presidential Signing Statements, 2001–2006 (2007), available at http://papers.ssrn.com/sol3/papers. cfm?abstract_id=1022202.

98. Pub. L. No. 109-435, 120 Stat. 3198 (2006).

99. 39 U.S.C. § 502.

100. Statement on Signing the Postal Accountability and Enhancement Act, 42 WEEKLY COMP. PRES. DOCS. 2196 (2006).

101. Id.

102. Kinkopf & Shane, *supra* note 97, at 178.

103. Statement on Signing the Intelligence Authorization Act for Fiscal Year 2002, 37 WEEKLY COMP. PRES. DOCS. 1835 (2001).

104. Pub. L. No. 107-108, § 305, 115 Stat. 1398 (2001), codified at 50 U.S.C. § 413a.

105. Statement on Signing the Syria Accountability and Lebanese Sovereignty Restoration Act of 2003, 39 WEEKLY COMP. PRES. DOCS. 1795 (2003).

106. Pub. L. 108-175, § 5(a)(b), 117 Stat. 2482, 2487–88 (2003).

107. Pub. L. 107-117, § 8098, 115 Stat. 2230, 2268 (2002).

108. Statement on Signing the Department of Defense and Emergency Supplemental Appropriations for Recovery from and Response to Terrorist Attacks on the United States Act, 2002, 38 WEEKLY COMP. PRES. DOCS. 46 (2002).

109. Kinkopf & Shane, *supra* note 97, at 178.

110. Gerhard Casper, *An Essay in Separation of Powers: Some Early Versions and Practices*, 30 WM. & MARY L. REV. 211, 240–42; Jerry L. Mashaw, *Recovering American Administrative Law: Federalist Foundations 1787–1801*, 115 YALE L.J. 1256, 1284–87 (2006).

111. Kinkopf & Shane, *supra* note 97, at 178.

112. See, e.g., Statement on Signing the Ronald W. Reagan National Defense Authorization Act for Fiscal Year 2005, 40 WEEKLY COMP. PRES. DOC. 2673 (2004), objecting to Pub. L. 108-375, § 1207(b)(1), 118 Stat. 1811, 2085 (2004).

113. See, e.g., Statement on Signing the Coast Guard and Maritime Transportation Act of 2004, 40 WEEKLY COMP. PRES. DOC. 1518 (2004), objecting to Pub. L. 108-293, §§ 217, 708(c)(2), and 803(c)(11), 118 Stat. 1028, 1038, 1077, 1081 (2004).

114. Pub. L. 107-279, § 115, 116 Stat 1940, 1948 (2002).

115. Id. at § 11, 116 Stat. 1944, codified at 20 U.S.C. § 9511.

116. Id. at § 115, 116 Stat 1948.

117. Statement on Signing Legislation to Provide for Improvement of Federal Education Research, Statistics, Evaluation, Information, Dissemination and for Other Purposes, 38 WEEKLY COMP. PRES. DOCS. 1995 (2002).

118. Pub. L. 108-465, §1408A(d), 118 Stat. 3882, 3886 (2004).

119. Statement by President George W. Bush upon Signing H.R. 3242, 40 WEEKLY COMP. PRES. DOC. 3009 (2004).

120. Pub. L. No. 109-435, § 1010, 120 Stat. 3198, 3262 (2006), amending 39 U.S.C. § 404.

121. Statement on Signing the Postal Accountability and Enhancement Act, 42 WEEKLY COMP. PRES. DOCS. 2196 (2006).

122. S. Res. 22, 110th Cong., 1st Sess. (2007).

123. See generally Elena Kagan, *Presidential Administration*, 114 HARV. L. REV. 2245 (2001).

Chapter Six

1. *Bush: "I'm the decider" on Rumsfeld*, CNN.com, April 18, 2006, available at http://www.cnn.com/2006/POLITICS/04/18/rumsfeld/.

2. JERRY L. MASHAW, RICHARD A. MERRILL, & PETER M. SHANE, ADMINISTRATIVE LAW—THE AMERICAN PUBLIC LAW SYSTEM 4–6 (5th ed. 2003).

3. Exec. Order No. 12,044, § 2(d), 43 Fed. Reg. 12661 (1978).

4. See JOHN QUARLES, CLEANING UP AMERICA: AN INSIDER'S VIEW OF THE ENVIRONMENTAL PROTECTION AGENCY 117–42 (1976).

5. Inflation Impact Statements, Exec. Order No. 11,821, 39 Fed. Reg. 41501 (1974).

6. Exec. Order No. 12,044, 43 Fed. Reg. 12661 (1978).

7. John D. Graham, Paul R. Noe, & Elizabeth L. Branch, *Managing the Regulatory State: The Experience of the Bush Administration*, 33 FORD. URB. L.J. 953, 958 n.26 (2006).

8. Exec. Order No. 12,044, § 2(d), 43 Fed. Reg. 12661 (1978).

9. Exec. Order No. 12,291, 46 Fed. Reg. 13193 (1981).

10. Proposed Executive Order Entitled "Federal Regulation," 5 O.L.C. 59, 63 (1981).

11. Id.

12. Regulatory Planning Process, Exec. Order No. 12,498, § 2(a), 50 Fed. Reg. 1036 (1985).

13. Id., § 3(a), 50 Fed. Reg. at 1037.

14. Executive Order No. 12,291, §6, 46 Fed. Reg. at 13196.

15. Peter M. Shane, *Political Accountability in a System of Checks and Balances: The Case of Presidential Review of Rulemaking,* 48 ARK. L. REV. 161, 165–74 (1994).

16. Nicholas Bagley & Richard L. Revesz, *Centralized Oversight of the Regulatory State,* 106 COLUM. L. REV. 1260, 1310–12 (2006).

17. Bob Woodward & David S. Broder, *Quayle's Quest: Curb Rules, Leave "No Fingerprints,"* WASH. POST, Jan. 9, 1992, at A1.

18. Id.

19. Regulatory Planning and Review, Exec. Order No. 12,866, 58 Fed. Reg. 51735 (1993).

20. Id., § 1.

21. Id., § 9.

22. For a comprehensive review of the differences between the Clinton order and its Reagan predecessor, see Shane, *supra* note 15, at 174–92.

23. Elimination of One-Half of Executive Branch Internal Regulations, Exec. Order No. 12,861, 58 Fed. Reg. 48255 (1993).

24. Elena Kagan, *Presidential Administration,* 114 HARV. L. REV. 2245, 2282–84, 2295 (1991).

25. Id. at 2251.

26. Id.

27. Neil Kinkopf & Peter M. Shane, Signed for Under Protest: A Database of Presidential Signing Statements, 2001–2006 (2007), at 178, available at http://papers.ssrn.com/sol3/papers.cfm?abstract_id=1022202.

28. Agency Responsibilities with Respect to Faith-Based and Community Initiatives, Exec. Order No. 13,198, 66 Fed. Reg. 8497 (2001).

29. Equal Protection of the Laws for Faith-Based and Community Organizations, Exec. Order No. 13,279, 67 Fed. Reg. 77141 (2002).

30. Address to the Nation on Stem-Cell Research from Crawford, Texas, 37 WEEKLY COMP. PRES. DOCS. 1149 (Aug. 13, 2001).

31. 42 U.S.C. § 282.

32. Testimony of Sally Katzen Before the House Committee on the Judiciary, Subcommittee on Commercial and Administrative Law, 110th Cong., 1st Sess. (Feb. 13, 2007).

33. John D. Graham, *The Evolving Role of the U.S. Office of Management and Budget in Regulatory Policy* (AEI-Brookings Joint Center for Regulatory Issues Working Paper No. 07-04, Feb. 2007).

34. Tarek Maassarani, *Redacting the Science of Climate Change: An Investigative and Synthesis Report* (Government Accountability Project, Mar. 2007), available at http://www.whistleblower.org/doc/2007/Final%203.28%20Redacting%20Climate%20Science%20Report.pdf.

35. Bithika Khargarhia, *Cooney Defends the Changes He Had Made in Climate Reports*, MONEY TIMES (Mar. 20, 2007), available at http://www.themoneytimes.com/articles/20070320/cooney_defends_will_to_may_changings_he_had_made_in_climate_reports-id-103138.html.

36. Further Amendment to Executive Order 12866 on Regulatory Planning and Review, Exec. Order No. 13,422, 72 Fed. Reg. 2763 (2007).

37. Jim Rutenberg, *Bush Uses Recess to Fill Envoy Post and 2 Others*, N.Y. TIMES, Apr. 5, 2007, at A1.

38. Exec. Order No. 13,422, § 5(b), 72 Fed. Reg. at 2764.

39. See Peter L. Strauss, *Presidential Rulemaking*, 72 CHI-KENT L. REV. 965 (1997).

40. Edward Rubin, *The Myth of Accountability and the Anti-administrative Impulse*, 103 MICH. L REV. 2073 (2005).

41. 5 U.S.C. § 553.

42. 5 U.S.C. § 552(b)(5).

43. See United States v. Nixon, 418 U.S. 683 (1974).

44. Public choice theorists typically invoke Arrow's Theorem to "prove" that a legislature governed by majority rule cannot reach an optimal "resolution among three or more mutually exclusive alternatives that are voted on pairwise." WILLIAM N. ESKRIDGE, JR., & PHILIP P. FRICKEY, CASES AND MATERIALS ON LEGISLATION: STATUTES AND THE CREATION OF PUBLIC POLICY 50 (1988). Given presidential candidates who represent dozens of alternative policy positions on matters of interest to voters, it is surely even less plausible that an electoral victory for a single candidate represents an optimal resolution of voter disagreements on all of those issues. On the "practical impossibility in our political system of ascertaining mandates" through presidential elections, see NELSON W. POLSBY & AARON B. WILDAVSKY, PRESIDENTIAL ELECTIONS: STRATEGIES OF AMERICAN ELECTORAL POLITICS 268–74 (6th ed. 1984).

45. In a wonderfully original and provocative analysis, John Rohr has suggested that the Senate was imbued with significant executive powers—and, indeed, conceptualized by the Framers as possessing a partly executive character—to compensate, in part, for the nonrepresentative character of the presidency. JOHN A. ROHR, TO RUN A CONSTITUTION: THE LEGITIMACY OF THE ADMINISTRATIVE STATE 28–39 (1986).

46. See, e.g., ROBERT DAHL & DOUGLAS RAE, WHO GOVERNS? DEMOCRACY AND POWER IN AN AMERICAN CITY (2d ed. 2005).

47. Bagley & Revesz, *supra* note 16, at 1285–91.

48. As one noted commentator has said: "[A]ny suggestion that resisting specialized appeals is best done by concentrating power in the President is clearly counterfactual, as the Framers themselves recognized." Jonathan R. Macey, *Comment: Confrontation or Cooperation for Mutual Gain?* 57 LAW & CONTEMP. PROBS . 45, 50 (1994).

49. For an argument that public interest groups assist in this dynamic, see Daniel A. Farber, *Politics and Procedure in Environmental Law*, 8 J.L. ECON. & ORG . 59 (1992).

50. THE FEDERALIST No. 10, at 78 (James Madison) (Clinton Rossiter ed., 1961).

51. William V. Luneberg, *Civic Republicanism, the First Amendment, and Executive Branch Policymaking*, 43 ADMIN. L. REV. 367, 403–04 (1991); see also Michael Fitts, *The*

Vices of Virtue: A Political Party Perspective on Civic Virtue Reforms of the Legislative Process, 136 U. PA. L. REV. 1567 (1988).

52. THE FEDERALIST No. 70, at 427–28 (Alexander Hamilton) (Clinton Rossiter ed., 1961).

53. Abner S. Greene, *Checks and Balances in an Era of Presidential Lawmaking,* 61 U. CHI. L. REV. 123, 178–79 (1994).

54. Bagley & Revesz, *supra* note 16, at 1310–12.

55. Prominent economist Paul Portney, in a 1984 paper, estimated these direct costs of OMB-OIRA oversight at $17–$25 million, which, in Fiscal Year (FY) 2001 dollars, would have amounted to $29.9–$47.4 million. Stuart Shapiro, *Assessing the Benefits and Costs of Regulatory Reforms: What Questions Need to Be Asked* (AEI-Brookings Joint Center for Regulatory Studies, Regulatory Analysis No. 07-01, Jan. 2007), available at http://www.aei-brookings.org/publications/abstract.php?pid=1146, *quoting* Paul Portney, *The Benefits and Costs of Regulatory Analysis,* in V. KERRY SMITH, ED., ENVIRONMENTAL POLICY UNDER REAGAN'S EXECUTIVE ORDER (1984). (I have derived all inflation-adjusted figures using NASA's New Start Inflation Index Calculator, available at http://cost.jsc.nasa.gov/inflation/nasa/inflateNASA.html, and am using the FY 2001 baseline because OMB currently uses 2001 dollars to state the annual costs and benefits of the regulation it reviews.) This sounds like a large figure, but OMB, in a draft 2007 report to Congress on the costs and benefits of federal regulations, estimated the annual costs in FY 2001 dollars of the major rules adopted in FY 2006, to be $ 3.7–$4.2 billion. Office of Management and Budget, Draft 2007 Report to Congress on the Costs and Benefits of Federal Regulations 2, 11 (Mar. 9, 2007), available at http://www.whitehouse.gov/omb/inforeg/2007_cb/2007_draft_cb_report.pdf. Assuming the direct costs of the program have remained the same since 1984, the high $47.4 million estimate of direct costs entailed in regulatory review amounts to just over 1 percent of the low estimate of the annual costs associated with the FY 2006 major rules. In other words, if we assume a ten-year lifespan for the new rules and if centralized oversight reduced the annual costs of what would otherwise have been the agencies' regulatory proposals by about one-tenth of 1 percent over the life of the rules, a very low target, the system would pay for its own direct costs.

The problem, however, is that there are also indirect costs, and the most obvious of these is the cost of delay. OMB's estimate, in FY 2001 dollars, of the annual benefits associated with the its major rules in FY 2006 was $6.3–$44.8 billion. Id. Any reduction of benefits attributable to delays in issuing rules that result from the centralized process of regulatory review should obviously count as a cost of regulatory oversight. There is, of course, very frequently some considerable delay between an agency's proposal of any rule and the promulgation of the rule in its final, legally binding form. The question is how much of this delay, for major rules, can be reasonably attributed to the OMB/OIRA review process that recent presidents have imposed.

A recent study of administrative rule making during both the second Clinton and first Bush 43 Administrations provides a reasonable basis for estimating this delay. Stuart Shapiro, *Presidents and Process: A Comparison of the Regulatory Process Under the*

Clinton and Bush (43) Administrations (Sept. 29, 2006), available at SSRN: http://ssrn. com/abstract=933678. The two Administrations have remarkably similar records with regard to the time elapsed between proposed and final rules. In both cases, the mean lapse for all rules between proposal and promulgation was roughly eleven months, while the mean lapse for rules reviewed by OMB was seventeen to twenty months. Id. at 31. This suggests as a reasonable estimate that the OMB process may add six months to the process for the typical rule it reviews. (This number is based on a calculation of rule-making length that compares the date of issuance of a final rule with the formal date of issuance of the rule in proposed form. Well before agencies publish rules in proposed form, however, those rules are still the subject of internal agency deliberation. A better measure of when that process starts might be the appearance of a rule-making initiative in the so- called Unified Agenda of pending regulatory efforts that the federal government publishes every six months. Making that comparison, it would appear that OMB review added three months to the rule-making process during the Clinton Administration, but nearly nine months during the first Bush 43 Administration. Id. at 18–20. Because of the small sample size, one cannot comment confidently on the trend, but these numbers also suggest that a six-month overall estimate is reasonable.)

If this is the case, then the cost of OMB review for the rules it reviewed in FY 2006 could have been in the order of $3.2–$22.4 billion, or half of the benefits estimated for any single year the rules would be in effect. Assume, again, that these regulations remain in place, on average, for ten years. OMB review would then have to reduce the costs of the rules by $320 million to $2.2 billion per year to compensate society for the benefits forgone. Given the annual cost estimate for these rules of $3.7–$4.2 billion, we can get a conservative estimate of the cost savings OMB would need in order to break even, by comparing the lower estimate of the costs that OMB imposes through regulatory delay ($320 million) with its high estimate of the overall cost of the rules ($4.2 billion). Making this comparison, the $4.2 billion price tag would have to have been over $4.5 billion without the review, in order for the cost of the review to be justified in light of the foregone benefits of 6 months' delay in implementing these significant rules. In other words, the review process would have had to shave off up to 7 percent of the total cost of the rules for the review itself to be cost justified. This assumes that the costs of delay are low and the overall price tag of the rules is high.

We can do the same exercise at the other end of the range in order to get a more generous estimate of the cost savings OMB would need to achieve in order to justify the review process. If OMB is correct in its high estimate of benefits but at the low end of the cost range, then the annual cost of six months' delay in implementation would have been $2.2 billion, and, in order for the review to be cost justified, the pre-review cost of the regulations would have had to have been $ 2.2 billion higher than the estimated $3.7 billion in post-review regulatory costs. This would have required a cost reduction based on OMB review of up to 37 percent. Routine gains in cost reduction in this range of magnitudes seems utterly implausible, unless there some reason to think that agencies are not just overregulating—they are regulating recklessly.

Defenders of OIRA might try to brighten the picture by suggesting that centralized review not only reduces costs, but maximizes benefits. From this perspective, judging the value of review entirely by cost reduction may understate the benefits of White House involvement in agency rule making. However, there is virtually no evidence that OIRA review ever focuses significantly on benefit enhancement as opposed to cost reduction. Bagley & Revesz, *supra* note 16, at 1270. Thus, it seems unlikely that administrative rules will yield greater benefits because of OIRA review than would otherwise be realized through decentralized efforts alone. The point is underscored by the relatively light review extended to any rule making proposal that is deregulatory in nature and the utter inattention to regulatory inaction as a problem in terms of potential opportunities forgone for social benefit. Id. at 1271–80. For example, between January 2001 and April 2007, the Occupational Safety and Health Administration issued exactly one major safety rule and one significant health standard—the latter under a mandate from a federal court. Stephen Labaton, *OSHA Leaves Worker Safety Largely in Hands of Industry,* N.Y. Times, Apr. 25, 2007, at A1. Given the ongoing advances in occupational safety and health science, it defies reason that OSHA could not have found more regulatory improvements that would have realized significant benefits at some lower regulatory cost. Yet, the White House has done nothing to stimulate more strategic regulatory thinking by OSHA. That is because Presidents have focused almost entirely on limiting regulatory cost, not increasing regulatory benefit.

56. Bagley & Revesz, *supra* note 16, at 1282–1304.

57. See generally William A. Niskanen, Jr., Bureaucracy and Representative Government (1971).

58. Daryl J. Levinson, *Empire-Building in Constitutional Law,* 118 Harv. L. Rev. 915, 932–34 (2005) (discussing the political literature critiquing Niskanan).

59. Bagley & Revesz, *supra* note 16, at 1294–96.

60. Frank Ackerman, Lisa Heinzerling, & Rachel Massey, *Applying Cost-Benefit Analysis to Past Decisions: Was Environmental Protection Ever a Good Idea?* 57 Admin. L. Rev. 155, 158–59 (2005).

61. Id. at 160–72.

62. Bagley & Revesz, *supra* note 16, at 1301.

63. Id. at 1302–04..

64. Id. at 1287–88.

65. Id. at 1288, quoting Cary Coglianese, *Litigating Within Relationships: Disputes and Disturbance in the Regulatory Process,* 30 Law & Soc'y Rev. 735, 743 (1996).

66. Id. at 1324–28.

67. *White House Interferes with Smog Rule,* OMB Watch (Mar. 18, 2008), available at http://www.ombwatch.org/article/articleview/4195/1/132.

68. Government Accountability Office, Chemical Assessments: Low Productivity and New Interagency Review Process Limit the Usefulness and Credibility of EPA's Integrated Risk Information System (Report to the Chairman, Committee on Environment and Public Works, U.S. Senate) (March 2008), available at http://www.gao.gov/new.items/d08440.pdf.

69. H. Josef Hebert, *EPA Scientists Complain About Political Pressure*, AP News (Apr. 23, 2008), available at http://talkingpointsmemo.com/news/2008/04/epa_scientists_complain_about.php.

Chapter Seven

1. THE FEDERALIST No. 10, at 83 (James Madison) (Clinton Rossiter ed., 1961).

2. Id.

3. THE FEDERALIST No. 68, at 412 (Alexander Hamilton) (Clinton Rossiter ed., 1961).

4. See Allen Buchanan, *Political Legitimacy and Democracy*, 112 ETHICS 689 (2002).

5. These ideas are developed further in Peter M. Shane, *The Electronic Federalist: The Internet and the Institutionalization of Democratic Legitimacy*, in PETER M. SHANE, ED., DEMOCRACY ONLINE: THE PROSPECTS FOR POLITICAL RENEWAL THROUGH THE INTERNET 65 (2004)

6. See generally Steven G. Calabresi, *Some Normative Arguments for the Unitary Executive*, 48 ARK. L. REV. 23 (1995)

7. Transcribed from a video of the interview, available at http://www.comedycentral.com/motherload/player.jhtml?ml_video=84011&ml_collection=&ml_gateway=&ml_gateway_id=&ml_comedian=&ml_runtime=&ml_context=show&ml_origin_url=/shows/the_daily_show/videos/celebrity_interviews/index.jhtml%3FplayVideo%3D84011&ml_playlist=&lnk=&is_large=true.

8. THE FEDERALIST No. 1, at 33 (Alexander Hamilton) (Clinton Rossiter ed., 1961).

9. GORDON S. WOOD, THE CREATION OF THE AMERICAN REPUBLIC 1776–1787, at 605 (1969).

10. THE FEDERALIST No. 52, at 327 (James Madison) (Clinton Rossiter ed. 1961).

11. THE FEDERALIST No. 64, at 414 (Alexander Hamilton) (Clinton Rossiter ed. 1961).

12. THE FEDERALIST No. 78, at 469 (Alexander Hamilton) (Clinton Rossiter ed. 1961).

13. Calabresi, *supra* note 6, at 34.

14. Joshua Ferguson, Linda Babcock, & Peter M. Shane, *Behind the Mask of Method: Political Orientation and Constitutional Interpretive Preferences*, 32 LAW & HUM. BEHAV. 502 (2008).

15. Nicholas Bagley & Richard L. Revesz, *Centralized Oversight of the Regulatory State*, 106 COLUM. L. REV. 1260, 1324–28 (2006).

16. Pub. L. No. 110-175, 121 Stat. 2524 (2007).

17. S. 2533, 110th Cong., 2d Sess. (2008).

18. S. 564, 104th Cong., 1st Sess. (1995).

19. 5 U.S.C. § 553.

20. See Report of the American Bar Association Task Force on the Future of Electronic Rulemaking (2008).

21. 5 U.S.C. § 552(b)(5).

22. The Reagan Administration successfully defended efforts to withhold from public disclosure any information regarding which actions by the Food and Drug Administration were still under review by the Secretary of Health and Human Services or the Office of Management and Budget. Wolfe v. Department of Health and Human Services, 839 F.2d 768 (D.C. Cir. 1988) (en banc). The status of proposed actions under OMB review can now be tracked at http://www.reginfo.gov/public/do/eoPackageMain.

23. The Web site, called Thomas (for President Jefferson), appears at http://thomas.loc.gov.

24. The Supreme Court first formulated the doctrine in Chevron, U.S.A. v. Natural Resources Defense Council, 467 U.S. 837 (1984).

25. Vieth v. Jubelier, 541 U.S. 267 (2004).

26. JEFF MANZA & CHRISTOPHER UGGEN, LOCKED OUT: FELON DISENFRAN-CHISEMENT AND AMERICAN DEMOCRACY 76 (2006).

27. Human Rights Watch & The Sentencing Project, Losing the Vote: The Impact of Felony Disenfranchisement Laws in the United States 5 (1998), available at http://www.sentencingproject.org/tmp/File/FVR/fd_losingthevote.pdf.

28. Christopher Uggen & Jeff Manza, *Democratic Contraction? The Political Conse-quences of Felon Disenfranchisement in the United States,* 67 AM. SOC. REV. 777 (2002).

29. Abby Goodnough, *Florida Governor Is Hoping to Restore Felon Voting Rights,* N.Y. TIMES, Apr. 3, 2007, at A1.

30. "A Gallup Poll conducted in the wake of the aforementioned 2000 election showed that a majority of Americans (61%) would support amending the Constitution so that the candidate receiving the most popular votes would win the election. Little more than a third (35%) preferred keeping the Electoral College system as it is. Gallup asked the question again last month and found that nearly four years later, public opinion on this question is virtually the same." Darren K. Carlson, Public Flunks Electoral College System (Nov. 2, 2004), available at http://www.gallup.com/poll/13918/Public-Flunks-Electoral-College-System.aspx.

31. JOHN R. KOZA ET AL., EVERY VOTE EQUAL: A STATE-BASED PLAN FOR ELECT-ING THE PRESIDENT BY NATIONAL POPULAR VOTE (2006).

32. Wesberry v. Sanders, 376 U.S. 1 (1964).

33. NORMAN J. ORNSTEIN, VITAL STATISTICS ON CONGRESS 2001–2002, at 69 (2002).

34. Id. at 32–34.

35. Id. at 28–29.

36. Such an amendment is proposed in JESSE L. JACKSON, JR., A MORE PERFECT UNION: ADVANCING NEW AMERICAN RIGHTS 425 (2001).

37. Katrina vanden Heuvel, *Bring Democracy Home,* NATION, Nov. 3, 2006, available at http://www.thenation.com/doc/20061120/kvh.

38. Demos, Tools for Democracy: Election Day Registration 2 (Sept. 1, 2006), available at http://www.demos.org/pubs/EDR%20Toolkit%20070506.pdf.

39. Reynolds v. Sims, 377 U.S. 533, 563 (1964).

40. See Federal Election Commission v. National Right to Work Committee, 459 U.S.

197, 207 (1982) (upholding legitimacy of government interest "to ensure that substantial aggregations of wealth amassed by the special advantages which go with the corporate form of organization should not be converted into political 'war chests' which could be used to incur political debts from legislators who are aided by the contributions").

41. Peter M. Shane, *Key Issues in Telecommunications Reform,* 3 ISJLP 1, 5 (2007).

42. JACOB S. HACKER & PAUL PIERSON, OFF CENTER: THE REPUBLICAN REVO-LUTION AND THE EROSION OF AMERICAN DEMOCRACY 196–200 (2005).

43. S. 1497, 108th Cong., 1st Sess. (2003).

44. FCC, Do Local Owners Deliver More Localism? Some Evidence from Local Broadcast News (Unpublished Working Paper 2004), available at http://hraunfoss.fcc. gov/edocs_public/attachmatch/DOC-267448A1.pdf; Adam Marcus, *Media Diversity and Substitutability: Problems with the FCC's Diversity Index,* 3 ISJLP 83, 88–92 (2007); Peter DiCola, *Do Radio Companies Offer More Variety When They Exceed the Local Ownership Cap?,* in BENTON FOUNDATION, DOES BIGGER MEDIA EQUAL BETTER ME-DIA? FOUR ACADEMIC STUDIES OF MEDIA OWNERSHIP IN THE UNITED STATES 38 (2006).

45. C. EDWIN BAKER, MEDIA CONCENTRATION AND DEMOCRACY: WHY OWN-ERSHIP MATTERS 73 (2007).

46. Id. at 97–123; Marcus, *supra* note 44, at 96–100, 105–09.

47. The doctrine and its history are recounted in Syracuse Peace Council v. F.C.C., 867 F.2d 654 (D.C. Cir. 1989).

48. BAKER, *supra* note 45, at 73.

49. Peter Muhlberger & Peter Shane, Prospects for Electronic Democracy: A Survey Analysis, Version 1 (Unpublished Paper, 2001), available at http://www.geocities.com/pmuh178/MarkleFinal.doc.

50. Peter Muhlberger, *The Virtual Agora Project: A Research Design for Studying Democratic Deliberation,*" 1 J. PUB. DELIBERATION, Art. 5, available at http://services.bepress.com/jpd/vol1/iss1/art5.

51. A catalogue of examples appears in an early, but still influential paper, Stephen Coleman & John Gøtze, Bowling Together: Online Public Engagement in Policy Deliberation 36–45 (2001), available at www.bowlingtogether.net. The British Council Germany and the German Web zine politik-digital.de have collaborated in the creation of an online database that links viewers to dozens of such projects, available at http://www.e-participation.net/.

52. BRUCE ACKERMAN & JAMES S. FISHKIN, DELIBERATION DAY (2004).

53. http://www.drinkingliberally.org (last visited September 5, 2008).

54. Id.

55. Peter Muhlberger, *Access, Skill, and Motivation in Online Political Discussion: Testing Cyberrealism,* in DEMOCRACY ONLINE, *supra* note 5, at 225.

56. See Muhlberger & Shane, *supra* note 49.

57. It has been argued, based on computer modeling, that liberalizing public policies allowing new entrants in telecommunications markets to offer video services encourages the deployment of broadband networks to low-income neighborhoods because video

represents a service that low-income families are willing to prioritize. George S. Ford, Thomas M. Koutsky, & Lawrence J. Spiwak, *The Impact of Video Service Regulation on the Construction of Broadband Networks to Low-Income Households,* 3 ISJLP 13 (2007).

58. FCC, Availability of Advanced Telecommunications Capability in the United States (Fourth Report to Congress FCC 04-208, GN Docket No. 04-54) 41 (Sept. 9, 2004).

59. Organization for Economic Co-operation and Development, OECD Information Technology Outlook 2006, at 186 (2006).

60. FCC Note of Inquiry, In the Matter of Inquiry Concerning the Deployment of Advanced Telecommunications Capability to All Americans in a Reasonable and Timely Fashion, and Possible Steps to Accelerate Such Deployment Pursuant to Section 706 of the Telecommunications Act of 1996 (GN Docket No. 07-45) 16 (Statement of Commissioner Michael J. Copps), available at http://hraunfoss.fcc.gov/edocs_public/attachmatch/FCC-07-21A1.pdf

61. Communication Workers of America, Speed Matters: A Report on Internet Speeds in All 50 States 2 (2007), available at http://www.speedmatters.org/document-library/sourcematerials/sm_report.pdf.

62. Organization for Economic Co-operation and Development, *supra* note 59, at 103 (2006); Michael Dell, Transcript of Keynote Address to the 2007 Consumer Electronics Show, available at http://media.podtech.net/media/2007/01/PID_001851/Podtech_v_1875-ces-2007-dell-launches-.html (on file with the author).

63. Id.

64. iN2015 Steering Committee, Innovation, Integration, Internationalisation 9 (2006), available at http://www.ida.gov.sg/doc/About%20us/About_Us_Level2/20071005103551/01_iN2015_Main_Report.pdf.

65. Parks Associates, Press Release, Offline Americans see Internet of Little Value (Mar. 22, 2007), available at http://www.parksassociates.com/press/press_releases/2007/nat_scan1.html (on file with author).

66. John Horrigan & Katherine Murray, Pew Internet and American Life Project Data Memo Re: Rural Broadband Internet Use 3 (Feb. 2006), available at http://www.pewinternet.org/pdfs/PIP_Rural_Broadband.pdf.

67. Id.

68. The Federalist No. 51, at 322 (Clinton Rossiter ed., 1961).

Index